DATE DUE

GAYLORD			PRINTED IN U.S.A.

FOOTPRINTS
OF THE
WELSH INDIANS

FOOTPRINTS

OF THE

WELSH INDIANS

Settlers in North America
before 1492

William L. Traxel

Algora Publishing
New York

Library of Congress Cataloging-in-Publication Data

Traxel, William L.
  Footprints of the Welsh Indians: Settlers in North America before 1492. /
William L. Traxel.
    p. cm.
  Includes bibliographical references (p.   ) and index.
  ISBN 0-87586-299-3 (trade paper : alk. paper) — ISBN 0-87586-300-0 (hard
cover : alk. paper) — ISBN 0-87586-301-9 (ebook)
  1. America—Discovery and exploration—Welsh. 2. Explorers—Wales—
History. 3. Welsh—America—History. 4. Welsh Indians—History. 5. Indi-
ans of North America—History. 6. America—Discovery and exploration. 7.
Explorers—America—History. 8. America—Antiquities. 9. Southern
States—Antiquities. I. Title.

  E109.W4T73 2004
  970'.0049166—dc22
                          2004006342

Front Cover: Viking Longship Replica Sailing at Sunset
A replica of a Viking longship, built by Danish boy scouts, sails along the Jut-
land peninsula of Denmark at sunset.

© Ted Spiegel/CORBIS
Photographer: Ted Spiegel
Date Photographed: ca. 1980

ACKNOWLEDGEMENTS

I want to mention those people who generously gave me their time and expertise. Without them this book would be an incomplete shadow of what it became with their assistance. This listing is generally in the order that I met with them and not in the importance of their contribution.

I sincerely thank Carolyn Hendon of De Soto Falls State Park, John Perry of Berea College, Berea, Kentucky, Helen McGuire of Beattyville, Kentucky, Olga Palmer of Tallega, Kentucky, Charles H. Faulkner of Knoxville, Tennessee, Pauline Nez of Four Bears, North Dakota, Billy Fredericks and Mark Halvorson of Bismarck, North Dakota, Edwin Benson of Halliday, North Dakota, Joe Benthal of Madisonville, Tennessee, and Gerald and Clyde Franklin of Prairie du Rocher, Illinois.

I also want to express appreciation to Donal Buchanan of the Epigraphic Society Occasional Publications, William R. Iseminger of the Cahokia Mounds Historic Site, Mary Sears of the Harvard University Library, Nick Honerkamp of the University of Tennessee-Chattanooga, Stephen D. Cox of the Tennessee State Museum, LuAnn Patton of the Kensington RuneStone Museum, Daniel Boudillion of the New England Antiquities Research Association, Julian Fell of San Diego and Edward Bochnak of New Jersey. I give a special heartfelt thanks to Jackie Thomas and her staff at the Poplar Bluff, Missouri, Public Library for the indispensable work they did helping me to acquire reference materials.

For their editing assistance I thank Helen Mountjoy of Owensboro, Kentucky and John Stanard and my wife Mary of Poplar Bluff, Missouri.

I especially give thanks to my good friend and colleague Wendell McChord of Dayton, Ohio, who got me started and directed my research in many ways.

Dr. William L. Traxel

DEDICATION

I dedicate this book to the *Nu'eta* people, the Mandan-Hidatsa, who I believe are descendants of the original settlers who sailed to America with Prince Madoc of Wales in 1170, 450 years before the *Mayflower*.

Dr. William L. Traxel

LIST OF ILLUSTRATIONS

Figure

1. Skull Shapes

2. (A and B) Dolmen (2 photos)

3. (A and B) Alban Longhouse Remains (2 photos)

4. A Modern Boat-Roofed House

5. Diana Island Stone Beacons

6. Map of Alban Beacons and Longhouses

7. The Zeno Map

8. Map of Leif Eriksson's Saga

9. Map of Thorfinn Karlsefni's Saga

10. (A and B) The Kensington RuneStone

11. Map of Wales

12. Route of the Welegens

13. (A and B) Cave Chambers at De Soto Falls (2 photos)

14. Inside the Chambers at De Soto Falls

15. View from Fort Mountain

16. (A, B, and C) The Stone Walls at Fort Mountain (3 photos)

17. Mounds at Etowah

18. Map of Welegen Country

19. Route of the Asgens

20. (A and B) The Thruston Tablet (2 photos)

21. Map of the Falls of the Ohio

22. The Welsh Coat of Arms

23. The Brandenburg Stone

24. Map of the Asgens Territory

25. The Big Four Railroad Bridge

26. The Cahokia Mississippian Culture Site

27. Fort Ancient Artifacts from Fox Field

28. Indian Fort Mountain Wall Remains

29. Indian Fort Mountain Ambush Area

30. (A and B) Indian Fort Mountain View and Cliffs (2 photos)

31. The Pinnacles Area

32. (A and B) Mandan Style Houses (2 photos)

33. A Mandan "Bull Boat"

34. Fort Mandan

35. Catlin's Map of Mandan Migration

36. Chief Ma-to-toh-pa (Four Bears)

37. The Treeless Windswept Plains

38. The Garrison Dam

39. (A and B) Lake Sakakawea (2 photos)

40. Fort Union

41. The Author and Pauline Nez

42. Round Depression from an Earthen House

43. Billy Fredericks and the Author

44. The Gwenan Gorn on the Ohio

45. George Catlin, Self Portrait

46. The Okipa Ceremony

47. Evans' Map

48. Rose Island

49. L'Anse aux Meadows

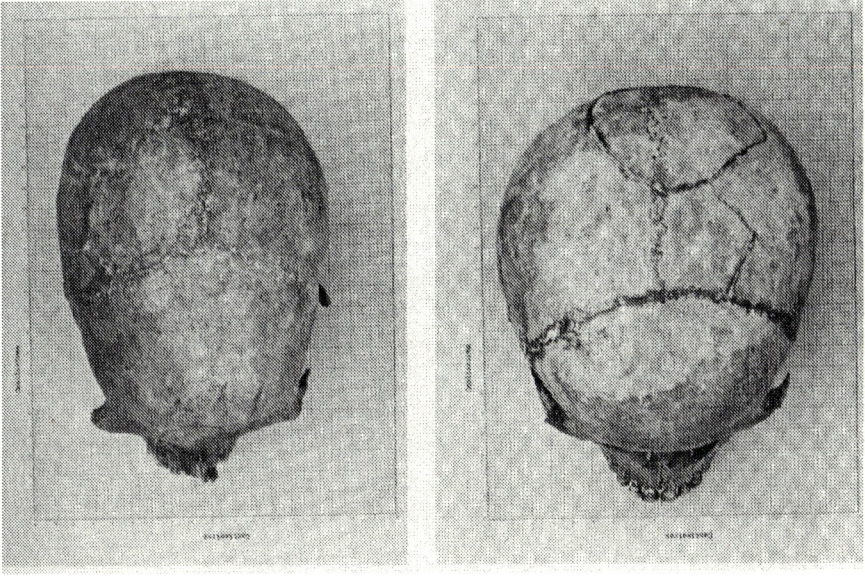

(Fig 1) Dolichocephaly (skull long and narrow) - left and Brachycephaly (skull short and broad) - right. One means used by anthropologists to classify ancient skeletal remains is the shape of the skull. The Paleo-Americans were typically dolichocephalic; the Red Indians were typically brachycephalic. (Photos by Walter Eitel, from *Bronze Age America* by Barry Fell)

(Fig. 2A and 2B) Dolmens come in all sizes. (A) is a relatively small one. It was discovered near Westport, Massachusetts. (Photo by James Whittall, from *Bronze Age America* by Barry Fell). (B) is a ninety ton boulder supported by five stones. It is situated in a valley in North Salem, New York. (Photo by Edward Bochnak)

(Fig. 3A and 3B)   Two views of a reconstructed longhouse. The roof was an upturned boat. The site is on Pamiok Island near the western shore of Ungava Bay. Carbon dating shows that the house was inhabited between AD 1200 and 1300. (From *The Farfarers...*, by Farley Mowat)

(Fig. 4) A modern boat-roofed house in the Orkney Islands. (From *The Farfarers...*, by Farley Mowat) (Fig. 5) A cluster of archaeological findings along the western shore of Ungava Bay and surrounding islands reflect the presence of the Alban people. Pictured are three stone beacons on Diana Island, the largest of which is thirteen feet high. Included in the picture is Robert Lee, son of archaeologist Tom Lee. (From *The Farfarers...*, by Farley Mowat)

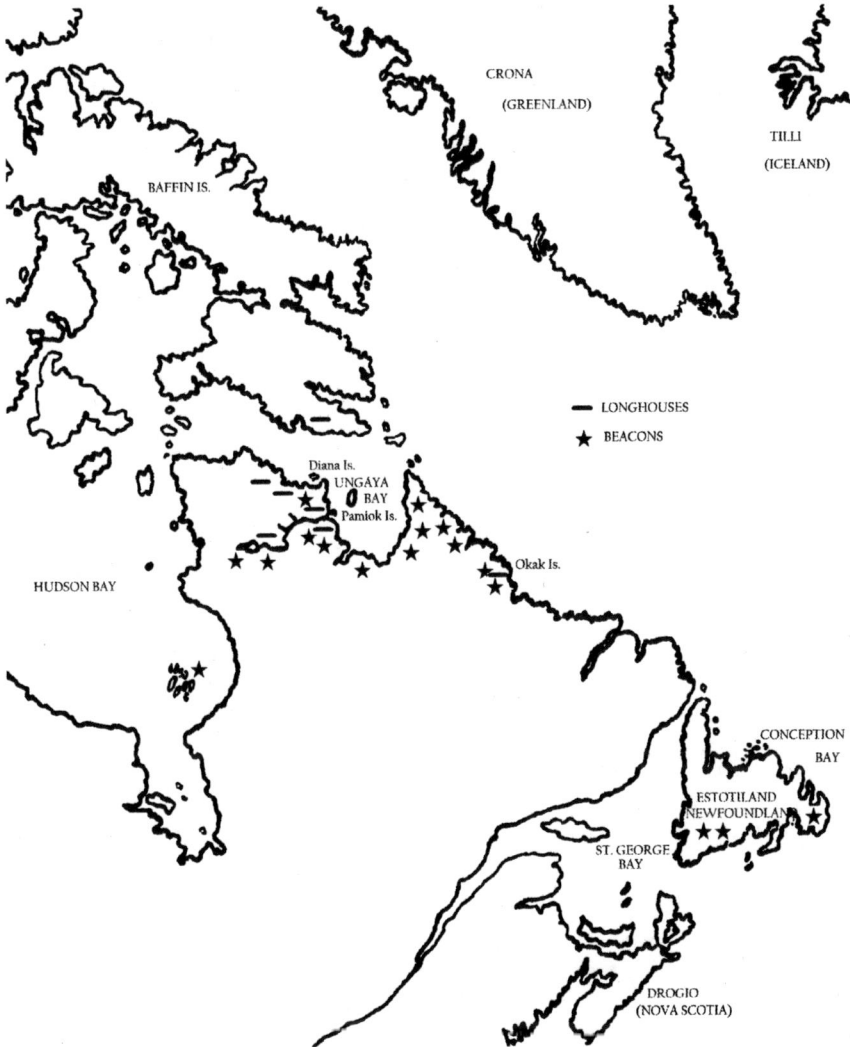

(Fig 6) This map shows the location of Alban longhouses and stone beacons that have been discovered in northeastern Canada. Before coming to Canada, the Alban people had migrated to Iceland and Greenland, where they preceded the Norse.

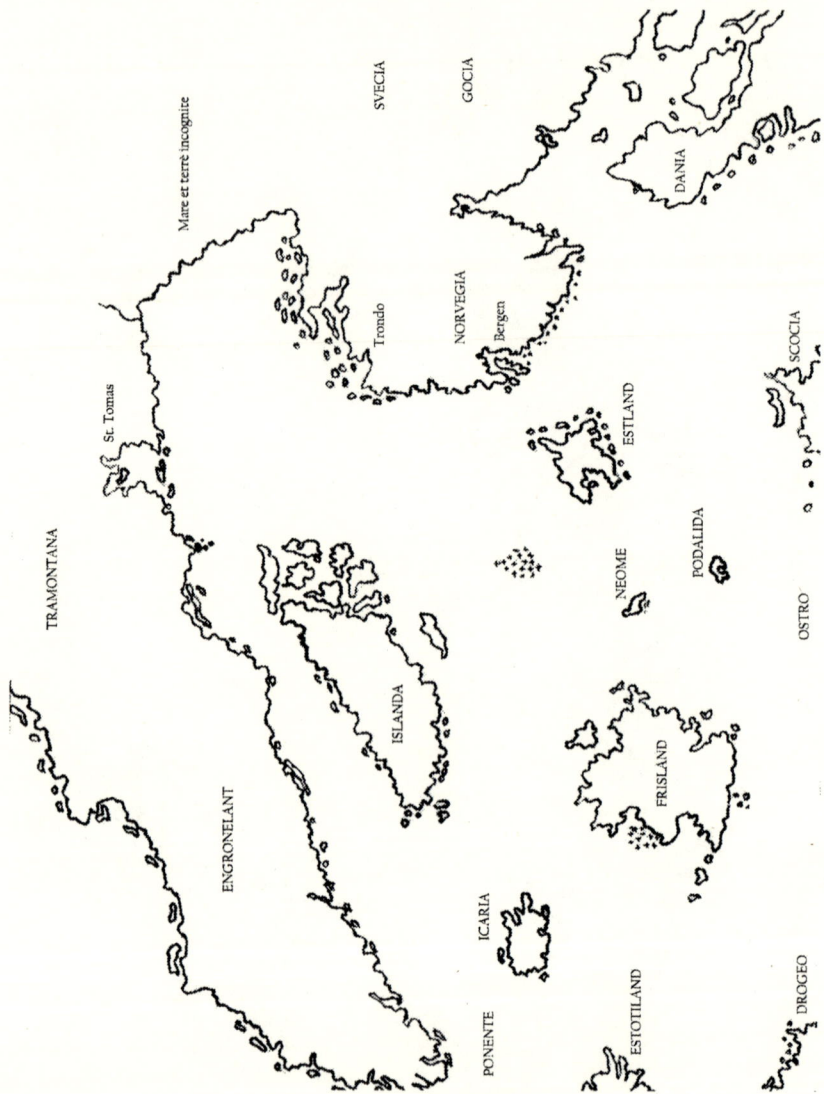

(Fig. 7) The Zeno Map. This is the map drawn from the experiences of the Zeno brothers in the late fourteenth century. The Zeno brothers' placements of Greenland (Engronelant), Iceland (Islanda), Scotland (Scocia), Norway (Norvegia), Denmark (Dania), and Sweden (Svecia Gocia) reveal their extensive travels. The Zeno Map was by far the most accurate map of the North Atlantic in the sixteenth century and was the standard relied upon by navigators at that time. On the map Estland is the Shetland Islands and Frisland probably represents the Faeroe Islands, although their size has been greatly exaggerated on the map. Icaria is Newfoundland and should have been labelled "Estotiland" to match the description the fisherman gave to Prince Henry Sinclair. What is labelled "Estotiland" on the map is Nova Scotia and matches the Drogio of the fisherman. Antonio Zeno never saw what he labelled Drogeo and the cartography of Drogeo was drawn only from descriptions given to Zeno by Sinclair and the fisherman. The land labelled Drogeo on the map is New England.

(Fig. 8) This map defines the AD 1000 voyage described in Leif Eriksson's Saga and that of Leif's brother Thorvald about two years later. Leif's Camp was known to the Norse as Leifsbudir. Thorvald, Thorfinn Karlsefni, and Leif's half sister Freydis are believed to have spent time there on their trips to Vinland.

(Fig. 9) Thorfinn Karlsefni led the largest Norse expedition to Vinland. It consisted of four ships and included women and cattle. Karlsefni spent most of his time at a mountainous area he named Straumsfjord, and on Straumsey, an island at the mouth of Straumsfjord. Straumsey may have been Mount Desert Island. He journeyed farther south with about forty men and spent several months at a place he founded and named Hop. The description for Hop given in his saga is consistent with either the Pettaquamscutt River basin off Narragansett Bay in Rhode Island, or Follins Pond at the base of Cape Cod. Karlsefni returned to Straumsfjord after a skirmish with the Indians. Karlsefni's son Snorri was born at Straumsfjord and is the first white child documented to have been born in the New World.

(Figs. 10A - on the preceeding page and 10B - above) The Kensington RuneStone was discovered in 1898 by Olaf Ohman, a Minnesota farmer. A controversy regarding its authenticity has raged since it was first discovered. The inscription is in fourteenth century Scandinavian. It has been engraved on the front and continued on one side. It tells of an exploration (acquistion business) by twenty-two Northmen and eight Goths in the year 1362. (Photo courtesy of the Kensington RuneStone Museum)

(Fig. 11) Wales is a mountainous, relatively unfertile enclave in Great Britain where native peoples were able to resist invasion. Thus could the Welsh under Owain Gwynedd hold out against Henry, the Norman King of England. The close proximity of Wales to the sea, its unfertile soil, and the Viking, Keltic, and Alban ancestry of its people, made them fishermen and seafarers.

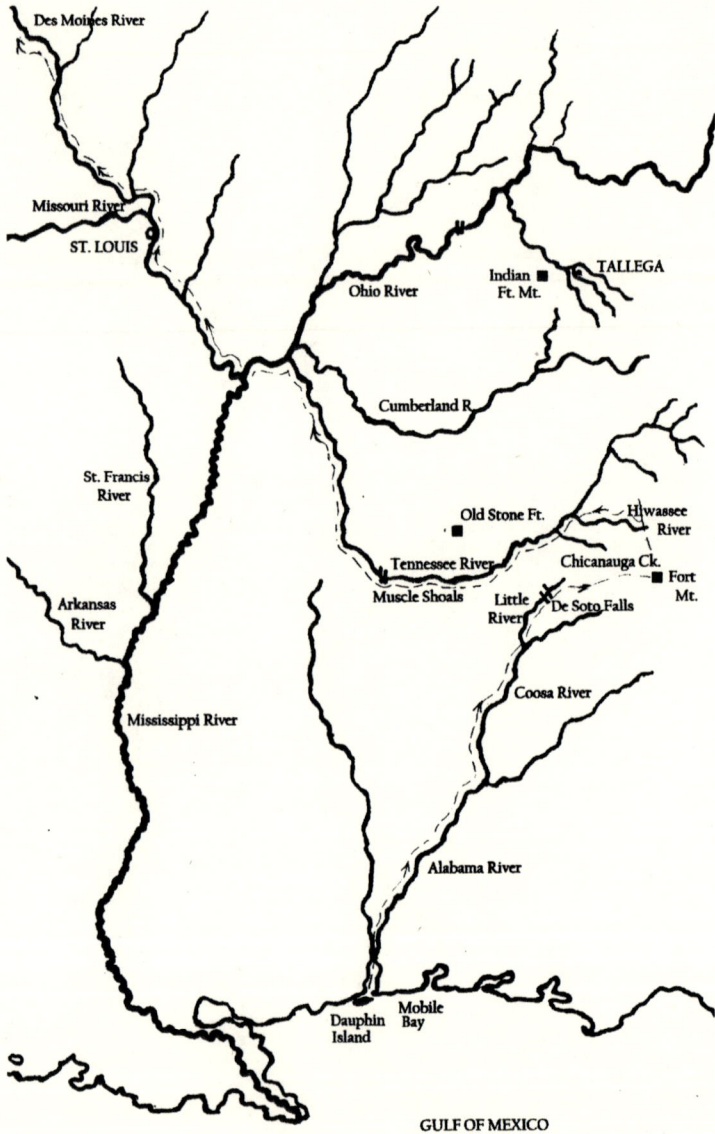

(Fig. 12) One of the landing places for Madoc's ships was Mobile Bay. From there the Welsh settlers traveled up the Alabama, Coosa, and Little Rivers to DeSoto Falls. They later sought refuge at Fort Mountain before going to sites in Tennessee. In about 1500, they were defeated by the Cherokee in battles at Chicamauga and Muscle Shoals. They were forced to leave the area, never to return.

(Fig. 13A and 13B - on the next page) The walls of the fort at DeSoto Falls have been dismantled, but the chambers that were chiseled into the face of the cliff remain and are shown here. A narrow, one-man path along the edge of the cliff leads to five chambers which are 150 feet above the river. The peril in which the fort's inhabitants found themselves can be appreciated from the selection of the cliff-faced site.

(Fig. 14 - above) The five chambers at DeSoto Falls interconnect. Some open onto the cliff-face, others are in the interior of the cliff and can only be entered by going through another chamber. (Fig. 15 - below) The view provided by the 2832 foot high summit of Fort Mountain alerted defenders of an approaching enemy.

(Figs. 16A, 16B, - both on the previous page, and 16C - above) The walls at Fort Mountain, Georgia are truly impressive even to this day. Although the walls collapsed long ago, the stones reveal that they were once at least six feet high. A foxhole and a redoubt can be seen in the pictures. The entrance (not pictured) is clearly visible to the visitor. The wall is an astounding 885 feet in length.

(Fig. 17 - above) The Mississippian site at Etowah, Georgia, is not far from Fort Mountain. It was inhabited by a Muskogean-speaking people until some time after the arrival of the Cherokee to the area in the thirteenth century. The mound pictured is the smallest of three. The photo was taken from atop the largest mound.

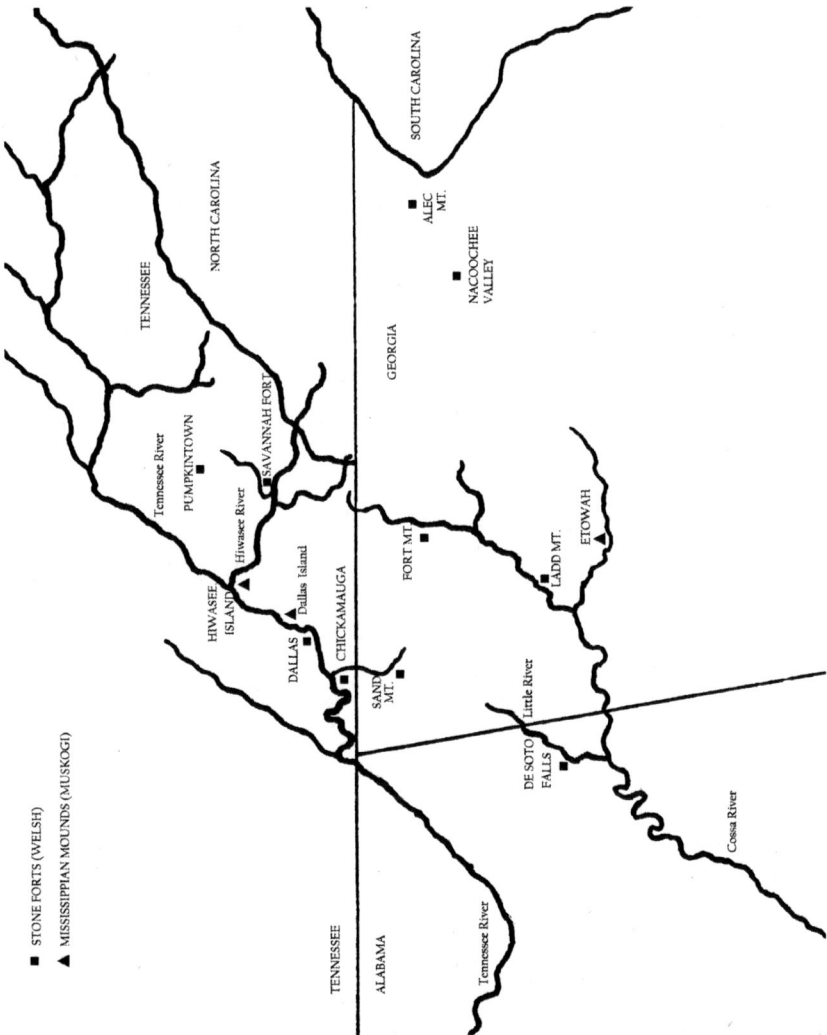

(Fig. 18) This map shows Welegen Country, the home of the Welsh Indians who landed at Mobile Bay. Shown are the major findings at De Soto Falls and Fort Mountain and also less well known stone fortifications at Ladd Mountain, Alec Mountain, and Sand Mountain, Georgia. In Tennessee the sites include (1) Savannah Fort on the Hiwassee River, (2) Dallas, now under the waters of Lake Chickamauga and built on the site of the first court house of Hamilton County across from the Creek Indian village at Dallas Island, (3) Chickamauga, at the mouth of Chickamauga Creek where the first treaty with the Cherokee was reached with the Welsh agreeing to leave the area, and (4) Pumpkintown, now the city of Athens. Pumpkintown was known to the Indians as Ei-ya-ga-u-gi. There have been several Red Indian villages with the same name.

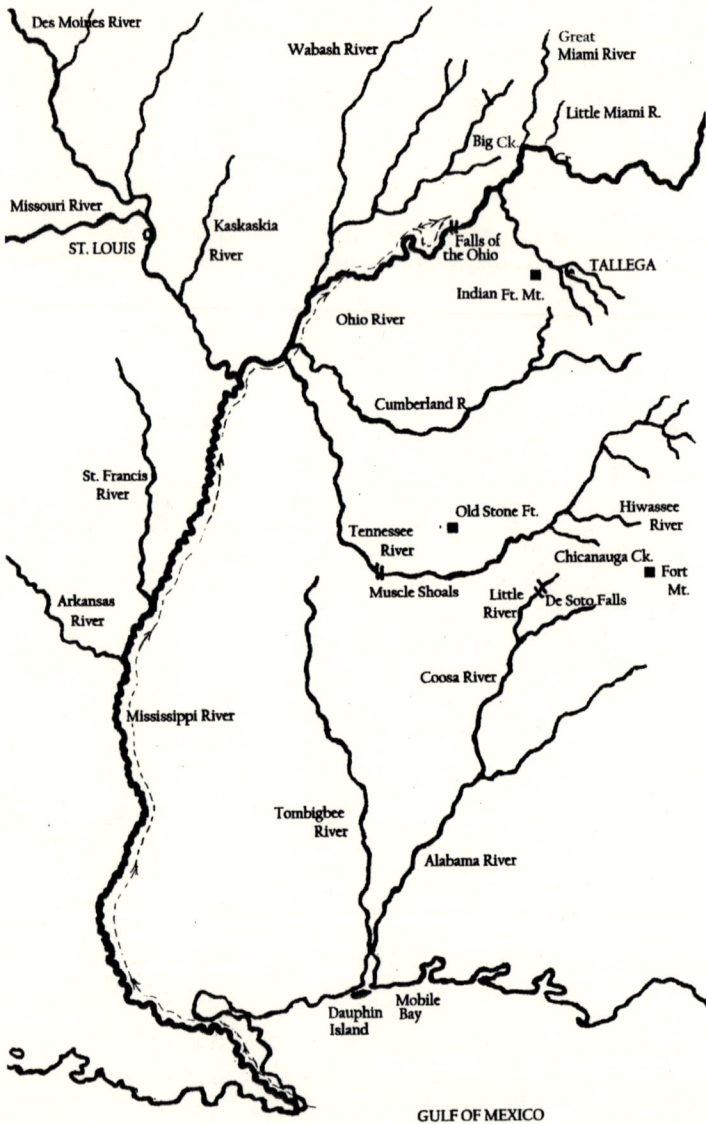

(Fig. 19) The other landing place for Madoc is believed to be the mouth of the Mississippi River. From there the group traveled to the Falls of the Ohio River. A Welsh gravestone found at the Falls was inscribed with the date 1186. In 1660 or shortly thereafter, allied Red Indian forces defeated a strong and vibrant colony of Welsh Indians. After their crushing defeat, remnants of the tribe may have existed for over a century near Kaskaskia in Southern Illinois.

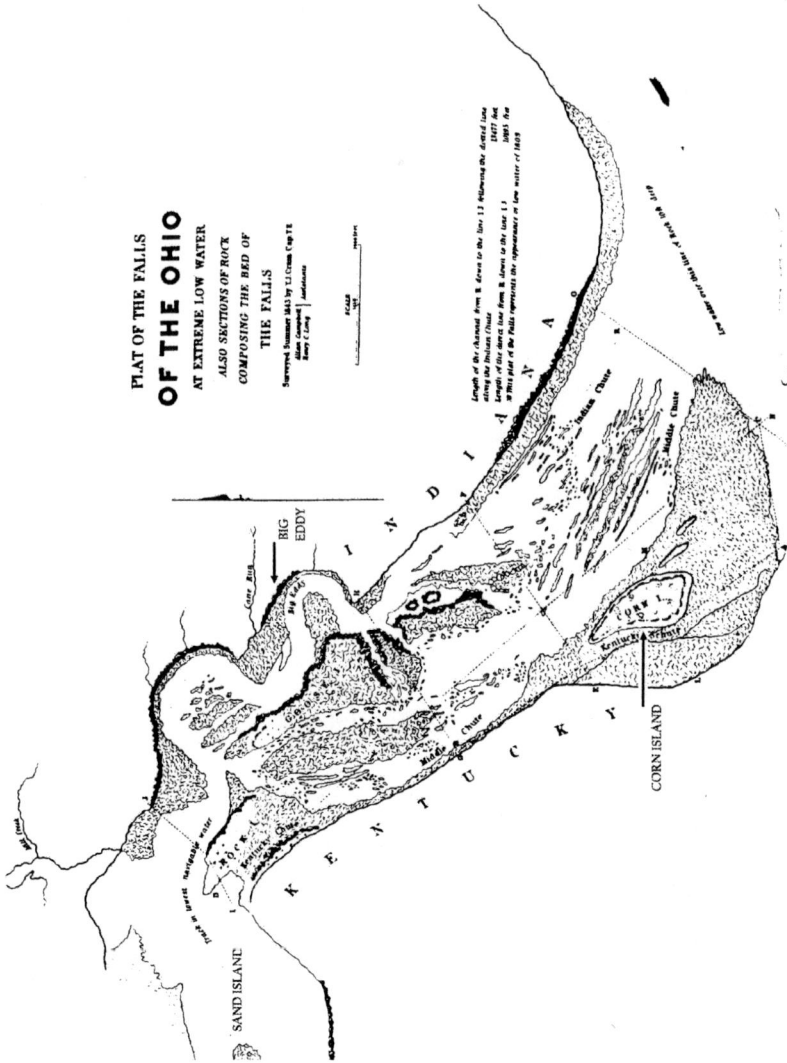

(Fig. 21) This is a map of the Falls of the Ohio as surveyed by T. J. Cram in 1843. It shows the extent of rock exposures before the dams were built.

(Figs. 20A and 20B) Pictured here are a photograph and a drawing of the Thruston Tablet, which was found near Castalian Springs, Tennessee, in 1874. On the left is depicted a battle between round-eyed and almond-eyed warriors. On the right the two are seen making peace. At the top is a Viking-style ship with a square sail and oar holes. At the bottom right, the spear of the fallen-round-eyed warrior is bent, suggesting it was made of metal. (Photo courtesy of the Tennessee State Museum, Tennessee Historical Society Collection, photography by June Dorman)

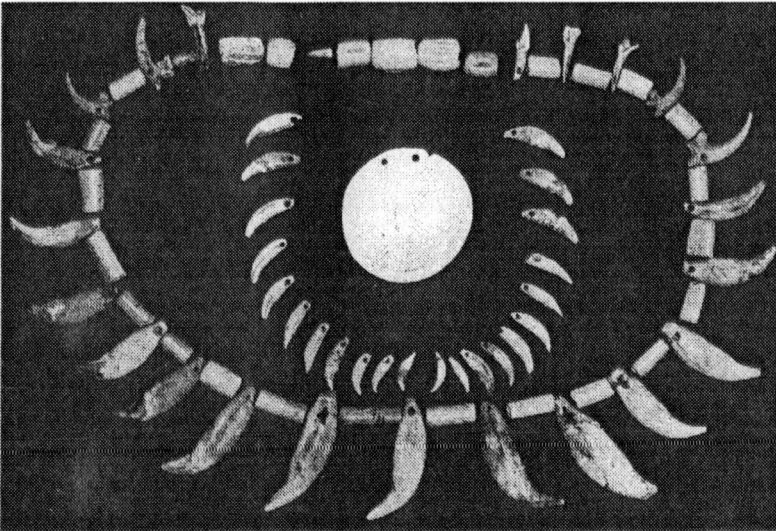

(Fig. 22 - above) The Welsh coat of arms contains a harp and a mermaid, the mermaid signifying a mariner under the charge of Madoc. (Fig. 27 - below) Fox Field in Mason County, Kentucky, contains many artifacts of the Fort Ancient Culture such as these pictured from the collection of S.A. Glass. Other findings at the site reveal that another people inhabited the site for a short period. This is shown by the stone lined underground passageway to nearby Lee's Creek, stone lined graves, and the finding of a bear's tooth with the distinct etching of a Maltese cross. (photograph courtesy of S. A. Glass)

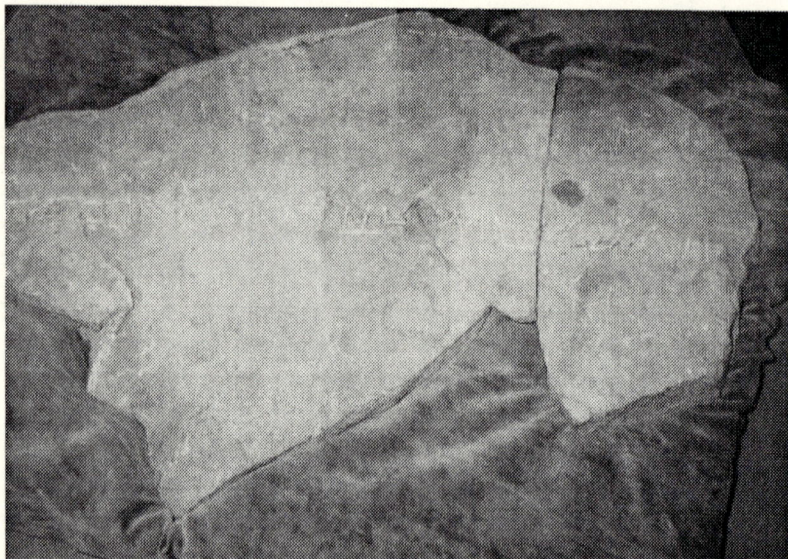

(Fig. 23 - above) The Brandenburg Stone was discovered in 1912 near the banks of the Ohio River in Meade County, Kentucky. The script is in ancient Coelbren as used in Wales. The translation of the stone has been interpreted as a land boundary marker between heirs. (Fig. 25 - below) This is a recent photo of the Big Four Railroad Bridge which connects Louisville, Kentucky, and Jeffersonville, Indiana. The foundations for the bridge were constructed from stones taken from the walls and a quarry at Great Stone Fort (Rose Island). The bridge was completed in 1895.

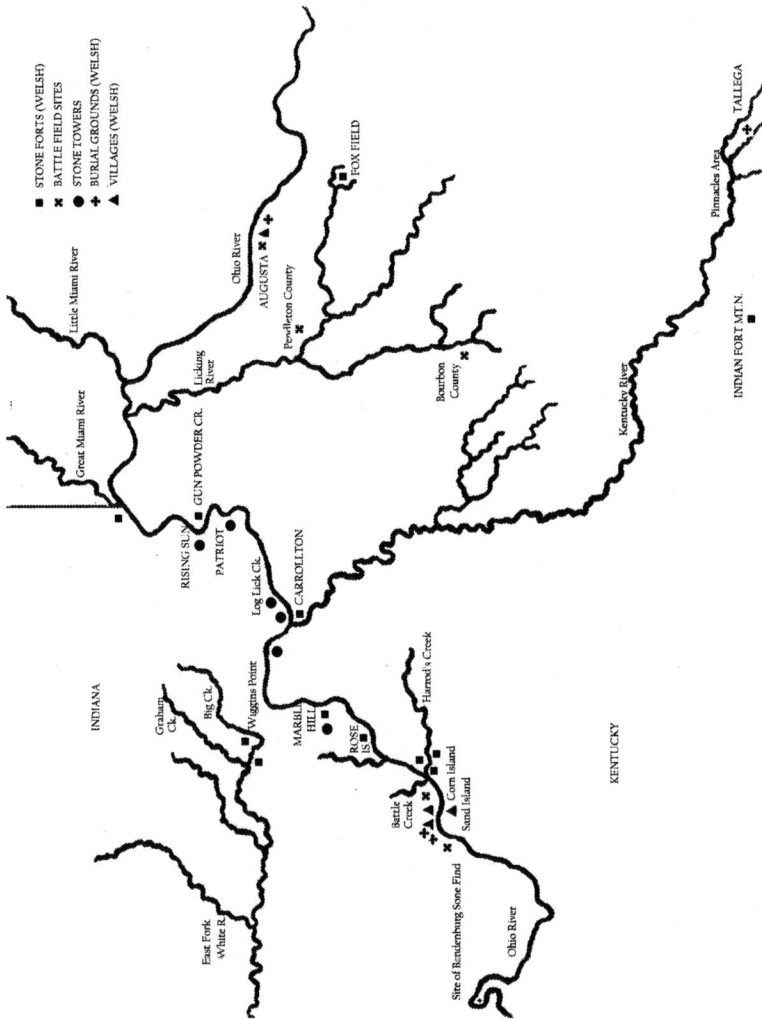

(Fig. 24) Asgens was the Shawnee name for the Welsh who landed at the mouth of the Mississippi and established a formidable nation with its stronghold at the Falls of the Ohio. From this base they sent out colonies into Kentucky, Indiana and Ohio. The map shows known sites of stone forts, stone towers used for communication, villages, battlefields, and burial grounds. Around 1660 a coalition of Indian forces extinguished the flourishing colony in what may have been the bloodiest battle ever to have taken place on American soil.

(Fig. 26) The Mississippian Culture was at its peak at Cahokia from 1050 to 1150 A.D. The community is estimated to have had a population of about twenty thousand people during that time. The influence of meso-American cultures is shown by the truncated pyramids. The huge mound in the background is Monk's Mound, on top of which was a large government building and the home of the chief. Cahokia was protected by a palisaded wall. The community was abandoned in about 1350. (A photograph of an L. K. Townsend painting of Cahokia, Courtesy of Cahokia Mounds State Historic Site)

(Fig. 28 - above) The ancient stone walls described by Bennett Young and mapped by W. G. Burroughs on Indian Fort Mountain are not preserved, but one can make out some of their remains. Pictured are what appear to be remains of a wall on the approach to the East Pinnacle. (Fig. 29 - below) The path to the East Pinnacle at Indian Fort Mountain contains large stone outcrops and overlooks that are ideal for ambush and defense.

(Fig. 30A - above and 30B - top of the next page) These two photos show the commanding view and steep cliffs at Indian Fort Mountain near Berea, Kentucky.

(Fig. 31 - below) The Pinnacles area in western Lee County, Kentucky, contains peaks which tower 1000 feet above the Kentucky River. According to county folklore, the peaks served as lookouts by a people of unknown origin and descent.

(Fig. 32A and 32B) Two round earthen Mandan-style houses. (A) is located at Fort Lincoln State Park. (B) is at the Knife River National Historic Site. Both are in North Dakota.

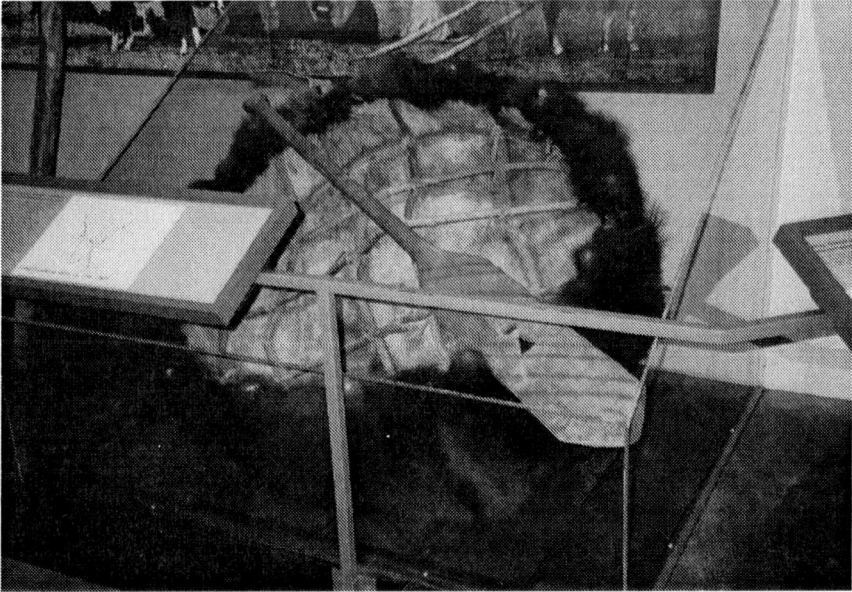

(Fig. 33 - above) This is a 'bull boat' as used by the Mandan, Hidatsa, and Arikara tribes. This one is on display at the North Dakota Heritage Center in Bismarck. The only other places in the world that boats such as this were in use are Wales and Ireland, where they are called coracles. (Fig. 34) Approaching reconstructed Fort Mandan where Lewis and Clark spent the severe winter of 1804-1805. The original Fort Mandan was located across the river from the lower village of the Mandans.

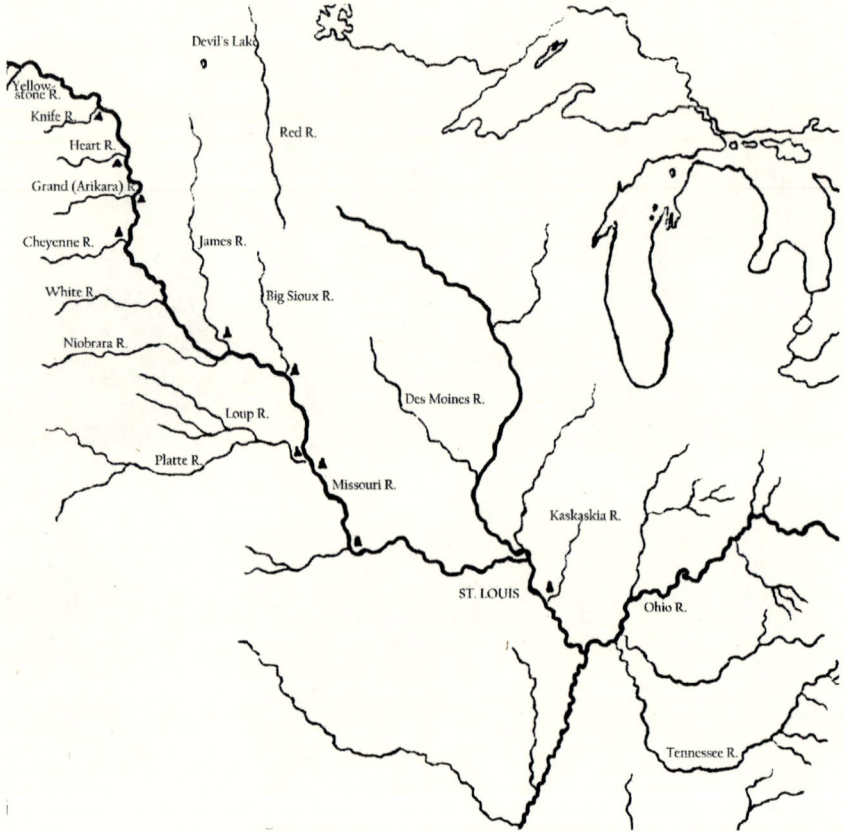

Fig. 35) In 1832, George Catlin located the Mandans far up the Missouri River near the Knife River in what is now North Dakota. In his travels on the Missouri, he identified the ruins of six or seven abandoned villages that he considered to be Mandan. These sites are indicated on the map by a triangle.

(Fig. 36) Chief Ma-to-toh-pa. Painting by George Catlin. (Property of The Smithsonian Institution)

(Fig. 37 - above) The treeless, windswept plain of the Fort Berthold Indian Reservation.
(Fig. 38 - below) The Garrison Dam and spillway.

(Fig. 39A and 39B) Lake Sakakawea.

(Fig. 40 - above) The reconstructed Fort Union. George Catlin spent several weeks in the tower pictured, painting members of the Crow, Blackfeet, and other tribes.
(Fig. 41 - below) The author and Pauline Nez.

(Fig. 42 - above) Round depressions in the ground such as this reveal the locations of the round earthen houses in the old villages of the Mandan and Hidatsa.
(Fig. 43 - below) Billy Fredericks and the author.

(Fig. 44 - above) The Gwenan Gorn on the Ohio River. (Original painting by the author)
(Fig. 49 - below) The National Park at L'Anse aux Meadows, Newfoundland, contains recreations of buildings that were part of the Norse settlement there. Eight complete house sites and one fragmentary one have been excavated by a team led by Anne Stine Ingstad, who estimated the population to have been about seventy. Also found at the site were a smithy and four boat sheds. This site is believed to have been Leif's Camp (Leifsbudir). (Photo courtesy of Parks Canada; André Cornellier, photographer, from *The Viking Discovery of America* by Helge Ingstad and Anne Stine Ingstad).

(Fig. 45) A George Catlin, self portrait done in 1824.

(Fig. 46) This is Catlin's drawing of a grotesque part of the Okipa ceremony. Here, young men of the tribe are hung by rawhide thongs until they lose consciousness. The rawhide is tied to skewers that have been run through their skin and muscles.

(Fig. 47) This is a section of the map drawn by John Evans for the Spanish Governor of Louisiana in 1798. It shows the big and little villages of the Mandans and the villages of the Big Bellies (Gros Ventres, Hidatsa or Minatarees). It is accurate, except for the coordinates. Evans' 46th parallel is actually 45.35, his 47th parallel is 46.20, and his 48th parallel is 47.15. The Copper River is the Heart River and the R a la Bomb is the Cannonball River. South of the mouth of the Cannonball River, Evans has drawn two triangles which he has labelled the 'old village of the Dog Indians." South of this section of map is the Dog River, which corresponds to the Cheyenne River. (From *Madoc and the Discovery of America*, by Richard Deacon. The original map is the property of the Library of Congress.)

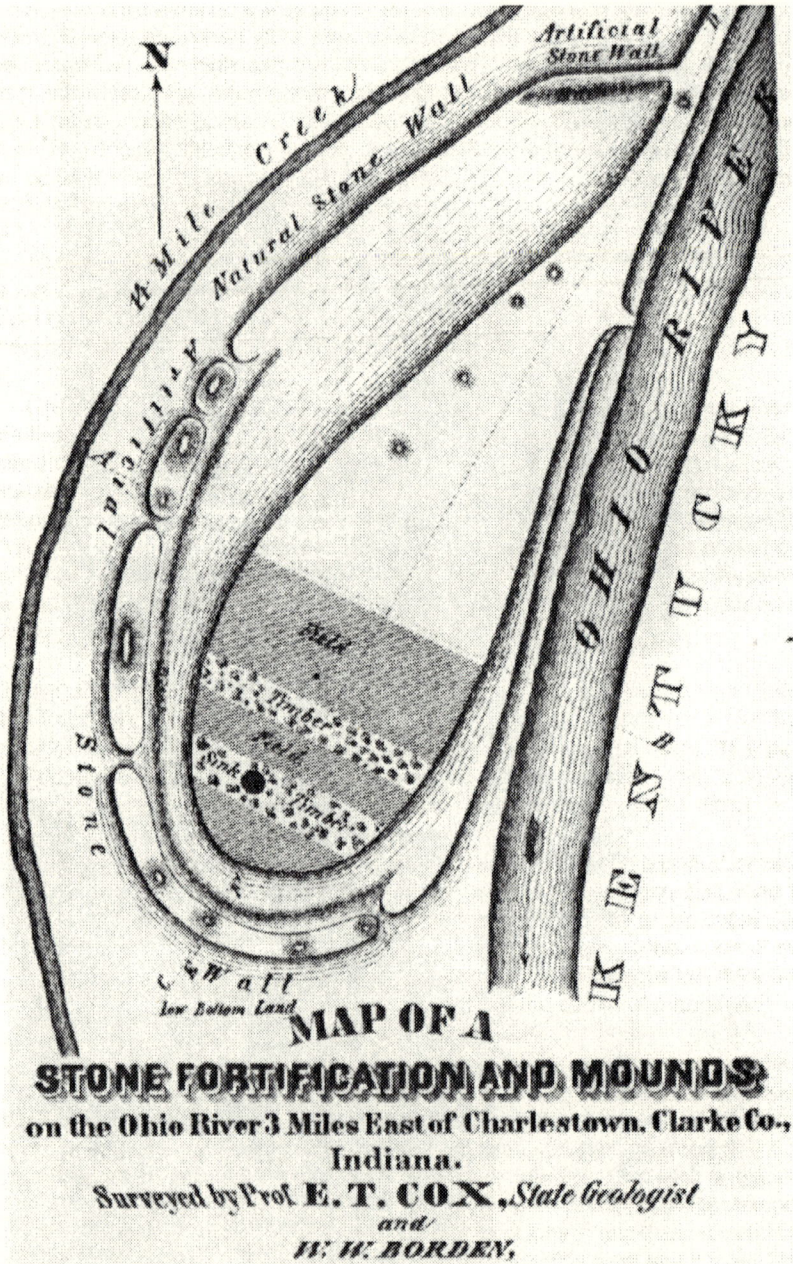

(Fig. 48) Rose Island as seen by Indiana State geologists E. T. Cox and W. W. Borden in 1874. The drawing designates which sections of the walls were considered natural and which sections were considered artificial. (From *The Legend of Prince Madoc and the White Indians*, by Dana Olson)

TABLE OF CONTENTS

FOREWORD
MY STORY   1

PROLOGUE
IN THE BEGINNING   5

BOOK I
THE PATHFINDERS   9

CHAPTER I
THE PALEO-AMERICANS   11

CHAPTER II
THE PHOENICIANS   15

CHAPTER III
THE KELTS   23

CHAPTER IV
THE ALBANS   27

CHAPTER V
ST. BRENDON AND ST. FINBARR   39

CHAPTER VI
THE VIKINGS   41

BOOK II
MADOC THE BOLD   55

CHAPTER VII
TALES FROM WALES   57

CHAPTER VIII
THE VOYAGES   63

BOOK III
  THE WELSH INDIANS   69

CHAPTER IX
  UP THE COOSA RIVER   71

CHAPTER X
  TO THE FALLS OF THE OHIO   89

CHAPTER XI
  THE RED INDIANS   101

CHAPTER XII
  EASTERN ENCOUNTERS   121

BOOK IV
  THE MANDANS   129

CHAPTER XIII
  WESTERN ENCOUNTERS   131

CHAPTER XIV
  FOLLOW YOUR DREAM   147

CHAPTER XV
  LANGUAGE   157

CHAPTER XVI
  THE HIDATSA AND THE ARIKARA   165
    The Hidatsa   165
    The Arikara   170

CHAPTER XVII
  1837   175

CHAPTER XVIII
  THE FATE OF THE MANDAN   181

CHAPTER XIX
  RETRACING THE DREAM   185

EPILOGUE
  CONCLUSIONS   197

BIBLIOGRAPHY   212

INDEX   215

FOREWORD

MY STORY

Thursday, May 21, 1998. On this day my story begins.

My wife and I were visiting our good friends Wendell and Pam McChord in Dayton, Ohio. That evening Wendell showed me his study which also serves as his library. Wendell is a dentist and a quintessential history buff with a special interest in eighteenth century events in Kentucky and Ohio. He also delves into genealogy and has found that his wife and I are distant cousins. That evening he was showing me excerpts from his well stocked and well organized collection of historical literature. One subject caught my eye; it had a byline that included the *White Indians.* There followed a brief text; it was only a paragraph or two, but it piqued my interest. Somewhere, sometime, I've long forgotten where or when, I had previously read something about the White Indians. It had been only an anecdote, no more than a written rumor. But now the text in front of me teased me and led me on by giving a reference. The reference was to a book by Richard Deacon, titled *Madoc and the Discovery of America.*

I soon obtained Deacon's book and read it with intensity. I found it to be a fascinating and well-documented story about Madoc, a Welsh prince who brought hundreds of settlers to America in 1170 and 1171. Other books followed and Wendell fed my new obsession by sending several articles that he had located, some in obscure places. As I read about these people, their story became a puzzle to me: a puzzle in which some of the pieces did not fit. I became convinced that there were misinterpretations, inaccuracies, and faulty

1

conclusions in the accounts of these people, which conflicted with what I regarded as reliable facts. Slowly a picture began to take form in my mind as to who these people were, where they had been, the lives they had led, and the battles they had fought. The picture gradually cleared and solidified and old contradictions that appeared to disprove a point vanished.

In time historical accounts get lost, legends become mystified, and physical evidence deteriorates or is destroyed. I wanted to see what remained firsthand. in Alabama, Georgia, Tennessee, Kentucky, and Indiana, sites where the Welsh are thought to have been. Wendell and I hit the road; and our wives would not be left behind. We visited historical sites, libraries and museums and I called on select local people for their information about the subject. Some of my discoveries were exciting, such as Fort Mountain, Georgia, where a state park has preserved the ruins, and De Soto Falls, Alabama, where cave chambers appear as they must have centuries ago. But most other sites of Welsh Indian occupation reflect little or nothing of the descriptions given by observers in the eighteenth and nineteenth centuries. Most of these sites have suffered from plowing, dismantling, or paving over and are unrecognizable. Some are obliterated forever.

Chasing evanescent physical evidence can be like chasing rainbows, as I recall one search:

> The shadows were growing long when we crossed the Hiwassee River heading north on Route 411. I stopped at a restaurant fortuitously named The Savannah Grill, because then I knew I was near the site I was seeking, the old Savannah Fort on the north bank of the Hiwassee. The fort and a nearby ford were named by the family whose nineteenth century farm contained the fort.
>
> I was disappointed that no one in the restaurant was aware of the old fort, but I proceeded to drive along the narrow road by the river, looking for a sign or a suspicious cairn. Before long, I entered the Hiwassee River Recreation Area and spotted a ranger. I could see that the engine of Ranger Crawford's truck was running and he was preparing to leave for the day, so I quickly approached him and inquired about the fort. He thought for a minute, then called another ranger at his headquarters, but neither was aware of the old fort. After a moment, he mentioned that an archaeological dig had taken place across the highway at the old Savannah Farm, which is now a tree farm. I saw a ray of hope and followed his truck across the highway to the entrance to the tree farm. The gate was closed that Sunday evening, but when I returned the next morning it was open and I entered.

The office staff at the tree farm suggested that I contact Joe Benthal, an archaeologist who had examined the site in 1986 and 1987. Vainly hoping for an impossible sighting, I slowly drove down the narrow gravel road by the river.

The next day I spoke with Benthal, who told me that the area had been a site of habitation for millennia, dating to the Archaic period and possibly before. When English settlers first arrived, it was occupied by the Chero-kee. The early eighteenth century history of the area is sketchy, and includes tales of French explorers from Fort Toulouse on the Tallapoosa River in Alabama, tales of English soldiers and tales of Indian wars. Before that, the history is more vague turning into legend. The Savannah Fort may be entering the legend stage, because I found that it no longer exists. It may have been destroyed when a levee was built on the river. Benthal had heard of the fort but had not found any evidence of its existence on the property. But I still hope that someday, someone will find the location of the old fort because the lower thirty-seven and one half acres, down by the river, are owned by the Archaeology Division of the State of Tennessee and Benthal has done no digs there...

Numerous references that I read had linked the Mandan Indian tribe to the Welsh Indians and at last I decided to go to North Dakota, home of the Mandans. I visited there in June, 2003. Before leaving for North Dakota I had begun writing and had completed seventeen chapters. The trip was so elucidating that I subsequently added two more chapters and rewrote several others.

In relating the story of Madoc and the Welsh Indians, I begin with events that occurred far back in time. This is to show that the discovery of America by Europeans as well as Asians was a continuum and related discoveries took place many times well before 1492. This is not to belittle the accomplishment of Christopher Columbus. Columbus discovered America, but his was a rediscovery; he was not the first European to do so. I am confident in declaring that he was preceded by thousands of others.

In this book I have avoided using the term "Native American" to describe any group; I consider the term confusing. The term has become a political term and does not mean what it says. I am a native American. I was born in America, as were my father and my grandfather. But in applying for a position with government or to a university, should I claim that I am a native American, I could be charged with fraud and any advantages would be taken away. In its place I have used the older term, "Red Indians." This term may have been used first by John Cabot and the English to describe the Beothuks of Newfoundland who

3

painted themselves with red paint. Also "Red Indians"" conveniently contrasts with "White Indians," which is one of the terms used for the Welsh tribes of Madoc.

I have found it disheartening that scientists are sometimes so singularly devoted to their own field that they neglect all others. This is true in nearly all branches of science and includes historians, archaeologists, anthropologists, paleontologists, geneticists and linguists. Their self-imposed blinders result in incomplete and inaccurate conclusions, which unfortunately may become generally accepted.

The legend of Prince Madoc and the Welsh Indians is a remarkable story of a brave, resourceful and intelligent people and the footprints they left in the New World. It is a story that needs to be told and needs to be heard for it has been scorned and neglected by modern historians. It is not a happy story, but it can grip the beholder with intrigue and emotion. At times the Welsh Indians enjoyed tremendous success, but at their peaks they encountered enemies they could not overcome in the form of large and powerful Red Indian forces that devastated them and a tiny virus that decimated them.

It was not my intention to write about the history of these people in an academic style and historians may fault what I say, but the facts are presented and I believe that what they have told me is true. The physical evidence is real, the legends persist, and the personal accounts are documented. These things comprise the footprints of the Welsh Indians and this is the story that they tell.

PROLOGUE

IN THE BEGINNING

Scientific studies on human DNA have succeeded in tracing the roots of the human race. Mitochondrial DNA is inherited only from the mother. From studies on this material it has been shown that *Eve*, the maternal ancestor of us all, lived a little more than 200,000 years ago. The Y chromosome is passed only from father to son. From this chromosome it has been shown that *Adam* was a much more recent individual, who lived about 65,000 years ago. The discrepancy that created a much older Eve than Adam is explained by Adam and his male ancestors having multiple wives.

Adam was born in Africa, probably in Ethiopia or the Sudan, and he is the ancestor of all men alive today. The genetic evidence for this man being the original Adam exists in markers on the Y chromosomes of men from all over the world. The time of Adam's existence is determined by extrapolation from a known mutation rate, which creates the markers. These mutations are discoverable using newer techniques of genetic research. Peter Underhill and his colleagues at Stanford University have discovered enough markers of these mutations on the Y chromosomes of men living today that the ancient migrations of our ancestors can be traced. Spencer Wells has described these migrations in his book, *The Journey of Man.*[1] Using this data I have brazenly condensed 65,000 years of human pre-history into the next few paragraphs.

---

1. Wells, Spencer, The Journey of Man: A Genetic Odyssey, Princeton University Press, Princeton, New Jersey, 2003.

Humans were a few small bands living in the Rift Valley of northeastern Africa 65,000 years ago, when the mutation that begot Adam occurred. Not long after that a mutation occurred that produced a man carrying a marker called M-168. His Y chromosome is carried by all non-African men living today. It was only a few thousand years later that a small group of these M-168 people left Africa for the coast of Arabia. This is indicated by a marker on the Y chromosome of these people called M-130. The M-130 people migrated along the coasts of Arabia, India and Southeast Asia. They crossed the water to Australia and Melanesia. Today, the purest descendants of these people are the inhabitants of the Andaman Islands in the Bay of Bengal. They are small with dark-skin and resemble Africans. They are called *Negritos*.[2]

About 45,000 years ago another migration of people carrying the M-168 marker occurred. These people left Africa and entered the Levant (eastern Mediterranean area). They have been identified by a marker on their Y chromosome designated M-89. They were not the first people to leave Africa for the Levant. Findings in caves in Israel reveal the presence of humans as early as 110,000 years ago, but these earlier people were few in number and their existence was not sustained.[3]

The M-89 people had better methods of survival than those who preceded them; they hunted cooperatively and practiced a pattern of seasonal migrations in order to follow a food source. They increased in numbers and their tribes divided and moved on. Some migrated to Central Asia, where about 35,000 years ago one tribe became three, as again indicated by markers on their Y chromosomes. The M-20 group migrated south to Pakistan and India. The M-175 group went east into China, and the third group, the M-45, became the ancestors of Europeans. For the purposes of this story, it is remarkable that the M-45 group also spawned the Siberians, who are the ancestors of more than ninety percent of the Red Indians of America.[4]

During the Ice Age the northern and mountainous areas of Europe were covered with ice, but it was much warmer in places like Jericho in the lower Jordan valley and along the shores of the Dead Sea. These places were below sea level, and the warmer climate allowed many more varieties of trees and other plants to grow. The oldest urban settlement ever excavated dates to 8500 B.C. and is at Jericho.[5]

---

2. Wells, p.75.
3. Wells, p.98.
4. Wells, p.118.

About 8000 B.C. the world began experiencing a sudden transition from hunting and gathering to a settled life. This happened about the same time in several independent locations.[6] Gordon Chiles placed the hub of this transition north of the Black Sea.[7] Archaeologist Marija Bimbutas located it in the Russian steppes and Ukraine, and Colin Renfrew, a linguist, located the center of this transition in Anatolia.[8] Central to these areas is the Black Sea.

During the colder times of the Ice Age, the Black Sea lost most of its affluent waters, which at other times flowed into it from the north. The headwaters of the Danube, Dniester, Dnieper and Don Rivers were frozen and these rivers emitted but a trickle downstream. The Black Sea was a large freshwater lake that was losing more water by evaporation than it took in from the frozen rivers and it began to shrink. The Bosporus Channel was not in existence and there was a land bridge between Europe and Asia in its place. The River Sakarya, which had been the effluent channel from the Black Sea to the Mediterranean, dried up. The river valley of the Sakarya filled with earth and became a meadow, then a forest. As the level of the Black Sea sank, its coastline receded, exposing a flood plain, which at one time was as much as three hundred feet below the present sea level. This warm, fertile area became a magnet for settlement. In time the people living in this salubrious clime learned to build houses with stone, wood, earth and mud bricks. They congregated into groups and divided the duties of labor among themselves. Towns sprang up. Being coastal dwellers, they learned to build boats with which they could fish and travel. They began planting trees and plants that were useful to them and they learned to domesticate several animals. Civilization was born.[9]

But by 8000 B.C. the Ice Age was ending. The ice was melting and the levels of the oceans and the Mediterranean Sea were rising. One day a wise old man perched on a mountain overlooking the River Bosporus, which cascaded into the Black Sea, noted that the level of the Sea of Marmara to the south was considerably higher than that of the Black Sea to the north. He could see that the waters to the south were lapping against the isthmus, threatening to come tumbling into the River Bosporus and on into the Black Sea. We know him as Noah. About 5600 B.C. (7600 years ago), it happened. Torrential rains and

---

5. Wells, p.148.
6. Wells, p.149.
7. Wells, p.164.
8. Wells, p.165.
9. Mallory, J. P., In Search of the Indo-Europeans, Thames and Hudson, London, 1989.

perhaps an earthquake (the North Anatolian fault runs directly through the area) so weakened the narrow land bridge separating the Sea of Marmara from the headwaters of the River Bosporus that the floodgates opened. At first only a trickle, but soon a torrent of salt water came rushing down into the freshwater lake carving a deep gorge in the floor of the Black Sea immediately to the north of the newly formed strait. The people of the fledgling civilization surrounding the Black Sea had to seek higher ground quickly or perish, because in the shallow areas the shore line advanced as much as one mile a day. A diaspora of these people ensued. A group of tribes known as Indo-Europeans migrated up the Danube and into Europe; other Indo-European tribes journeyed east and settled in Iran and India. Other tribes of the Black Sea peoples went to Egypt and became the predynastic Egyptians. Into the Middle East went people who became the Semites, and into Central Asia went the Tocharians. The Black Sea people brought their knowledge with them to every place they went.[10]

The sudden mass outpouring of these people upset living relations all over the Eurasian continent. With their superior methods and larger tribal groups, the new arrivals were able to push out, and onward, the former inhabitants of an area. In the Balkans there is evidence of a protracted struggle between the autochthonous people and the Indo-European invaders between 4500 and 3500 B.C. The earlier skeletal remains found in the Balkans are of a physically smaller people than those found after 3500 B.C. After that date, the villages showed evidence of fortification and were located much closer together indicating a larger population. The pottery and other artifacts also reflect a shift in the population.[11] In Central Asia the Siberian clan was forced to migrate to the east. Some of the Siberians may have become aware that others had crossed the waters in the east and entered a new land. What had been a trickle of infrequent arrivals to Alaska by small groups of wanderers during the Ice Age, grew into a wave that followed wave.

---

10. William Ryan and Walter Pitman, Noah's Flood, Simon and Schuster, New York, 1998.
11. Mallory, p.238-242 and p.260.

BOOK I

THE PATHFINDERS

CHAPTER I

THE PALEO-AMERICANS

Men occasionally stumble onto the truth, but most pick themselves up
and hurry on as if nothing had happened.
                                                        Winston Churchill

In July of 1996, two college students were walking along a shallow area of
the Columbia River at Kennewick, Washington when they discovered a human
skull. A nearly complete skeleton was found nearby. The sheriff initially thought
it was a case of homicide, and the coroner's first impression was that it was the
skeleton of a 19th Century American settler. One finding made him change his
mind. That was the discovery on x-ray of an ancient Cascade type spear point
embedded in the pelvis bone. The spear head was clearly Cascade as it had a
serrated edge, convex base and was unnotched. Radio carbon dating placed the
skeleton at 9500 years old, or dating to 7500 B.C. Anthropologists found him to
be typical of the earliest Americans, deemed Paleo-Americans, and classified him
as Caucasoid. They have been unanimous in declaring that he is definitely not
associated with any Red Indian group, all of which are classified
anthropologically as Mongoloid. (Fig. 1)[12]

Before a complete scientific examination could be done, the Department of
Interior acceded to demands by several Indian tribes and the remains were

---

12. Fell, Barry, Bronze Age America, Little, Brown and Company, Boston,1982, p.93.

confiscated. The site of the discovery was then covered over with rock by the Army Corps of Engineers.

Kennewick Man has become the thirty-ninth example of Paleo-American remains discovered in the U.S. The skeleton of Kennewick Man was nearly complete, and like the thirty-eight others does not classify as a match to any people alive today. His closest living relatives appear to be the Ainu of Japan, the Australian Aborigines and the Polynesians, all descendants of the Coastal people, who left Africa over 50,000 years ago as shown by the M-130 Y chromosome marker that they carried. These people migrated along the coasts of Arabia and India to Southeast Asia, and then up the coast of Asia to the Bering Strait. They are generally thought to have entered America about 15,000 years ago, but some believe that they arrived much earlier than that. The Monte Verde site in southern Chile has been excavated by Tom Dillehay of the University of Kentucky and has been carbon dated at thirty thousand years. Sites in Pennsylvania, Virginia and South Carolina have been dated to fifteen to twenty thousand years.[13]

The skulls of the Paleo-Americans were defined as "Caucasoid" because they were the longer or dolichocephalic skulls typical of Europeans. But these people were not Caucasians, nor were they members of the Siberian clan, which begot the Red Indians. Their journey from Africa can be traced by their anthropology and the M-130 markers on the Y chromosomes of their kinsmen, the Ainu, Australians and Polynesians.

The Paiute Indians of Nevada and California have a legend that their ancestors exterminated a race of red haired giants whom they called the *Sitecah.* The Paiutes described these people as being warlike. According to the legend, the last of the Sitecah were driven into a cave in front of which the Indians piled brush which they ignited, burning and suffocating the cave's occupants. Remains of a relatively tall people with the skulls of Paleo-Americans have been found near Lovelock, Spirit Cave, Pyramid Lake, and in the Humboldt Lake Basin, all in Nevada. Carbon dating of the mummified remains of the Spirit Cave Man placed him at 10,700 years old.[14]

---

13. Chatters, James C., Ancient Encounters, Kennewick Man and the First Americans, Simon and Schuster, 2001; and, Nugent, John, 'Who Were the Original Native Americans?' The Barnes Review, v.5 no.3 p.5, 1999; and, Editorial, The Barnes Review, v.5 no.3, 1999.

14. Chatters, James C. and McNallen, Steve, "Indian Tribal Folklore Reveals Evidence of a Vanished Tribe of Caucasoids in North America," The Barnes Review, v.5, no.3, p. 9, 1999.

The Horn Shelter site in Texas is another place where well preserved skeletal remains of Paleo-Americans have been found. It contained the skeleton of a middle aged man and a girl of about twelve years.[15]

Migration across the Bering Strait by Paleo-Americans as well as the Red Indians was not a one time event but occurred in waves. Migrations by the Paleo-Americans occurred during interstadial or warmer periods, when they could walk across the Bering Strait, and ceased when the ice returned. With each subsequent migration, earlier arrivals moved farther south, eventually to the tip of South America. This pattern was also followed by the Red Indians. For example, the Maya have been shown to have been living in Oregon in 5000 B.C.[16] Evidence points to the Paleo-Americans being a marine people and depending on seafood for their survival. This is reflected by their coastal migration routes in Asia, and it explains their migratory route along the west coast of America. The East Coast sites are explainable by the crossing of the cordillera in Central America and subsequent migration up the Atlantic shore.

Skeletal evidence shows that the Paleo-Americans led a precarious existence; the skeletons of the men exhibit multiple fractures and head wounds. The women have all been small in stature and with a delicate body build. All examples of the women have shown them to be relatively young at the time of their death, indicating a short life span. The skeletons of various Paleo-Americans are not only markedly different from any existing people, but they are also significantly different from each other. This fact and the wounds that reflect battles with other men are consistent with the migration of different, however related small tribes of Paleo-Americans across the Bering Strait at different times.[17]

The present interstadial, or interglacial warm period, began about 8000 B.C. For most of the period before that, ice would have prevented penetration into America. This isolated and protected the Paleo-Americans from invasion until around 7000 B.C. All remains of ancient Americans that have been carbon dated to 9000 years old (7000 B.C.) or older are of the dolichocephalic type. In North America, most remains found that date to 6000 B.C. or later are of the brachycephalic or Red Indian type. The arrival of the Indians is presumed to have prompted the eventual extinction of the Paleo-Americans either through warfare or failure to compete.

---

15. Chatters, p.196.
16. Duncan, James, personal communication, 2002.
17. Chatters, Chapter Nine.

In South America, the Paleo-Americans were able to survive for a longer period and evidence suggests that they did not become totally extinct until the time of Christ.[18]

The demise of the Paleo-Americans may be due in large part to the size of their tribes. The Paleo-Americans lived in small groups consisting of no more than several related families, and they never developed a large population. Their numbers were limited by their migratory hunter-gatherer culture, their propensity for warfare against each other, and perhaps most importantly by a low birth rate of about 2.8 children per adult female. Their low birth rate is reflected by lines (called "Harris lines") in the long bones of children, which indicate the age of weaning. For Paleo-Americans this age has been placed at an average of three and one-half years and sometimes as late as five years. A short life expectancy in the precarious environment in which they lived led to an exceedingly slow population growth rate. Any disaster could spell extinction.[19]

A lack of genetic diversity among the Red Indians reveals that a small population or genetic bottleneck occurred at some point in their migrations. But the Siberians who spawned the Red Indians were well adjusted to living in Arctic and Subarctic climates. Their superior food gathering skills, as exemplified by cooperative hunting and seasonal migrations, allowed their numbers to increase rapidly into the thousands after they entered Alaska and western Canada.[20]

The various peoples that crossed the Bering Strait in antiquity were diverse. There is skeletal evidence that a population of prognathic pygmies once lived in America. Their remains have been unearthed in Tennessee, California and elsewhere. They resemble a similar people living in Malaya and the Philippines today, who are thought to have originated in southern Mongolia. The site in Tennessee has been carbon dated to 2160 B.C. Pygmy remains at that site were found adjacent to those of Red Indians. The skull of an adult pygmy was comparable in size to that of an average seven-year-old child. These people came to America much later than the Paleo-Americans and were not their contemporaries, but the presence of their remains underscores the diversity of the early immigrants to America.[21]

---

18. Chatters.
19. Chatters, Chapter Nine.
20. Wells, Spencer, The Journey of Man, a Genetic Odyssey, Princeton University Press, 2002, p.141.
21. Fell, p.87.

CHAPTER II

THE PHOENICIANS

Some Phoenicians came, notorious sailors, rogues, and brought all kinds of geegaws in their black ship. Now in my father's house there was a Phoenician woman, large and comely... who knew how to do fine work too.

The Phoenicians led her astray... and seduced her by the empty ship... (The woman stated,) "I am proud to come from Sidon, the town rich in ore, and I am the daughter of Arybas, who is very rich..."[22]

I made for a ship and begged the Phoenician crew for mercy, paying those decent hands a hearty share of plunder... but a heavy galewind blew them way off course... they'd no desire to cheat me.[23]

Homer

Homer was well acquainted with the Phoenicians. To him they were fine sailors, skilled artisans, crafty merchants and entrepreneurs, and slavers.

The Phoenicians were a Semitic people who migrated to Mesopotamia after the Great Flood. Later they settled in the eastern Mediterranean area (the Levant) bringing with them their culture and customs. By the beginning of the Bronze Age in 3500 B.C. they had founded the city states of Byblos, Sidon and Tyre.[24] Being on the Mediterranean and in the Fertile Crescent, the Phoenician city states were at the center of trade in the ancient world. The contribution of

---

22. Herm, Gerhard, The Phoenicians, The Purple Empire of the Ancient World, William Morrow and Co., New York, 1975, p.161.

23. Homer, The Odyssey, Book 13, line 305-315.

24. Miller, Madeleine S. and Miller, J. Land, Harper's Bible Dictionary, Harper and Rowe, New York, 1973, p.553-556.

Phoenicia to civilization is daunting, especially considering that they not only served as a conduit for the spread of innovations and advancements, but they actually were the inventors of many of the cultural and technical innovations of the times. They are credited with inventing the Greek alphabet and the sail; they developed shipbuilding, metallurgy, cloth and dye production, glass making, lumber products, and agricultural products. It is the Phoenicians who are responsible for the legend of the Great Flood.

Phoenician sea captains guarded their maps carefully and controlled the trade of the world through ruthless commercial tactics. They blockaded the Pillars of Hercules (Strait of Gibraltar) to prevent competitors from discovering their sources of trade. From a historian's standpoint their Achilles heel is that they were so overwhelmingly bent on acquiring wealth that they became ultra secretive and totally unsharing with their knowledge. As a result we are only aware of their explorations, routes and destinations through indirect evidence and the writings of Greek historians.

Phoenicia emerged as a nation of traders and seafarers when the sail came into use around 3500 B.C. They developed trading monopolies in North Africa, western Europe and on the west coast of Africa. They found copper deposits on Cyprus and developed the tin mines of Cornwall. They were renowned shipbuilders and built and captained the ships of the navies of Solomon in 960 B.C. and later the huge navy of Xerxes, which battled the Greeks in the Aegean Sea in 480 B.C. The Greek historian Herodotus, in the fourth book of his History, describes Phoenician sailors sailing around Africa in 600 B.C., two thousand years before the Portuguese. They accomplished this feat by sailing clockwise around the continent, beginning in the Red Sea. Herodotus also wrote: "The Phoenicians could sail for thousands of miles without falling off the edge of the earth."[25]

Phoenicians were the first to utilize the North Star for navigation and could determine their latitude at a very early date. In 335 B.C., Aristotle wrote that Phoenicians had discovered an island in the Atlantic, many days journey from the Pillars of Hercules, with navigable rivers, woods and succulent fruits.

Plutarch, a Greek historian living around A.D. 100, found some old parchments in the ruins of the Phoenician city of Carthage. He translated them as saying, "Sail westward from Britain and you will pass three island groups on a

---

25. Deacon, Richard, Madoc and the Discovery of America, George Braziller, New York, 1966; and, Cahill, Robert E., New England's Ancient Mysteries, Old Saltbox Publishing House, Salem Massachusetts, 1993, p.6.

northwest bearing, where the sun sets in midsummer. These are equidistant from one another, and also from an island called Ogygia, which lies in the arms of the ocean five days sailing from Britain." This is an accurate summary of the proximity of the Orkney, Shetland, and Faeroe Islands to one another, and to Iceland, which is Ogygia.

Plutarch's translation continues, "If you continue to sail westward for another 5000 stades, you will reach the northern coast of a continent, Eperios, that rims the great ocean... if you sail along this coast in a southward direction, you will pass a frozen sea and come to a land where Greeks have settled." Plutarch apparently did not believe the sea was frozen and formed the opinion this was an old and confused notion. However, the southern part of Davis Strait between Labrador and Greenland becomes an impassable mass of floating ice during the summer season, although far-northern navigation can be performed.[26]

The Phoenicians established colonies in Africa, Europe and presumably America as well. At one time Carthage, a North African Phoenician colony, was losing so many of its people from emigration that its rulers put to death sailors who returned with stories that told of finding favorable new lands.[27]

There is evidence that the Mayan Indians and the Olmecs before them may have had considerable exposure to people of the old world, especially Phoenicians. Frances Gibson, the author of *The Seafarers*, has described many parallels between the Mayas and the Phoenicians, and as Gibson states, "coincidence stretches only so far; there are too many analogies."[28] In 500 B.C. there were only two places in the world where the sciences of mathematics and astronomy were advanced. Those places were Babylon and Maya. Olmec and Mayan sculptures depict men of a variety of races, some are Oriental, some Negroid and there is especially a bearded Semitic type. All are male. The Mayan rain god, Tlaloc, sports a handlebar moustache and beard and holds a thunderbolt as does his Phoenician counterpart. Indians do not have beards or moustaches. Mayan sculptures also reflect similarities to Hindu and Buddhist idols. The Mayan pyramids at Teotihuacan and other places suggest contact with Egyptians. In addition several languages, including those of the Zuni, Pima

---

26. Olson, Dana, The Legend of Prince Madoc and the White Indians, Jeffersonville, Indiana, 1987, p.viii.
27. Gibson, Frances M., The Seafarers: Pre-Columbian Voyages to America, Dorrance and Co., Philadelphia, 1974, Chapter Two.
28. Gibson, p.108.

and Micmac Indians, have been shown to have roots in North Africa, including Egypt and Carthage. If the Olmecs and Mayas did have exposure to diverse peoples from the old world, the Phoenicians, as the traders and sea travelers that they were, would have had the singular ability to bring these peoples to the New World.[29]

Following the founding of Carthage in 814 B.C., a western Phoenician Empire was built in Northwest Africa and on the Iberian peninsula. Iberian Phoenicia was populated not only by Phoenicians, but also by their predecessors. According to Gibson, there was a considerable amount of intermarriage between the Phoenicians and the native people of Iberia (Tartessians, Iberians and Basques). Fell considers the autochthonous people of Iberia to be Basque. The Basques were related to the Picts of Brittany and to the aborigines of Britain, whom Mowat calls the *Albans*. In 1101 B.C., nearly three centuries before the founding of Carthage, Phoenicians traders established Cadiz, the oldest city in Europe, and the Phoenician script spread throughout Iberia.[30] The Kelts arrived in Iberia about 800 B.C.[31] The Punic Wars with Rome began in 264 B.C. and ended with the destruction of Carthage in 146 B.C. After that, Rome was able to close the Mediterranean to Phoenician traders. The historian Robert Ellis Cahill reports that after the defeat of Carthage, Phoenicians sailed away from North Africa in great numbers, never to be seen again. Their destination has never been discovered.[32]

In West Virginia three separate stone tablets have been dated to 800 B.C. One of these tablets, "The Grave Creek Stone", is a grave stone that was discovered in 1838. The stones have inscriptions that originally were thought to be of Viking origin, but now are identified as Iberian-Phoenician as has a birch bark manuscript from A.D. 272 found in New England. A burial mound stone found in the 1880s along Bat Creek in east Tennessee is inscribed in ancient Hebrew or Aramaic and has been dated at A.D. 100.[33]

The Phoenicians may have ventured as far north and west as Lake Superior in ancient times. An old Menominee Indian legend tells of white men, called

---

29. Deacon; and, Olson.

30. Gibson, p.131.

31. Fell, Barry, Bronze Age in America, Little Brown and Co., Boston, 1982, p.248; and, Mowat, Farley, The Farfarers: Before the Norse, Steerforth Press, South Royalton, Vermont, 2000.

32. Cahill; and, Angel, Paul Tudor, 'Who Built New England's Megalithic Monuments?' The Barnes Review, 1997, v.3, no.11, p.17.

33. Fell, p.256; and, The Brandenburg Stone Exhibit, Meade Co. Ky. Public Library, on loan to the Charlestown, IN. Public Library, 2001.

Marine Men, who were travelers from across the Sunrise Sea. The legend states that long ago they arrived in great canoes to upper Michigan. There they "sinned by wounding Mother Earth, digging into her flesh to tear out her shining bones which they then carried back across the sea." Similar legends exist among the Attiwandeton and Chippewa tribes. Punic and Keltic inscriptions are said to have been found "by the score" in the Michigan copper area.[34]

Indeed there was a colossal mining enterprise on the Keewenaw Peninsula of Upper Michigan and on Isle Royale in Lake Superior. Activity at these mine sites has been carbon dated as beginning suddenly about 3000 B.C. and ending suddenly about 1200 B.C., dates which correspond to the European Bronze age. (Bronze is an alloy composed mostly of copper with a small percentage of tin). A huge amount of copper was removed from pit mines and trenches amounting to between 250,000 and four million tons in eighteen centuries of mining.[35]

During the European Bronze Age, the Paleo-Indians in the Lake Superior area were few in number and had a primitive hunter-gatherer culture. Farming, ceramic pottery and the bow and arrow were unknown to them. They did use float copper, which is exposed, relatively pure copper found on the surface, to make trinkets and an occasional spearhead. There is no way these people could be responsible for the colossal mining enterprise in upper Michigan and on Isle Royale, although some Indians may have worked as laborers.

At the site of one mine, ten wagon loads of well made stone tools were removed in 1848. It has been estimated that ten thousand men would have been needed to work the mines during the summer months for the eighteen centuries that it was in operation.[36]

The miners were astute at identifying subterranean ore and sophisticated in removing it by heating large underground boulders of copper with fire and then cooling it suddenly with water. This fractured the rock and allowed them to remove it. The northern Michigan and Isle Royale ore deposits were rediscovered in the 19th century and are mined to this day, however there have

---

34. Angel, Paul Tudor; and Joseph, Frank, 'More Evidence for a Lost Civilization in Ancient America,' The Barnes Review, v.7 no.5 p. 11.

35. The Aboriginal Research Club, Detroit, compilers of Ancient Copper Mines of Upper Michigan, ca. 1941; and Slaymaker, J.S., 'Rediscovering the Forgotten White Ancestors of Many American Indians,' The Barnes Review, v.7, no.5, p. 5; and, Fell, p. 261; and, Corliss, William R., Ancient Infrastructure, Remarkable Roads, Mines, Walls, Mounds, Stone Circles, The Sourcebook Project, Glen Arm, Maryland, 1999, p. 109-113.

36. Joseph, Frank, 'More evidence...,' p.11.

not been any new leads discovered that were not previously mined by the ancients.[37]

At Rock Lake in southern Wisconsin the winters are much milder than at Keewenaw. Ancient funeral mounds that contain mining tools and remains of a people who are not thought to be Indian date to the period of the European Bronze Age. The stone sepulchres at Rock Lake are now mostly under water as the lake level has risen for the past four millennia. Also near Rock Lake is a stone monolith not unlike those found in Britain and western Europe. Stone petroglyphs are also present at this site. These petroglyphs are of undetermined origin although one may be Indo-European (Keltic).

Winters on the Keewenaw Peninsula and Isle Royale are severe to the point of threatening survival. It has been postulated that the miners spent the winters at Rock Lake where they buried their dead as there are no ancient burial grounds on Keewenaw or Isle Royale.[38]

One route for the copper trade appears to have been through the Great Lakes. A site near Toronto has been found that contained a thousand or so copper artifacts. Radio carbon dating has indicated the site was occupied around 3000 B.C.[39]

During the Bronze Age, Europe and the Middle East were in a frenzy of copper trading. Old world sources for the metal, such as Cyprus, were sparse and of low quality unlike the Michigan source. It is thought that the bulk of the large amount of copper utilized in Europe during this time came by ship from the upper Michigan and Isle Royale mines. When the Bronze Age ended suddenly about 1200 B.C., the miners would have been left stranded. Indian legends of the Chippewa and Attiwandeton tribes have it that the Marine Men were exterminated in a series of bloody clashes with native tribes.[40]

A French missionary in the mid 18th century described an idol of worship in an area Indian tribe as being a one foot high statue of pure copper. It was a statue of a man with a beard.[41]

In 1877 the Nez Perce Chief Joseph was captured. Found in his medicine bag was a cuneiform tablet that dated to 2042 B.C. The chief claimed that it was

37. The Aboriginal Research Club, Detroit, compilers of Ancient Copper Mines of Upper Michigan, ca.1941; and, Joseph, Frank, 'More evidence...,' p.11.

38. Joseph, Frank, 'Wisconsin's Sunken City,' The Barnes Review, v.6 no.6 p.63.

39. Fell, p.130.

40. Slaymaker, J.S., p.5.

41. Angel, Paul Tudor, p.17.

an inheritance from his white ancestors that brought great knowledge to his people eons ago.

How could ancient Phoenicians or Europeans discover copper mines located so far inland? Perhaps, some time before 3000 BC, European mariners landed on the East Coast and discovered Indians wearing copper ornaments. The Indians could have directed them to the copper rich area where mining began about 3000 B.C. With the close of the Bronze Age in 1200 B.C. a dark age period came over Europe that lasted five hundred years. During this time the mines and the stranded miners would have been forgotten.[42]

---

42. Joseph, Frank, 'More evidence...,' p.11.

CHAPTER III

THE KELTS

By 2000 B.C. the Kelts had emerged as a distinct people.[43] The La Tène Culture, which was located in Germany, appears to have been their immediate progenitor.[44] From this base the Kelts began spreading toward western Europe between 1500 and 600 B.C. There is considerable evidence that around 5600 B.C. there was an opening of the Bosporus Channel and an inundation of the flood plain of the Black Sea. William Ryan and Walter Pitman of Columbia University believe that this was the Biblical flood of Noah, and that a flourishing, advanced civilization had previously resided in the flood plain. As the flood plain filled there was a diaspora of the population to all directions. The Indo-Europeans may have been the largest group of these displaced people. Some Indo-Europeans migrated to Central Europe, then continued into Western Europe; others migrated to the east and into Asia.[45] These people are the progenitors of nearly all native Europeans and a significant portion of Asiatics. They include the Kelts, Italians, Germanic peoples, Slavs, Balts, Iranians, Armenians, Tocharians, and some of the people of Anatolia and India.[46]

The Kelts were at their peak in 300 B.C. At that time they occupied territory extending from Spain to the Black Sea and from the North Sea to the

43. Gibson, Frances M., The Seafarers: Pre-Columbian Voyages to America, Dorrance and Co., Philadelphia, 1974, p.128.
44. Mallory, J.P., In Search of the Indo-Europeans, Thames and Hudson, London, 1989, p.105.
45. Ryan, William, and Pitman, Walter, Noah's Flood, Simon and Schuster, New York, 1998.
46. Mallory, p.164.

Mediterranean. They included the Gauls of France, the Gaels of Scotland and Ireland, the Britons of England and Brittany, and the Galatians of Spain, Poland and Asia Minor. In southern Spain, the Kelts overwhelmed the Phoenicians, who had taken over the region from a non-Indo-European people called Tartessians.[47] With the Keltic influx the Keltic language became dominant in Spain. The takeover was apparently amicable as much of the Phoenician language and many of their skills were maintained and the two peoples allied themselves against Rome in the Punic Wars. Mutual respect must have been present as both the Phoenicians and the Kelts were able seafarers and ship builders as were the Tartessians. Other autochthonous non-Indo-European people who inhabited Spain prior to the Keltic invasion were the Basques in the north and their relatives the Iberians on the Mediterranean coast.

In Britain the Kelts replaced a native people that are relatively unknown. Farley Mowat has researched and written about these people whom he calls the *Albans*. Alba is the ancient name for Great Britain and is not derived from the Latin word, which means "white"; rather it is associated with the name of the indigenous people of Europe. The Albans and their kin, including the Basques of Spain and the Pictones of France, were these indigenous people. When the Kelts arrived, they pushed these peoples westward to the edge of the continent and beyond.

Prior to the Keltic invasion of western Europe any European explorers to America that were not Phoenician had to have been the Albans or their kin. These people were experienced mariners and furthered their explorations of the Atlantic as a result of the invasion of the Kelts.

In A.D. 1154, the Arab geographer Al Idrisi described the territory beyond Greenland as "Albania" or "Greater Ireland." He was also aware of the fishing banks near Newfoundland and of whale bone huts built by the Inuit. He described an island in the western Atlantic where natives were beardless, smoked tobacco and wore only a covering of leaves. This geographer had an unusual knowledge of the world at that time and it indicates that he was aware of stories related by explorers who had been there.

The major evidence of a prehistoric Keltic presence in America comes from New England, where beginning in the late 1600s, Colonists began discovering ancient underground stone buildings and large, man made stone megaliths. At least 275 of these structures have been identified in New England. Some of the

---

47. Gibson, p.131.

structures resemble ancient old world sites such as Avebury and Stonehenge in England and sites in Phoenician Iberia as well. *Dolmens* are stone structures that are found in western Europe and New England. These are tables made of a large stone slab supported by three to five legs of smaller stones. They usually contain scriptural incisions.(Fig. 2)[48]

Other stone structures in New England consist of: (1) Stone lined underground rooms or cellars that some of the British Colonists later used as root cellars, (2) Stone circles with astronomical placement of the stones not unlike Stonehenge, (3) Large stones with a sculpted hole in the center called "men-a-tols", (4) A large stone block thought to be a sacrificial site, (human sacrifice was practiced by both the Kelts and the Phoenicians.), (5) Phallic symbols with Ogamic inscriptions related to fertility and embryos, (Ogamic was a written language used by the Kelts.), (6) Inscribed stones with inscriptions in Ogamic and Iberian Phoenician dedicated to the Keltic Sun God, Bel, or the Phoenician Sun God, Baal.

Many of the inscribed stones served as grave markers. Inscriptions with both Phoenician and Ogamic have been found side by side on the same stone. When both languages are present, it is presumed that the people were Iberian, for it was there that these two peoples existed together and presumably explored and colonized together.[49]

At one megalithic site in New Hampshire called "Mystery Hill," the inscription has been identified as a Punic style that was used from 800-500 B.C. Carbon dating at the same site has indicated human presence there in 2000 B.C., 1690 B.C. and 995 B.C. Clearly the site was occupied for a long period of time.[50]

Ancient ceramic olive jars of Iberian design have been pulled out of coastal waters in Maine and Massachusetts. Those found in Massachusetts and on the Maine seacoast were carved faces with the likeness of a Druid.

An Ogamic-inscribed stone on Manana, a small island ten miles off the Maine coast near Monhegan Island, is translated as saying "Ships from Phoenicia: Cargo Platform." The island appears to have served as a port for Phoenician trading vessels.[51]

---

48. Cahill, Robert Ellis, New England's Ancient Mysteries, Old Saltbox Publishing House, Salem Massachusetts, 1993; and, Fell, Barry, Bronze Age America, Little, Brown, and Company, Boston, 1982, p.57.

49. Angel, Paul Tudor, 'The Mysterious Megaliths of New England,' The Barnes Review, v.3 no.10, 1997, p.3; and, Angel, Paul Tudor, 'Who Built. New England's Megalithic Monuments?' The Barnes Review v.3 no.11, p.17, 1997.

50. Angel, Paul Tudor, 'The Mysterious...'

In 1975 an inscribed stone called the Bourne Stone was found in Massachusetts. It was translated as saying: "A proclamation of annexation. Do not deface. By this Hanno takes possession." In fact, Hanno was a known Phoenician explorer who was also a king in southern Iberia with a home port at Cadiz, which was founded by the Phoenicians. He explored the African coast and the Atlantic in about 500 B.C., and according to Plutarch, he circumnavigated the North Atlantic in 480 B.C. The inscription on the Bourne Stone is in the style of southern Iberia.[52]

Coins have been found in New England that were designated as payment to Greek and Iberian soldiers in the army of Carthage. Other coins, which were found on a beach in Massachusetts, depict fourth century B.C. Roman Emperors. Similar coins have been unearthed all across New England.

It is postulated that, for a long period of time, New England harbored a colony of Keltic and Phoenician settlers, the first of whom were Iberian with later arrivals of British and Irish origin. Phoenician sailors maintained an active trade with this colony for a time.

Some tribes of Algonquian Indians in the northeast have displayed Mediterranean Caucasoid physical characteristics. When Samuel de Champlain met with the Micmac tribe in 1609, he found them taking notes as he spoke to them. When examined, the notes were written in the hieroglyphics of Egypt and Libya and could be easily translated.

Many Algonquian words are phonetically the same as or similar to the same words in Gaelic including the words for fish stream, deep water, white stone, cold pond and many others.[53]

What happened to these people? Were they destroyed in wars with the Algonquians? Were they decimated by a natural disaster or epidemic, or were they assimilated into the Algonquian tribes and Culture? No one knows. We know only that the evidence that they existed is compelling.

---

51. Cahill; Robert E.,; and, Fell, Barry, p.57.
52. Cahill; and, Fell, p.57.
53. Cahill; and, Fell, p.57.

CHAPTER IV

THE ALBANS

The archaeologist employed by the National Museum had made a remark-able discovery on Pamiok Island that he described as a "huge rectangular structure measuring 85 feet long by 20 wide... the walls, which were collapsed, were made of stone."
Most of a decade had slipped away with no evidence of further interest in the site by the museum. When asked why, a friend at the museum surrepti-tiously replied that "certain quarters felt it could turn out to be archaeolog-ically embarrassing, so he had decided to leave it alone..."
"...*Lickspittle scholarship!*" snorted Tom Lee, a talented archaeologist who had been blacklisted for speaking out.
I sensed it was a favorite expression of his when he referred to his colleagues who publicly only admitted finding things that their superiors wanted found.

Farley Mowat, *The Farfarers*[54]

The first inhabitants of Great Britain entered between 8000 and 7000 B.C. Rare remains of campsites in Scotland attest to the presence of a small population of humans around 7000 B.C. Not long prior to that ice had engulfed Britain and made the islands uninhabitable. The first inhabitants of the British Isles were a non-Indo-European hunter-gathering people who are thought to have originated in Iberia and were relatives of the Basques, Iberians and

---

54. Mowat, Farley, The Farfarers, Steerforth Press, South Royalton, Vermont, 2000, p. 2, 202.

Tartessians. In Britain they began farming between 4000 and 2500 B.C. Between 2500 and 700 B.C. another wave of immigration to Britain occurred. These people were probably of similar origin to their predecessors. The new arrivals introduced metalworking skills of the Bronze Age and appear to have assimilated without evidence of conflict.[55]

Keltic tribes began invading Britain as early as 700 B.C. and drove the aborigines to Scotland and northern Ireland. The original inhabitants of Britain are called *Albans* by Farley Mowat, Alba being the ancient name for Great Britain.[56]

When the Kelts began their migration into western Europe the indigenes were pushed to the west, where they became the Basques, Iberians and Tartessians of Spain, the *Pictones* (Picts) of France and the Albans of Britain. Relatives of these people had also inhabited Asia Minor and North Africa and were pushed into remote mountainous enclaves and other physically difficult areas by the Indo-Europeans.[57]

The Albans and their kin were a small, dark complexioned non-Indo-European Caucasian race. They have been associated with the construction of Stonehenge and Avebury and megalithic sites in Brittany. It is suspected that Phoenician priests who traveled to Britain and France were responsible for the Druid religion practiced by the Albans and later by the Kelts in pre-Christian Britain.[58] In Britain the Kelts pushed the Albans into northern Ireland and northern Scotland. The Kelts called the people living in these areas *Cruithne*, Cruithne being the name of an Alban king. The Romans referred to them as the Caledonians.[59]

Prior to the Roman invasion the population of Gaul consisted mostly of Keltic tribes, which were allied into groups. The Romans called the war-like tribes of northern Gaul *Armoricans.* In 51 B.C., following a period of bitter warfare, the Romans conducted a mass slaughter of these people. The *Pictones* (Picts) were a non-Keltic tribe who lived on the western edge of Armorica along the shores of the Bay of Biscay from Brittany to south of the Loire.[60] The Pictones

---

55. Jones, Gwyn, The Norse Atlantic Saga, Oxford University Press, London, 1964, p.4; and, Duncan, John, 'The Origin of the Picts,' www.scotshistoryonline.co.uk/origin1.html.

56. Mowat, p.60.

57. Mowat, p.47.

58. Ryan, William and Pitman, Walter, Noah's Flood, Simon and Schuster, New York, 1998; and, Gibson, Frances, The Seafarers: Pre-Columbian Voyages to America, Dorrance and Company, Philadelphia, 1974, p.143.

59. MacDonald, Lorraine, 'The Picts,' www.siliconglen.com/Scotland/11_5.html.

were a marine dependent people who had excellent sailing abilities and large ships. They escaped annihilation by the Romans by sailing away; they steered their ships north and away from the Roman Empire. The Kelts refused them entry into England and Ireland, but the Albans allowed them to settle in southern Scotland. The Albans had an ulterior motive, intending to use the Picts as a buffer against the Kelts.[61]

The Romans invaded England in A.D. 43 and remained until the Picts, aided by troubles in Rome, forced their departure shortly after A.D. 400. By A.D. 700, the Kelts had driven the Picts back to Scotland. By A.D. 565 Keltic Christian priests from Ireland had begun arriving in northern Scotland and converting the Cruithne (Albans and Picts).[62]

Following renewed Keltic attacks, the Albans and Picts united to battle the Kelts, the Anglo-Saxons, and their most fierce, most feared, and most detested foe, the Vikings. The confederation of Albans and Picts was joined by some Keltic tribes who had come to Scotland from Ireland, and who were called *Scotti*. These new allies made up what became known as the Pictish Kingdom.[63] Viking attacks began in the Shetland and Orkney Islands and soon spread to the Hebrides, Scotland and Ireland. The attacks were vicious, and the pillaging, burning and slaughtering that the Vikings practiced took a tremendous toll on their victims. As a result, by A.D. 900 the Pictish Kingdom had disappeared, and the Albans were effectively eliminated from Scotland for the first time in six thousand years.

Some of the Cruithne (Albans and Picts) were able to flee to Iceland. Pytheus, a geographer, astronomer, and mathematician from the Greek colony of Massalia (Marseilles), ran the Phoenician blockade at the Pillars of Hercules and visited Iceland (*Thule*) between 330 and 300 B.C. Pytheus found the island inhabited by a primitive people who lived on millet, herbs, fruit and roots and had little in the way of domestic animals. [64] He was guided there by the Albans of Great Britain and Ireland who sailed there in their small skin-covered sailing vessels. There they fished, hunted and gathered.

In 860 when the Norse began arriving in Iceland, they found a Christian people had preceded them. The Norse considered these people to be Irish and

---

60. MacDonald, Lorraine.
61. Mowat, p.60.
62. Mowat, p.105.
63. Duncan, John.
64. Mowat, p.124; and, Jones, Gwyn, p.4.

called them the *Papar*, meaning monks.[65] The Norse definition of "monk" was someone who was a land lubber and unaccustomed to ocean voyaging.[66] According to Cahill they were also known as *Culdees* and their religion was a mixture of Christianity and Druidism.[67] The Papar had set up small farms called crofts in the more fertile areas and they fished. By the seventh century they had sailed west to Greenland to hunt for furs and ivory. In 1977, Peter Schledermann found a longhouse on the Kane Basin in northwest Greenland which dated to A.D. 700-900 and appears to have been a wintering place for Alban hunters from Iceland.[68] (Fig.3) The Alban longhouse is characteristic. It is a rectangular house with curving stone walls and no evidence of a roof, because the roof was made by an upturned boat. Similar houses exist in the islands near Scotland today. (Fig. 4) Forty-five longhouses of Alban or Norse origin have been discovered in Greenland and northern Canada. They range from forty to eighty feet long and all have a length to width ratio of 3:1 to 3.5:1.

The Alban sailing vessels were characteristic. Many of their vessels were small curraghs no longer than fourteen feet, but they also built larger ships over fifty feet in length. The Albans covered a wicker or wooden frame, not with planks, but with animal skins. They sealed the hull with tar made from walrus or seal oil. These vessels proved to be remarkably strong and reliable even on long voyages.

When the Norse began invading Iceland in the ninth century, the *Papar* began to leave. They went first to Greenland and then to the western shores of Ungava Bay in northern Quebec where the remains of longhouses, stone beacons, and two ancient European type skulls reveal their former presence. The Inuit have said that the stone beacons were built by "white strangers who came to Ungava in boats a long, long time before we did."[69] (Fig. 5)

Contemporary Icelanders believe themselves to be about 85% Norse and 15% Irish, the Irish component being derived from Keltic slaves imported by the Norse. Researchers have been surprised to find that Icelanders of today are also related to the Turks.[70] When the Indo-Europeans invaded the Balkans and Asia Minor one of the refuges for the indigenes was the mountains of Turkey and Iran.

65. Jones, p.9.

66. Pohl, Frederick J., The Viking Settlements of North America, Clarkson N. Potter, New York, 1972, p.271.

67.

68. Mowat, p.145.

69. Mowat, p.161,164; and, Tiffany, John, 'Did an Unknown 'Pre-Viking Culture Roam Canada?' The Barnes Review, v.7, no.5, 2001, p.37.

The indigenes who retreated to these mountains were at one time the same people as the Albans of Britain. The relation between the Turks and Icelanders is not so surprising if one accepts that the Turkish genetic component in today's Icelanders came from the Albans *(Papar)*.

In the Ungava Bay area the Albans commingled with a relatively unknown and now extinct people called the *Tunit* or *Dorsets*. When the climate changed and became colder, the Albans and the Tunit moved to Okak, Labrador, and to the St. George's Bay area in southwestern Newfoundland. The Tunit were well acquainted with Newfoundland and had begun living there intermittently before 1000 B.C. The forested lands of Labrador were known as *Markland* to the Norse. The Norse knew Newfoundland not only as *Vinland*, but also as *Hvitramannaland*, meaning "White Man's land." This may be a reference to the skin color of people they found living there, or it may be a reference to white robes worn by priests of the Christian (ex-Druid) Albans. (Fig 6)

The Norse found two separate population groups living on Newfoundland. In the west around St. George's Bay they found a population of Albans and Tunit. In the east around the Conception Bay they found a mixture of Albans from Greenland and Ungava Bay, Tunit, Beothuks, (an Algonquian Red Indian tribe also known as the *Innu)*, castaways, and possibly an early population of Albans or Kelts from Ireland.

The Inuit are the Eskimos of Greenland and eastern Canada. They described the Tunit as a people of large stature, who when attacked (by the Inuit) preferred to leave an area rather than fight. The Tunit were responsible for the artifacts archaeologists call the Dorset Culture. They were talented and performed well done wooden carvings with metal utensils. They are thought to have invented the ice house (igloo) and the kayak. We do not know what they looked like, but they were apparently decidedly different from the Inuit who named them *Tunit*, meaning "alien."[71] They are the earliest people known to have inhabited the eastern Arctic areas of North America.

Farley Mowat, a Nova Scotian, has extensively studied the Alban people and is convinced that during their habitation in Labrador and Newfoundland, they received trading vessels from Europe. Trading vessels to the New World must have begun with the Phoenicians and later involved the Kelts and Basques of Iberia. By the time the Albans had reached Newfoundland, there are references

70. Brown, Frederick N., The Voyage of the Wave Cleaver, http://www.vinlandsite.com/nutshell.htm p.1.

71. Mowat, p.154.

that European trading centers were in keen competition. Among such centers were: Bergen in Norway; the Orkney Islands; Bristol, England; and the German Hanseatic League.[72] The traders' route west took them to Iceland. Some ventured on to Greenland and Newfoundland. Mowat estimates that these traders were relatively few in number, and he is convinced they kept their destinations secret. He postulates that in some years as many as three trading vessels visited the Albans, who welcomed them and traded furs and walrus tusks in exchange for metal utensils. Depending on events in Europe, sometimes several years may have gone by with no traders making the long and dangerous trip.[73]

There is a report in the Norse Annals of Greenland of Ari Marson, a tenth century Icelander and a contemporary of Erik the Red, whose sailing vessel was blown off course to Hvitramannaland. Ari was captured by natives there sometime between 981 and 986. Because he was Norse it was expected that he would be executed; but the natives (presumably Alban who had been Christian since the seventh century) found that Ari had been converted (very recently) to Christianity. For whatever reason, Ari was spared and treated amicably by his captors. He became a de facto Alban and was later baptized.

Related to the story of Ari Marson is a report by an Icelandic merchant named Gudleif Gudlaugson who left Dublin late one summer about 1025 bound for Iceland and Greenland. He and his companions were blown far off course to the southwest where they at last sighted land. The landing is thought to have been at Conception Bay on the Avalon Peninsula of southeast Newfoundland, where stone beacons have been found indicating the presence of the Albans. Gudleif and his companions were taken prisoner by the natives. Some wanted the Icelanders executed, and they were brought before a meeting. As the natives were arguing, *a group of horsemen* rode up. One of these appeared to be a chieftain. He was described as an old man with a head of white hair, tall and courageous looking. The old man spoke to the mariners in Icelandic; Gudleif then stepped forward and replied that he was from Iceland. Gudleif and the old man discussed some older inhabitants of Iceland whom the old man had known. The old man then conversed with the rest of the tribe and convinced them that the mariners' lives should be spared, whereupon the old man told the mariners to leave soon, because "these people are tricky and hard to deal with and they think you have

---

72. Pohl, Frederick J., *Prince Henry Sinclair*, Clarkson N. Potter, New York, 1974, p. 93.
73. Mowat, p.250.

broken their laws." He further advised them that "strangers *like you*" (Norse) "should expect plenty of trouble here because there are people in this country more powerful than I who would show them no mercy."[74]

At that time, Newfoundland was inhabited by the Albans and their friends the Tunit. The Beothuks (Red Indians) lived on the island amicably with the Albans and Tunit. Gudleif did not describe his captors as Skraelings as would be expected if they had been Beothuks. Mowat thinks they were Albans or a mixed breed who lived in the Conception Bay area. The fact that they had horses leads credence to his opinion, as the Indians did not have horses until the Spanish arrived. The old man on the horse may well have been Ari Marson.[75]

There is another account, this by a fisherman from the Orkney Islands, who in 1371 was castaway with his fellows on the coast of what was probably Newfoundland (called *Estotiland* by the natives). The natives, (presumably Christian Albans), had a written language and books in Latin that they could not read. They took the fishermen in and cared for them. A few of the fishermen traveled extensively and became well acquainted with the island. After five years the natives with twelve vessels had the fishermen accompany them to the south to a land they called *Drogio*. During this journey the fishermen were again capsized, this time landing on the coast of the mainland. There they were captured by "savages" whom they described as cannibals and very primitive. Some were spared a gruesome death by teaching the Indians how to fish with nets. As word spread among the Indian tribes, the fishermen were passed from tribe to tribe. The fisherman relating the story claimed to have lived with twenty-five tribes in thirteen years of captivity, all the while teaching the Indians to fish with nets. One fisherman eventually was able to escape and found his way back to Drogio. (Drogio was Nova Scotia, inhabited by friendly Micmac Indians.) Three years after he arrived in Drogio vessels arrived from Estotiland and he returned to live with his old friends. He stayed in Estotiland for three more years trading and interpreting. He eventually became wealthy enough to buy passage or build his own ship and he returned to Orkney.

The fisherman told his story to Prince Henry St. Clair, the Earl of Orkney. Henry was also a Scottish Master Freemason, a group which evolved from the Knights of the Templar. The story made Henry eager to retrace the footsteps of the fisherman, but the fisherman died three days before Henry's expedition was

---

74. Mowat, p.243.
75. Mowat, p.281-3.

33

scheduled to depart.[76] But with the help of men who had traveled with the fisherman, Prince Henry embarked on his voyage. Henry's expedition deserves special mention as there is a considerable amount of evidence for it. The expedition consisted of thirteen vessels and about three hundred men, most of whom were from the Orkney and Shetland Islands and were of Norse descent. They departed on April 1, 1398. *The Zeno Narrative and Map* is a written account of the expedition, and consists of notes, maps and letters from Antonio Zeno to his brother Carlo in Venice. The surviving map was drawn by Antonio's great great great grandson from Antonio's notes and correspondence. (Figure 6) Antonio and his brother Nicolo were patrician Venetian sailors who had set off to explore the northern lands, Nicolo in 1390 and Antonio two years later. They became consorts of Henry St. Clair, whom they greatly admired and respected. The respect was mutual and Henry appointed Nicolo captain of his fleet. When Nicolo died in 1394, Antonio succeeded him.[77]

The Estotiland of the fisherman clearly appears to have been Newfoundland, home of the Albans, Tunit and Beothuks. In the fisherman's story there is a distinct difference made between the people of Estotiland who appear to have had European characteristics and the "savages" on the mainland.[78] Since the fisherman died before Prince Henry began his journey, Henry was denied his guidance and his identification of the island of Estotiland. Henry's first landing was on an island he called Icaria that fits the geographical description of southeastern Newfoundland and the natives seem to have been the same as those found by others in the Conception Bay area.[79] These natives must have mistaken Henry's group for pirates or Vikings of old, because they drove them away, their fury increasing "more and more, as though they were fighting for their existence."[80] They told Henry that they would be willing to take in one of his people and give him an honorable position among them if only for the sake of learning his language and finding out about the customs of his people. *They had already received people from ten different countries, who had come to their island and thereby they had linguists among them who could speak ten languages.*[81]

---

76. Sinclair, Andrew, The Sword and the Grail, Crown Publishing, New York, 1992, p.201-204.
77. Pohl, Prince..., p.99-104; and, Sinclair, Andrew, p.201-204.
78. Mowat, p.297.
79. Mowat, p.281-3.
80. Sinclair, p.206.
81. Pohl, Prince..., p.110.

Centuries before the arrival of Columbus, Newfoundland found itself as the host to European fisherman who had discovered the Grand Banks and used its shores to dry and salt their fish. The Avalon Peninsula is in position to receive fishermen and castaways as it juts into the Atlantic near the Grand Banks. When Cabot and Cartier arrived to Newfoundland, they found natives able to speak rudimentary forms of at least twelve languages including Basque, Beothuk, Breton, Catalan, English, Old French, Gascon, Irish (West Coast Gaelic), Italian, Norse (Icelandic), Portuguese and Provencal.[82]

Henry's next stop was Nova Scotia where he and some of his crew spent one winter. The Earl of Orkney is thought to have made a side trip to New England where he probably spent another winter before his journey home. Proof of his expedition exists in European records, Micmac (Mi'kmaq) Indian legends, an ancient Venetian ship's cannon found on a Nova Scotia beach, and the Massachusetts burial site of one James Gunn, a Scottish knight and a friend of St. Clair's. In 1401, less than a year after he returned, Orkney was attacked by the English and Henry was killed in battle. Antonio Zeno returned to Venice in 1406 and died shortly thereafter. In his notes Antonio described Henry as a man as "worthy of immortal memory as any that ever lived."[83] If there were any men from the expedition who stayed in the New World they were stranded and forgotten after Henry's untimely death.

On the Zeno Map Nova Scotia is mislabeled as Estotiland. According to the fisherman's description Drogio is south of Estotiland and the Zeno map places it there. In fact, the "Drogio" of the Zeno map was drawn only from the description given by the fisherman and possibly the description of New England as given by Prince Henry. (Fig 7) Zeno himself never went south of Nova Scotia as Henry sent him home with most of the men and all of the ships of the expedition a few weeks after landing in Nova Scotia. Henry kept only the oared boats and had to build a ship to carry himself and his crew home. The shipbuilding was accomplished on Advocate Bay, Nova Scotia, at the apex of the Bay of Fundy.[84]

The Greenland Norse had begun raiding the Alban settlements in Newfoundland around the year 1000. The Norse foothold on Newfoundland was at L'Anse aux Meadows, which was on a storm prone peninsula at the northern tip of Newfoundland.[85]

---

82. Pohl, Prince..., p.201.
83. Pohl, Prince..., p.181.
84. Pohl, Prince..., p.114.
85. Mowat, p.261.

According to the Icelandic Annals a priest named Jon was sent to Vinland. At that time the church was not interested in proselytizing "savages," whom they considered as not having souls to save. Eric Gnupson, a bishop of the Norse colony on Greenland *and neighboring regions*, is said to have arrived at a Norse colony on Vinland in 1118. It may be that Jon and Eric came to pastor the Christian Albans, because the Norse colonies in New England and L'Anse aux Meadows, Newfoundland, had been abandoned before 1118.[86]

The Tunit, being walrus and seal hunters, left Newfoundland when the climate warmed in the north. By 1500 AD, the Inuit had invaded the Ungava Bay area. The Tunit subsequently disappeared either from bloodshed or dispersal and assimilation, but the Albans on Newfoundland survived.

A Spanish slave raider to Newfoundland described the people he captured there in 1502; "They resemble Gypsies in color, features, stature and aspect. They are very shy and gentle but well formed... They will be excellent for labor and the best slaves that have hither to been obtained."[87]

In 1497, John Cabot set sail from the Bristol Channel for lands in the west that Bristol seamen had already visited. In June he passed Cape Breton Island and soon sighted the coast of southwestern Newfoundland. There he saw a "country very rich in pasture... a trail that went inland, a fireplace, and the manure of farm animals." Cabot then sailed east along the south coast of the island and described fields where he thought there might also be settlements, but he saw no people. I suspect the natives had seen him coming.[88]

The only Europeans who had contact with the native of North America and did not seem to abuse them were the Basques. Basque fishermen killed many whales in the Gulf of St. Lawrence and met and traded with the people of Newfoundland. The Basques were probably the ones who named the native Newfoundlanders *Jakatars*, a corruption of "Jainko tar," which in the Basque language indicates a follower of a Christian God.[89]

A few British merchants established themselves on St. George's Bay in the 1840s. They noted that the population consisted of nomadic Micmac Indians from Nova Scotia, some Acadian French and a dark skinned, dark eyed, dark haired native people called Jakatars. An Anglican minister at Sandy Point, St. George's Bay, on May 23, 1857 wrote, "Went to see a poor man... He and all his

---

86. Mowat, p.284.
87. Mowat, p.317.
88. Mowat, p.325.
89. Mowat, p.318.

family belong to a much despised and neglected race called 'Jack a Tars,' they speak an impure dialect of French and Indian (and are) of almost lawless habits."[90]

Jakatars can still be identified in the area around St. George's Bay. One told Farley Mowat:

> We have always adapted to the times. Intermarriage was never a prob-
> lem and we have a history of sharing as well as getting along with other
> people. We were always taught we were a mix of Micmac, possibly
> Beothuk, French and other European peoples, but we look different and act
> different than others.

Mowat, who was inquiring about the extinction of the Tunit and the Beothuks, received this reply from Leonard Muise, a Jakatar:

> All those early people, the Dorsets (Tunit), Red Indians (Beothuks), the
> ones you call Albans, Farley; they didn't just dry up and blow away, you
> know. Don't you believe it! Truth is they're all of them still round about. In
> St. George's, Port au Port, and Codroy too. One of these times, scientists
> will likely show up here looking to test our DNA to see whereabouts we
> come from. I don't doubt they'll be some surprised by what they find. But
> us Jakos, now... we won't be the smallest little bit surprised because, you
> see, we know just who we are.[91]

---

90. Mowat, p.319.
91. Mowat, p.334.

CHAPTER V

ST. BRENDON AND ST. FINBARR

St. Brendon (Brendan, Brandon) was born in the year A.D. 486 in the County Kerry in western Ireland. He became a monk and an abbot and founded many monasteries in Ireland during his long lifetime of ninety-one years. He was a great seafarer and went on lengthy journeys accompanied by some of his monks. His journeys are described in 120 manuscripts still in existence in various monasteries and museums across Europe. He is credited with traveling to islands in the North Atlantic including the Shetlands, Faeroes and Iceland.

The legend begins with the monk Barthinus telling Brendon that he had just returned from "The Land Promised the Saints." Brendon was a sixty year old accomplished sailor when he decided to find this land. In A.D. 546, he set out with fourteen to seventeen other monks in an Irish sailing vessel called a curragh. He thus began an epic seven year journey that took him literally around the North Atlantic Ocean. The legends regarding the journey of St. Brendon take him to Newfoundland where he encounters an iceberg, walruses and dense fog.[92]

Legend has it that another Irish monk named St. Finbarr had previously made this journey, though very little is known about St. Finbarr.

---

92. Chapman, Paul H. 'They Were Here First - St. Brendan and the Norsemen,' The Barnes Review, v.13, Oct.,1995, p.23; and, Gibson, Frances M., The Seafarers: Pre-Columbian Voyages to America, Dorrance and Co., Philadelphia, 1974 p.118.

In 1976, Tim Severin, a British navigator, and his companion Trondur Patursson duplicated a portion of St. Brendon's feat in a similar boat, an Irish type curragh with three sails. (Curraghs of today cover a frame with canvas. In St. Brendon's time they used animal skins). Severin and Patursson sailed from Ireland to Newfoundland.

After St. Brendon and his party reached Newfoundland they sailed south to a subtropical area of islands. There they were attacked by small, dark savages. After traversing a transparent sea, which some think was the Great Bahama Bank, they disembarked in a land with many fruits and a river where the land seemed to stretch infinitely beyond. St. Brendon also described the Sargasso Sea and Azore Islands in his encirclement of the North Atlantic.[93]

There is not a great deal of evidence to substantiate the journeys of St. Brendon and St. Finbarr. But the legends themselves are of tremendous significance because they were available to later seafarers, including the Vikings, Madoc, and Christopher Columbus, tempting these later explorers to sail to the west in search of what they believed others had previously found.[94]

---

93. Tiffany, John, 'Did Irishmen Discover America?' The Barnes Review v.7 no.5, 2001, p.9; and, Chapman, Paul H., p.23.

94. Deacon, Richard, Madoc and the Discovery of America, George Braziller, New York, 1966; and Tiffany, John, p.23.

Chapter VI

The Vikings

"Save us, oh Lord, from the fury of the Northmen. They ravage our lands. They kill our women and children."
(A 9th- and 10th-century monasterial prayer, northern France)

There is evidence that the Norse visited America in 1700 B.C. An inscribed stone found near Toronto known as the Peterborough Stone was written on petroglyphs in a prerunic alphabet called *Tifinagh*. It tells of a Norwegian king named *Woden-Lithi* who established a colony where the Norse traded with the Algonquians for copper. The copper is presumed to have been mined in upper Michigan or Isle Royale.[95]

Although the ancient Norse vessels were structurally sound and skilled sailors could cross the ocean with them, it was not until about A.D. 700 that the Vikings began to build truly seaworthy vessels. They built the *knorr*, a sturdy, wide trading vessel and the *longship*, a narrow, fast warship with sixteen pairs of oars. These vessels had decking, deeper keels, and a greater amount of freeboard than their previous vessels, making them more stable and therefore able to use larger sails. The Phoenicians and the Kelts had been builders of sturdy sea going vessels and the Norse copied their designs. The larger vessels of the Kelts were as long as 120 feet and surpassed the ships of Julius Caesar and Christopher

---

95. Fell, Barry, Bronze Age America, Little Brown and Company, Boston, 1982, p.102.

Columbus in length. With this in mind, one can easily appreciate that these peoples had ships with ocean crossing ability.[96]

According to paleontologist Barry Fell, the ocean crossing ability of the Norse was intermittent and dependent upon the weather. At times the northern route would have been impassible due to a large amount of floating ice. During the warmer periods, the route opened and the Norse were able to resume travel to the west.[97]

By A.D. 836, Norwegians had established a base at Dublin, which became the center of their slave trade. Not long after that, Norwegians took over Iceland, Danes occupied Normandy, and both Norwegians and Danes invaded the British Isles. In Britain and Iceland the Viking invasion resulted in the flight of the native Albans. By 950, the Norse population of Iceland had grown to thirty thousand and they were looking for new lands to pillage and to settle. The Norwegians sent a flotilla of sixty ships into the Mediterranean to Asia in the Crusades; their soldiers returned by land. Meanwhile Swedes were plundering Russia all the way to the Black Sea.[98]

The dates of notable deeds by the Norsemen have been recorded all over Europe. Among these recordings are annals known as the Icelandic Sagas. Included in the Icelandic Sagas are the Saga of the Greenlanders and Erik the Red's Saga. From these writings we learn that in 986, Erik the Red, who was a lawless thug even by Viking standards, led a flotilla from Iceland to Greenland to establish a colony. Erik did not leave Iceland willingly; he was banished. Erik's father had previously been outlawed from Norway for murderous feuding. In Iceland Erik continued his lawless legacy and evoked the wrath and fear of his neighbors. He was ousted from his district after he unleashed a landslide on the house of Valthjof, a neighbor; then he killed Valthjof's cousin. After leaving the district, he returned to raid the farm of Thorgest in a dispute over a bedstead. Thorgest and his friends gave chase, and in the ensuing melee Erik and his band killed two of Thorgest's sons and several of his friends. The names of two of Erik's feuding opponents suggest that they were more unsavory than Erik, those being Eyolf the Foul and Hrafn the Dueller. In 982 Erik left Iceland. having been banished for three years. With a band of adventurers Erik set off for Greenland

---

96. Mowat, Farley, The Farfarers: Before the Norse, Steerforth Press, South Royalton, Vermont, 2000, p.102.

97. Fell, p.289.

98. Gibson, Frances M., The Seafarers: Pre-Columbian Voyages to America, Dorrance and Co., Philadelphia, 1974, p.157; and, Mowat, p.231.

and marked out a settlement there. He returned to Iceland in 985 to persuade others to join him. Erik was a man of stern disposition, and in spite of his lawlessness he was not a common roughneck. His subsequent actions proved that he was an excellent sailor with marked leadership qualities and foresight. Erik lived under a code that required that one seek one's own justice, and when he felt he was wronged he did something about it. His ability to command confidence and respect is evident in that he was able to persuade enough people to fill twenty-five ships and follow him to Greenland in A.D. 986.[99]

Later in 986, Bjarni Herjolfsson was seeking to sail from Iceland to Greenland to join his father who had sailed with Erik. He was blown off course in waters unfamiliar to him and his crew. He discovered what are thought to be the coasts of Newfoundland, Labrador, and Baffin Island. He did not disembark and did a minimal amount of exploring because he was anxious to get to Greenland before winter began.

Norse accounts say that Leif Eriksson, a son of Erik the Red, sailed from Iceland to Norway in 999 at the age of twenty. Leif was converted to Christianity while in Norway, and his subsequent behavior lacked the brutality exhibited by his father, his brother Thorvald, and especially the malevolence of his half sister Freydis. (Freydis instigated the cold-blooded murder of an ship's entire crew. Her motives were jealousy and greed.)

In the year 1000, Leif sailed from Greenland on a journey to retrace Bjarni Herjolfsson's route of discovery. He located what he thought were the three land regions described by Bjarni. Leif named those regions: *Helluland*, a land of large flat stones (Baffin Island); *Markland*, a forested land (Labrador); and a region of forests, beaches, rivers, and estuaries, which he called *Vinland*. The actual location of Vinland as found by Leif is still in dispute. Some claim it was New England, but Ingstad and others believe it was Newfoundland. (Fig. 8)

Leif's description of his discovery of Vinland states that after leaving Markland his ship sailed on the ocean with a wind that blew from the northeast. They lost sight of land for two days; then they...

> ...came to an island, which lay north of the land, where they went ashore. In fine weather they found dew on the grass, that they collected in their hands and drank, and thought they had never tasted anything as sweet. Afterwards they returned to their ship and sailed into the sound,

---

99. Pohl, Frederick J., The Viking Settlements of North America, Clarkson N. Potter, New York, 1972, p.6; and, Wahlgren, Erik, The Vikings and America, Thames and Hudson, London, 1986, p.73.

which lay between the island and the headland that stretched out north-wards from the land. They rounded the headland and steered westward. Here there were extensive shallows at low tide and their ship was soon stranded, and the sea looked far away to those aboard ship. They carried their sleeping-sacks ashore and built booths. Later they decided to spend the winter there and built large houses. The land seemed so good that the livestock would need no fodder during the winter. The temperature never dropped below freezing and the grass withered only slightly.[100]

The days in midwinter were much longer than in Greenland. On exploring the land grapes and grapevines were found.[101]

The surrounding geography and voyage time given in this description of Leif's Camp *(Leifsbudir)* are a perfect match with the L'Anse aux Meadows site in northern Newfoundland. But the weather, length of day in midwinter, and presence of grapevines point to a site much farther south such as southern New England.

Leif left the following spring and never returned, but two years later his brother Thorvald with thirty men spent two summers exploring at the same location. Other exploratory and raiding expeditions from Greenland that visited Vinland were led by Thorfinn Karlsefni and Freydis, Leif's nefarious half sister. None stayed more than three years in Vinland.[102] The Sagas from these expeditions are just as revealing as Leif's Saga. Thorvald's vessel ran aground, breaking the keel. The ship took two months to repair. They left the old keel upright in the sand to identify the site, which they called *Kjalarnes* (Keel Point), which may have been on Cape Breton Island. Thorvald was killed in a battle with Skraelings, but a ship's keel was later found buried upright on the beach by Karlsefni.

In about 1009, Thorfinn Karlsefni led an expedition consisting of 160 men in four ships. Women were included in the venture, Karlsefni taking five in his ship. Karlsefni was a wealthy Icelandic merchant whose ancestors had been kings in Ireland and Scotland. He took livestock with him, having in mind to establish a colony. An ulterior purpose may have been to raid and plunder any settlements or trading vessels they might find. He offered his men an equal share of any wealth that was acquired.[103]

---

100. The Sagas of the Icelanders, numerous translators, Pehguin Books, New York, 2001, p.639.
101. The Sagas of the Icelanders, p.639.
102. The Sagas of the Icelanders, p.626-674.
103. Finnan, Mark, The Sinclair Saga, Formac Publishing Company, Halifax, 1999, p.32.

The report states they then spent two years at *Straumsfjord.* Although proof is lacking, from the descriptions given I suspect that Straumsfjord is a fjord in Maine. The fjord was described as having an island near its mouth they named *Straumsey,* which had so many birds that they could hardly walk without stepping on eggs. There were mountains there and a pleasant landscape. The grass grew tall and they found grapes and self sown wheat there. The winter was harsh. Mt. Desert Island may well have been Straumsey.

At one point Karlsefni took forty men and explored farther down the coast, spending one winter at a place he named *Hop,* which appears to have been in southern New England.[104] After a skirmish with *Skraelings* (natives or barbarians), they returned to Straumsfjord. (Fig. 9)

I suspect that the description of the mild weather at Leif's Camp in Leif's Saga was borrowed from Karlsefni's experience at *Hop.* L'Anse aux Meadows is located at the tip of a bleak, cold, desolate and windy peninsula at the northern tip of Newfoundland. The average temperature at the site is fifty-one degrees F. in July and August and fourteen degrees F. in January and February. Epaves Bay at L'Anse aux Meadows remains frozen and icebergs drift by the site until June. Therefore, it would seem that the dispute regarding the location of *Vinland* depends upon whether one is consulting the voyage of Leif or that of Karlsefni. Leif's 'Vinland' would necessarily be Newfoundland as there is no good indication that he visited lands farther south. On the other hand, Karlsefni probably stopped at Leif's Camp, considered the site unsuitable for settlement, and proceeded to New England, which he considered to be part of Vinland.

While at Straumsfjord, Karlsefni's group was approached by Skraelings who attempted to trade their furs for weapons, but Karlsefni refused to allow his men to give up their weapons and instead traded red cloth, milk, and curds. In the transactions a Skraeling was killed, reportedly trying to pilfer weapons. A few weeks later the Skraelings retaliated and attacked the Norse with a large war party. Shortly after that attack Karlsefni decided to return to Greenland. Karlsefni described one man among the Skraelings as "tall and fair, and he thought he might have been their leader."[105] Because the natives knew to approach the Europeans with furs for trading, it can be surmised that they had been in touch with European trading vessels in the past.

104.The Sagas of the Icelanders, Introduction by Robert Kellogg, p.xxxi-xxxiv.
105. Mowat, p.277.

Karlsefni's wife Gudrid told of meeting a small native woman described as having pale skin, chestnut hair and large eyes, who repeated Gudrid's comment, "*Ek heiti Gudridr* (My name is Gudrid)." It is doubtful that this woman spoke Norse or was named Gudrid; it is more likely that she was simply phonetically repeating Gudrid's statement.[106]

Gudrid, the wife of Karlsefni, gave birth to a son named Snorri while at Straumsfjord, the first White child documented to have been born in the New World. Snorri was nearly three years old when they returned to Greenland.

On the way back to Greenland, Karlsefni's ships again stopped at *Markland*, where Karlsefni's men captured two Skraeling boys and took them to Greenland.[107] The boys were well treated and learned to speak Norse. They told of a land across from theirs where the people were white like the Norse and carried white banners before them as they *screamed* (presumably in religious fervor).[108] The Norse presumed they were referring to *Hvitramannaland*. The captured boys had been accompanied by a man and two women who escaped capture. The man was described as bearded.[109]

Norse historians sometimes become defensive when the exploits of the Vikings are described in a critical manner. They point out that the Norse were essentially farmers and did not deserve the brutal pillaging, thieving, and murdering reputation that has been laid to the Vikings. But the thirteenth century writers of the Sagas were straightforward. The Sagas contain neither pity or remorse and they do not try to justify Viking attacks on moral grounds. They took the pre-Christian view that pillaging and murdering in foreign lands were simply what a Viking did. The author of *Egil's Saga* describes the raids of a young Norwegian named Thorolf:

> There was plenty of loot, so each of them had a good share. That's how things stood for a number of years: every summer they'd go out on viking expeditions and then spend winter at home with their fathers. Thorolf brought his parents back a lot of valuable things. In those days there was ample opportunity for a man to grow rich and famous.[110]

106. Jones, Gwyn, The Norse Atlantic Saga, Oxford University Press, London, 1964, p.157.

107. Bronsted, Johannes, The Vikings, Penguin Books, Middlesex, England, 1965, p.111-116.

108. Brown, Frederick N., The Voyage of the Wave Cleaver, Inc., http:// www.vinlandsite.com/ saga3.htm.

109. The Sagas of the Icelanders, p.672.

110. Roberts, David, with Krakauer, Jon, Iceland Land of the Sagas, Villard Books, New York, p.23.

The Icelandic sagas are filled with accounts of bloody feuds, constant lawlessness and crude behavior by the men who have been called peaceful farmers. The Norse apologists have a point however, as some of the Norsemen are known to have been exceptional and fair minded individuals. This is especially true after their conversion to Christianity. An example of self-sacrifice by a Norse is Bjarni Grimolfsson, who commanded a ship in the Karlsefni expedition. On the way back to Greenland his ship became infested with worms (molluscs) and began sinking. Lots were chosen because the after-boat could hold but half of the crew. Bjarni gave up his lot to a younger man he had promised to protect. Although he gave his place in the after-boat willingly, he included a comment to the man "as I see you put a high price on life and are very upset about dying." Obviously Bjarni did not condone the attitude of the younger man. Vikings did not die willingly, but they did not whimper over it.[111]

By the year 1075 Vikings had settled in the areas that they had been accustomed to raiding and become Christian. By that time most of them had stopped their fearsome depredatory practices and became traders.

The Albans and the Tunit (Dorsets) have been described as friendly and peaceful peoples except where the Vikings are concerned. The behavior of the men on Thorvald's and Karlsefni's expeditions reveal that they carried on their usual brutality of pillaging and killing. They enraged the native peoples, and as a result future Norse incursions into North America were bloody and met strong resistance.

I believe that the Norse settlement at L'Anse aux Meadows was Leif's Camp, however Karlsefni appears to have ventured much farther south. Frederick Pohl has claimed to have found mooring stones, remains of a palisade enclosure, remains of two longhouses and remains of two boat sheds at Follins Pond, a lake on the base of Cape Cod that drains into Nantucket Sound via the Bass River.[112] Others dispute his claim. Although Pohl believed that he had found Leif's Camp, the Follins Pond site is much more likely to have been Karlsefni's *Hop.* Cahill has reported that remains of a Viking longhouse measuring 54'x17' have been found near Buzzard's Bay, which is between Follins Pond and Narragansett Bay.[113]

---

111. The Sagas of the Icelanders, p.673; and, Wahlgren, p.73.
112. Pohl, The Viking..., p.195-208.
113. Cahill, Robert Ellis, Ancient Mysteries of New England, Old Saltbox Publishing House, Salem, Massachusetts, 1993, p.77.

Another site that matches the geographical description given for *Hop* is on the Pettaquamscutt River off Narragansett Bay, Rhode Island.[114] The remains of two (non Indian) stone structures are located on Point Judith, immediately to the south of the Pettaquamscutt River. Straumsfjord was described as being about halfway between Kjalarnes (Cape Breton Island) and Hop (Cape Cod or Narragansett Bay). That description is consistent with Mt. Desert Island being Straumsey.

There were two Norse colonies on Greenland: the Eastern Settlement at the southwestern tip of the island, and the smaller Western Settlement, which was located four hundred miles up the west coast. It is well established that these colonies existed. There are ruins from the buildings, and an account of trade with western Europe exists that tells of Greenlanders exporting furs and walrus tusks. The Norse colonies on Greenland lasted over four hundred years. At their peak in the eleventh and twelfth centuries the two colonies together had four thousand people, 380 farms, a monastery, a nunnery, sixteen churches and a bishop. (The Greenland settlers came from Iceland, which by law was converted to Christianity in the year 1000). From 1000 to 1025 the tiny colonies on Greenland were responsible for sending out the explorations and raids that have become renowned. But in reality the Greenland colonies were beyond the outer fringe of the habitable world. Unearthed human remains from the their settlements reveal that chronic disease and poor nutrition were rampant among the inhabitants and reflect the considerable hardships to which the Greenlanders were constantly exposed.

In 1261, the Greenland colonies came under the Norwegian crown. Iceland followed suit the next year. They relinquished their independence in return for the periodic arrival of trading vessels from Bergen. It was not a fair trade, because in many years no ships were sent due to problems, which included the plague, the decline of Bergen merchants from competition, and raids by Baltic pirates upon Bergen.[115] In order to keep their monopoly in Greenland, Norway expressly forbid the Colonists from building sea-going ships; but by 1261 the impoverished Greenland colonies were beyond controlling their own destiny. Greenland had no trees with which to build ships, and without ships the people no longer had a source for lumber.[116]

---

114. Brown, http://www.vinlandsite.com/coastal.htm p.6.
115. Pohl, The Viking..., p.235-242.
116. Jones, p.55.

Evidence that the Greenlanders had completely converted to a peaceful lifestyle exists in that not one sword or shield has been unearthed there.[117] Due to the perceived safety of their isolation, they lost the ability to defend themselves. The last people of the Greenland colonies disappeared rather suddenly between 1410 and 1500. The weather may have been a cause of the abandonment of the colonies; climatologists assert that between 950 and 1200, the climates of Greenland and Newfoundland were warmer than at present, but colder weather set in after that time. By 1300 the Inuit Thule Culture had begun invading southern Greenland from the north, and there are reports that some of their encounters with the Norse were bloody. In 1656 a ship visited Baffin Land and told of seeing a tall, well-built, fair complexioned people among the Eskimos. Another ship arrived at Coronation Gulf in far northern Canada and told of meeting a tribe of two hundred Tunit, fifteen of which were described as "fair European types." These meetings have been taken as evidence that the fate of some of the Greenland Norse was assimilation with the Eskimos, but the fair complexioned people living with the Tunit may have been Albans.[118]

The Inuit told of pirates who attacked and killed the Norse in Greenland and burned their buildings. This legend is consistent with a papal letter of 1448 that tells of foreign ships that came to the settlement where "the barbarians ravaged with fire and swords and destroyed the sacred buildings, and carried off the natives of both sexes into slavery."[119] English traders from Bristol, and other ports were common sites in Icelandic waters in the fifteenth century. Most were trading vessels, but some were adventurers and pirates, who were guilty of abduction, robbery and murder. Treaties between Denmark and England allude to the presence of these vessels in Greenland waters as well. [120] In July of 1627 Algerian pirates of the Barbary Coast are known to have attacked Heimaey, an island off the coast of Iceland. They killed or captured most of the inhabitants; a few escaped by hiding in caves.[121] The Greenlanders would have been frightened of a return by the pirates; they would have been tempted to flee to the north and join the Inuit. This theory is supported by the discovery of Norse carvings and Runic inscriptions in northwest Greenland, and the finding that the Inuit of

---

117. Ingstad, Helge. The Viking Discovery of America, Checkmark Books, New York, 2001.
118. Gibson, p.183-4.
119. Ingstad, p.24,28;, and, Jones, p.70.
120. Jones, p.70.
121. Roberts, p.55.

Greenland, unlike the Inuit in Canada, have an ancestry that is partially White.[122]

Since the Viking ships were capable of traveling 150 miles a day and it is only 200 miles across water from Greenland to Baffin Island, it would be surprising if the Norse had not discovered America. Now most experts agree that the Newfoundland colony did in fact exist. Proof of its existence is in the ruins at L'Anse aux Meadows, which were discovered by Helge Ingstad in 1960. He and his archaeologist wife Anne Stine spent the next seven summers investigating the site. The L'Anse aux Meadows site is congruous with the site called "Promontorium Winlandia," which was placed on two prominant maps drawn around 1600. The site consisted of nine buildings including a house and a 60' x 45' great hall with a hearth in the middle in the Viking manner. These buildings lacked stone foundations, which indicates they were built for temporary occupation.[123] Sixty to ninety individual sleeping places were located there. Four boat sheds and a smithy were also found, the iron ore having come from a nearby bog. (Fig. 49) Radio carbon datings from the site cluster near A.D. 1004, the latest being 1080. No one stayed long at L'Anse aux Meadows; there are no burial grounds there. It was an active colony only briefly and intermittently; its functions appear to have been to serve as a way station for travelers to Markland and Vinland and as a base for procurement by Viking raiders. The Tunit are thought to have temporarily lived at the site after the Vikings departed. The isolation and undesirability for habitation of the site allowed the remains at L'Anse aux Meadows to remain in existence without destruction or discovery for nearly a millennium.[124] Another Viking settlement has been discovered at Blanc Sablon, which is on the Labrador-Quebec border directly across the Strait of Belle Isle from the northern tip of Newfoundland.

A cadre of vocal and influential authoritarians has belatedly and begrudgingly accepted that the L'Anse aux Meadows site was inhabited by the Norse, who preceded Christopher Columbus. Despite the Sagas, Rune stones, and other artifactual evidence, some still claim that the Vikings ventured no farther south than the Gulf of St. Lawrence. It was more than a century after the events took place that the Sagas were first written down in Iceland. Before that the stories of the various voyages were passed on by word of mouth, and

---

122. Mowat, p.102.

123. Cohat, Yves, The Vikings Lords of the Seas, Thames and Hudson, p.258-161; and, Review of Birgitta Wallace article in Dossier of Archeology, No.27.

124. Ingstad.

mistakes undoubtedly occurred. Also, the descriptions of Vinland, Leif's Camp, Straumsfjord, Hop, and other sites are too brief to be exact and without controversy. A mixing of events occurs several times between the Sagas, giving the impression of contradictions, and in some places an obvious mysticism has been added. But with proper interpretation a locale and a story can be shown to fit the text of the Sagas quite well. Thus, although imperfect, the Sagas of the Greenlanders and Erik the Red are genuine historical documents and should not be regarded as entirely fictitious. The Vikings were a bold, adventurous and straightforward people. To ignore the Sagas is to underestimate their achievements in the discovery and exploration of the New World.

Norse accounts relate to Hvitramannaland (Newfoundland) as being *Irland Mikla*, or Greater Ireland. The Icarians described by Antonio Zeno claimed that their kings were descendants of Icarus, the first king of Scotland, who in turn was the son of Daedalus, a king in Ireland. Indeed the Gaels (Kelts) had a legend of Daedalus being an Irish king and the Gaels on Ireland were called "Scotti" by the Romans long before they invaded Scotland. Scotland derives its name from these people. The evidence becomes even stronger if a "c" is substituted for a "t" in *Estotiland*, for then it becomes *Escotiland*. The Albans were the inhabitants of Ireland before the Gaels (Kelts) arrived. Norse accounts admit that Newfoundland was inhabited by the Irish before the Norse arrived. This is suggestive that Albans or Kelts from Ireland had settled in Newfoundland before the arrival of the Albans from Labrador and Ungava Bay.[125]

When Giovanni da Verrazano visited the New England coast in 1524 he stopped near Newport, Rhode Island. There he and his men "spent many days with the natives who were friendly and generous, beautiful and civilized". He further described the local Indians as bronze and tawny and "some inclining toward whiteness." Other Indians that he met farther north were "dark and less civilized."[126]

Skeletons of the Narragansett Indians that date to pre-colonial days have shown a high incidence of resistance to an infestation of tuberculosis, unique among Indian tribes and indicating miscegenation with Europeans. There is no record of Norse from the Greenland colonies making excursions into Vinland (New England) after 1025, but the Norse from Greenland and Iceland continued their raids and most certainly obtained timber intermittently from Markland

---

125. Pohl, Frederick J., *Prince Henry Sinclair*, Clarkson N. Potter, New York, 1974, p.111.
126. Cahill, p.81.

and Vinland at least until 1261, when the Norwegian king prohibited them from building sea-going vessels.

Newport, Rhode Island, is on Narragansett Bay. Found there is a medieval thirty foot tall octagonal stone tower that contains five Rune stones. The tower was once owned by Benedict Arnold, who has been credited with building the tower to function as a windmill. But the tower was built long before Arnold's ownership and before the arrival of the Colonists, because it was described by Colonists as early as 1632.[127] The tower appears to have been built for use as a fort, an observatory, and a church. If Arnold did convert the tower to a windmill, he found it to be ill suited for that purpose. The eight points of the tower are aligned perfectly with the points of a compass. The arches, pillars and single and double splays in the sophisticated architecture reflect Freemasonry, which in turn reflects the presence of Prince Henry St. Clair's expedition. Verrazano called the Newport settlement *Norman villa* on his map. The St. Clair clan was originally Norse and came to Scotland from Normandy.[128]

The Narragansett Indians were a mixed breed. They could have been the progeny of sailors and lumberjacks from Iceland and Greenland who elected to stay in Vinland, and/ or stayovers from the Sinclair expedition. The Wampanoag Indians, who also lived on Narragansett Bay, have a tradition involving a battle with White invaders who sailed upstream in a large ship with a "house on the back."

A tribe of Indians as far south as Central America may have had a Viking origin. The Tule tribe of San Blas Indians of the Darien area of Panama was described by the Spaniards as being a band of White Indians with blue eyes and golden hair. (Thule is the early Norse name for Iceland). Linguists have described an Aryan structure in their language and have identified sixty words that equate to Norse. When the Spanish discovered these people, their name for their village, on the Atlantic side of Panama, was *Atlan*.[129]

At least seventy Viking artifacts have been found at various places in America that date from the tenth to the fourteenth centuries, and stand as proof of their presence. These artifacts are in the form of Rune stones, pictoglyphs, swords, axes, firesteels and mooring stones. The Rune stones are the most interesting and the most controversial of these finds. Runes are characters of the

127. Cahill, p.81.

128. The Sagas of the Icelanders, p.7; and, Cahill, p.81; and, Sinclair, Andrew, Prince Henry Sinclair, Crown Publishers, New York, 1992, p.145-6.

129. Gibson, p.183-4.

Runic Alphabet, used by the Norsemen of the time. Unfortunately for translators, the Runic Alphabet was changeable and at one point was even downsized from twenty-four to sixteen characters. This made several sounds overlap and gave Runic words more than one interpretation.

Perhaps the most famous Rune stone is the Kensington RuneStone, found in 1898 under tree roots in west central Minnesota by Scandinavian farmer Olaf Ohman. (Fig. 10) The finding was immediately branded a hoax by an "expert;" later it was said to probably be genuine; then it was scoffed again. Since carbon dating cannot be done on stone, that bit of proof is lacking. The inscriptions are definitely man made and consistent with the times. A letter published in the 2001 spring issue of the *Journal of Scandinavian Studies* by Richard Nielsen refutes linguists' objections to the stone and at this time it appears that the stone is genuine. A translation of the Kensington Rune Stone by Dr. Nielsen reads:

> Eight Goths [Swedes] and 22 Northmen [Norwegians] are on acquisi-tion [var. exploration] business from Vinland far to the west. We had encampment by two shelters one day's time north from this stone we were fishing one day. After we came home I found 10 men red from blood and dead. Hail Mary deliver from evil. I have 10 men by the sea to attend to our ship 14 days' journey from this wealth. Year of Christ 1362.[130]

Reinforcing the authenticity of the Kensington RuneStone is the finding of ten mooring stones in Minnesota with the characteristic Scandinavian triangular hole.[131]

Norwegian records from 1354 include a report that King Magnus ordered his knight Sir Paul Knutsson and thirty other men to Greenland, reputedly because the Greenlanders were turning pagan. Their exploratory party returned to Greenland and then to Bergen, Norway in 1364. They are thought to have explored to Hudson Bay, the Nelson River to Lake Winnipeg and the Red River of the North to Minnesota. Seven of them survived and returned to Norway.[132]

In the 19th century a steamboat ran aground on the St. Francis River in Arkansas. When the travelers disembarked, they discovered the ruins of an ancient fortified town with a citadel. The construction was of bricks and mortar. Large trees growing in the walls showed 300 annular rings. The type of

---

130. Martin, Stephen J. 'The Kensington Rune Stone,' The Barnes Review, v.8 no.2, 2002, p.5.
131. Gibson, p. 34 and p.175.
132. Pohl, The Viking..., p.147.

construction pointed to it being a European colony. There is no record of who built the site.[133]

Near the Arkansas River in eastern Oklahoma, six stones with Runic inscriptions have been discovered. The translations from these Rune stones have provided dates ranging from A.D. 1012 to 1024.[134]

The Spirit Pond Rune Stones are four in number and were discovered in 1972 near Popham Beach, Maine. They are written in Common Scandinavian, an old proto-Scandinavian language used in Iceland, with a penchant toward the Danish branch of that proto-language. One of the Spirit Pond Rune Stones has a map inscribed in addition to characters. The Runes tell of an exploratory trip by thirty-four Vikings in A.D. 1010 and 1011.[135] Those dates would correspond to the Karlsefni expedition.

The Norsemen were diligent in their record keeping and at least seventy-two descriptions of sailing directions exist that tell of accounts of early Norse explorations about North America.

---

133. Olson, Dana, The Legend of Prince Madoc and the White Indians, Jeffersonville, Indiana, 1987, p.64.

134. Pohl, Frederick J., The Viking ..., p.32.

135. Chapman, Paul H. 'The Spirit Pond Runestones: The Ultimate Crossword?' The Barnes Review v.7 no.3 p.67.

BOOK II

MADOC THE BOLD

CHAPTER VII

TALES FROM WALES

Although he had done no research of his own, the esteemed university professor considered himself the watchdog of his field, the moral guardian of scientific probity. But his verbal legerdemain and omission of contrasting studies in his reviews, his use of arguments that he knew had been disproven and his slanted analysis of research, pointed to an agenda pushing role. His indefatigable search for flaws in the reports of those who opposed his views had become, for most scientists in the field, the accepted way to refute and, in the end, the only way that meant anything.

William Wright, Born That Way

In the twelfth century A.D., Wales was divided into three kingdoms: Gwynedd in the north and west, Powys in the east and Deheubarth in the south. Each area had its own king or chieftain and each spoke a different dialect of Cymric, the Welsh language. Owain ab Gwynedd came to the throne of Gwynedd in 1138 and ruled until his death in 1169. His forefathers had ruled in Wales dating back to the year A.D. 350, and his mother was an Irish Viking Princess. Owain was a man of considerable ability. He was a sagacious diplomat, a prudent governor, and a brilliant soldier with no record of ever having been defeated. His reputation was such that he generally was regarded as King of Wales, although in actuality he ruled only in Gwynedd. Owain engaged in numerous internecine battles, but his chief enemy was Henry II, the Norman King of England, who repeatedly tried to invade and conquer Wales. One of Owain's goals was the unification of Wales. His reputation was great enough that he was able to forge an alliance with France against Henry, and French bards and minstrels were known to visit Owain's castles in Gwynedd. (Fig. 11)

Owain was a fierce ruler and gave out brutal penalties to those who he thought were disloyal, especially within his own family. He imprisoned his son Cynan and had one nephew murdered and another blinded and castrated. He was in constant warfare with his brother, Cadwaldr. Yet Owain was also described as generous and as having no desire for great wealth.

Owain had two wives: Gladwys, the mother of Iowerth, and Chrisiant, his first cousin and the mother of David. Owain also had a large number of mistresses. He is known to have sired at least twenty-seven children, most of whom were illegitimate. One of his concubines was Brenda, the daughter of an Irish Lord with Viking ancestry. Brenda bore Owain at least six sons, one of whom was Madoc, who was born sometime between 1134 and 1142.

Upon Owain's death, he was refused burial in the church cemetery as the church did not recognize his marriage to his first cousin Chrisiant, which it considered incestuous. It is significant that the marriage of cousins within the ruling families of Europe was common and possibly the rule. This preserved the thrones for an extended family for centuries.

Owain was a giant of a man, a trait he inherited from his ancestors; it was a trait he shared with his children.

Madoc was an outcast son of Owain, and Owain ordered him slain at birth. Whether this was due to suspected infidelity on the part of Brenda, a perceived birth defect (club foot), or to remove a future contender for the throne is not known. At any rate Brenda was able to smuggle the infant out of the court and to Ireland. Ieuan Brechfa, a 15th century Welsh bard wrote this verse of Madoc's childhood:

> Madoc, alive in truth, but slain in name,
> A name that could be whispered on the waves,
> But never uttered on the land.

It is likely that Madoc became an accomplished sailor at a young age. He may have returned to Wales on more than one occasion until at last he was no longer threatened by his father. He fell in love with Annesta, a handmaiden of Chrisiant. Annesta bore Madoc a daughter, Gwenllian, who is claimed as an ancestor by several people living in Wales today.

Following the death of Owain in 1169, Gwynedd was thrown into a bloody conflict between his heirs for succession to the throne. The oldest legitimate son was Iowerth, who was also known as "Edward with the Broken Nose." Iowerth was not in contention for the throne because of his facial deformity and simple mindedness. Iowerth's son Llewellyn did not share his father's handicaps and although young, qualified as a contender. A battle for succession to the throne began and raged until Howell, a son of Owain and Pyvog, stepped in and assumed the throne. David, a son of Owain and his first cousin, Chrisiant, made preparations to seize the throne from Howell, and things got out of control. Two years after he had taken the throne, Howell was slain by David, who then proclaimed himself king.

Not all of Owain's sons were as barbaric and ambitious as David, who is said to have slain two other brothers and ordered the slaying of Annesta, a handmaiden in his mother's court and the wife of Madoc. Rhodri, another of Brenda's sons, was exiled to the island of Anglesey. David may have encouraged Madoc's departure in order to be rid of him.

The historians of the time were court bards and minstrels. These troubadours wrote in verse and then put the words to song. They traveled throughout Europe and taught others their verses. The great libraries of Europe had accounts of Leif Ericsson's journey shortly after the year 1000. By 1250 these libraries had accounts of Madoc's journeys as told by the bards, although by 1282 the bards and their songs vanished temporarily, probably due to an epidemic of the plague.

The bard, Meredith ap Rhys (1430-1460), wrote:

> Madoc am I, who throughout my life will seek
> Upon the water, that which I have been used to.
> Madoc the bold, of expanding form,
> True whelp of Owain Gwynedd,
> Would not have land (my kindred soul),
> Nor great wealth, but the seas.

Guytin Owen, also in the fifteenth century, interpreted Madoc's naval prowess in a somewhat different verse:

> *Madoc am I, the son of Owain Gwynedd,*
> With stature large and comely grace adorned,
> No lands at home, nor store of wealth,
> My mind was whole to search the ocean.

A Dutch patron of poets, Lodewijk van Velthem, was impressed by legends of King Arthur, and commanded Flemish settlers and mercenaries in England and Wales to translate such legends into Flemish. Willem the Minstrel was one of these transplanted Flemings. Willem had written epics from the Welsh about the legends of King Arthur that had so impressed van Velthem. Willem lived in Wales and the nearby island of Lundy for a lengthy period during the late twelfth and early thirteenth century. He wrote many tales of Madoc that included his journeys and an account of a visitation by Madoc to the court of Louis VII of France dressed as a monk. This corresponds to a historical account of Owain sending two Welsh monks with letters to the French king offering his support against Henry II of England. Willem's narrative contained other material which would not have been generally known at the time, including a description of the Sargasso Sea. An Icelandic Saga that was written in the twelfth century describes a "Freeman from Wales" who sailed from the island of Lundy to the southern isles and Willem gives an accurate description of Lundy.[136]

A main source of knowledge about Madoc comes from Caradoc's work, *Historie of Cambria, Now Called Wales.* Caradoc died in 1157, and the work was then taken up by Humphrey Lloyd, whose desire it was to bring the work up to the year 1270. Lloyd died before he finished and David Powell then completed the work, which was published in 1568.[137]

Another often quoted source is the Reverend Richard Hakluyt (1552-1616), who was a distinguished man of letters. Hakluyt utilized multiple historical sources and wrote extensively of Madoc. His works were published in the late 16th century.[138] One of Hakluyt's sources was Guytin Owen, a Welsh bard, who in turn obtained information from records of the abbeys of Conway in North Wales and the Strata Florida in South Wales. Another Welsh Bard who wrote of Madoc was Cynfryg ap Cren. Meredith, Guytin and Cynfryg all wrote in the fifteenth century before Columbus discovered America.

Madoc, having lived in Ireland with his mother's family who were descended from Vikings, no doubt was familiar with the voyages of the Vikings

---

136. Armstrong, Zella, Who Discovered America? Lookout Publishing Company, Chattanooga, 1950; and, Deacon, Richard, Madoc and the Discovery of America, George Braziller, New York, 1966; and, Olson, Dana, The Legend of Prince Madoc and the White Indians, Jeffersonville, Indiana, 1987.

137. Durrett, Reuben, Traditions of the Earliest Visits of Foreigners, Filson Club Number 23, 1908 p.20-28; and, Deacon.

138. Durrett, p.20-8.

and their discovery of land to the west. It is also likely that he had heard the stories of St. Brendon and St. Finbarr. Due to his naval skills, he became the Commander of Gwynedd's fleet. With consideration of Madoc's nautical experience and his knowledge of the Norse journeys, the legends of his transoceanic voyages become credible.

Chapter VIII

The Voyages

Madoc, the sailor and commander of the naval fleet of Gwynedd, must have spent much of his youth and early adulthood at sea. He sailed to Ireland and France and touched other parts of Europe as well. He was known in Brittany and Provence. It is likely that he visited the Hebrides, Orkney, Shetland, and Faeroe Islands and Iceland. He is reported to have sailed to the "Southern Isles." Qualifying for that description would be the Canary, Madeira, Azore, and Cape Verde Islands. It seems safe to say that he was aware of the feats of Erik the Red and Leif Eriksson and their discovery of land to the west. In his travels it is conceivable that he may have conversed with others who were knowledgeable of ancient Phoenician and Keltic discoveries in the west.

There are only two seaways by which sailing vessels from Europe could successfully reach America. The northern route was by way of Iceland. This route skirted the southern tip of Greenland, then continued to Newfoundland. This was the route followed by the Irish Kelts, Albans, Vikings, and Prince Henry Sinclair. If one veered south of this course, he found himself in the Gulf Stream and would be carried back to the east. The Greenland Sagas describe this happening to Leif's brother Thorstein, who floundered in the Atlantic in an unsuccessful attempt to sail to Vinland. It also happened to Thorhall, who commanded a ship in the Karlsefni expedition. Attempting to return to Greenland, Thorhall and nine companions wound up in Ireland where they were imprisoned.

The second route to America led to the southwest following the equatorial trade winds past the Azore Islands to the West Indies, Caribbean, and Gulf of Mexico. This was the route taken by Madoc and Christopher Columbus. The amazing Phoenicians had utilized both the northern and southern routes to America.

In the latter half of the twelfth century, there was an exodus of the frightened and disillusioned populace from Wales to Ireland in order to escape the terror and turmoil brought about by the contention for the throne of Gwynedd. David had married Emma, the half sister of King Henry of England, and allied himself with England, the historical enemy of Gwynedd. He had killed his brother Howell, his chief rival for the throne, and imprisoned his brother Rhodri. Rhodri escaped and took exile on the island of Anglesey. Madoc and other kinsmen were seriously threatened.

Most historians give 1170 as the year of Madoc's initial expedition to North America. His return trip to America is said to have taken place the following summer. These dates appear to correspond to the dates of his voyages with ships that were crowded with Welsh men and women intent on settling in the New World. Those who have credited Madoc with only two expeditions to the New World appear to have taken a mistaken interpretation of Hakluyt. After reading the admittedly confusing account from Hakluyt as taken from the bard Guytin Owen, I agree with Chattanooga historian Zella Armstrong and others, that indeed there were three voyages.[139]

Madoc's initial voyage was necessarily a voyage of discovery that took several years. This voyage entailed fewer ships and no settlers were involved. The ships were manned by a crew of experienced sailors. There is evidence that Madoc's initial exploratory voyage landed in Mexico. The Toltecs passed down a legend to the Aztecs (who founded Mexico City in A.D. 1325), about giant white men whom they considered to be gods, coming from the east in ships with square sails. The sailors and the Indians were friendly and shared knowledge and skills. When Cortez arrived in Mexico City in 1520, he found Montezuma, the Aztec ruler, to be physically unlike other Indians; he was taller and had different features. Montezuma told the Spanish a legend that he and his forebears were descended from a race of fair-skinned visitors who had come from the east in ships with square sails and who were regarded as gods of the sea by the Indians.

---

139. Armstrong, Zella, *Who Discovered America?* Lookout Publishing Company, Chattanooga, 1950.

The fair-skinned sailors departed having promised to return. When the Spanish arrived in Mexico, they found natives who were apparently acquainted with Christianity and revered the cross.

Part of the text of Montezuma's speech to his people in 1520 follows:

> My predecessors and fathers [previous kings] and all descendants of my race since...we came from a far distant northern nation whose tongue and manners we have yet partly preserved...you have sprung from a race of free-men and heroes... our divines have instructed you of our natural descent from a people most renown upon earth for liberty and valor because of all nations they were, as our first parents told us, the only unsubdued people upon the earth, by that war-like nation, whose tyranny and ambition assumed the conquest of the world, but nevertheless our great fore-fathers checked their ambition and fixed limits to their conquests, although but the inhabitants of a small island, and but few in number, compared to the ravages of the earth, who attempted to conquer our great glorious and free forefathers,...[140]

Father Bernardino de Sahagun was one of the first Spanish historians in Mexico. He sought out the oldest and most learned of the natives and asked each to point out, in his own Aztec picture writing, as much as he could clearly remember of Aztec history, religion, and legend. His labors produced many volumes of Mexican lore including the epic *Song of Quetzalcoatl*. Here is a small part:

> All the glory of the godhead
> Had the prophet Quetzalcoatl;
> All the honor of the people.
> Sanctified his name and holy;
> And their prayers they offered to him
> In the days of ancient Tula,
> There in grandeur rose his temple;
> Reared aloft its mighty ramparts,
> Reaching upwards to the heavens.
> ....
> See, his beard is very lengthy;
> See, exceeding long his beard is;
> Yellow as the straw his beard is!

140. Diaz, Bernal, The Conquest of New Spain, Penguin Books, New York, 1963; and, Olson, Dana, The Legend of Prince Madoc and the White Indians, Jeffersonville, Indiana, 1987, p.33; and, Durrett, Reuben, Traditions of the Earliest Visits of Foreigners, Filson Club Number 23, 1908, p.135.

And his people, they the Toltecs,
Wondrous skilled in all the trades were,
All the arts and artifices,
So that naught there was they knew not;
And as master workmen worked they.
Fashioned they the sacred emeralds;
Fashioned they the precious turquoise;
Smelted they both gold and silver.
Other arts and trades they mastered;
In all crafts and artifices
Skilled were they as wondrous workmen.
And in Quetzalcoatl all these
Arts and crafts had their beginning;
In him all were manifested.
He the master workman taught them
All their trades and artifices[141]

....

Another chronicler of Mexican history was Juan de Torquemada, who in his summary of Quetzalcoatl, agreed that he was a White man with a long yellow beard.

It is unlikely that the entire Legend of Quetzalcoatl referred to Madoc since he was in Mexico much too briefly to accomplish all that is credited to Quetzalcoatl. It is more likely that the legend began with the Phoenicians who influenced the culture of the Olmecs and the Mayas in so many ways. A visit by Norsemen may have reinforced the legend. Madoc's contribution to the legend may have been considerable however, and would account for the description of Wales, the allusions to Christianity and the yellow beard. Some of the technological instructions that the Indians received may well have come from Madoc and his sailors.

Upon leaving Mexico, Madoc is believed to have sailed north to the Gulf Coast of the United States where he found a land that was inviting and appeared to be uninhabited. He sailed into Mobile Bay, where some of his party disembarked and elected not to return to Wales. Madoc would have made the return trip to Wales via the Gulf Stream current. By one account, Madoc's first journey to America and back took four years. Upon his return he told his countrymen of a world with many strange and wonderful things (Mexico), and a fruitful and uninhabited land (Mobile Bay). As word of Madoc's adventures

---

141. Olson, p.31.

spread, David and Emma began hearing tales that included a description of the mouth of the Mississippi River.

Back in Wales, Madoc gathered men and women who were anxious to leave their strife-torn country and settle in the new land. In 1170 he sailed with these men and women in ten or eleven ships from the mouth of the Afon Ganol, a small river in North Wales. His brothers Riryd and Einon and his sister Goeral accompanied him. Edwall, another brother, may have gone with him also. Although the British manned their vessels with 120 men per ship, the similar ships of Madoc could have been manned by as few as twenty-six. Estimates of the total number of people that Madoc took on the voyages varies from thirty to three thousand, but the most quoted estimates for each of the two latter voyages are between 200 and 250. The ships were Viking style, up to seventy-five feet long and were "clinker-built," or having the freeboard built with overlapping planks. They used staghorns instead of nails. They had a single mast with a large square sail, a deep straight keel and eight to sixteen pairs of oars. After a voyage lasting six to nine weeks, Madoc and his party arrived at Mobile Bay. There he found that many of the men he had left behind had perished. Whether this was at the hands of the natives or by natural forces is not known. With only enough men to man the ships, he returned to Wales, this time stopping at the island of Lundy in the Bristol Channel, a place familiar to Madoc, which was removed from the threat of his brother David and King Henry.

At Lundy, Madoc again filled his ships with future settlers anxious to leave Wales. In 1171, he set sail again in the same ten or eleven ships. He sailed southwest "leaving the coast of Ireland far to the north," and followed the trade winds of the equatorial current.[142]

Since Madoc did not return to Wales following this third and last voyage, the Welsh bards do not reveal whether or not all the ships successfully reached Mobile Bay or if they ever located the previous settlers. Spanish historian Antonio de Herrara stated that Christopher Columbus, on his fourth voyage to the New World in 1502, found a ship's mast and an iron pot on the island of Guadeloupe in the Windward Islands. There is also a tale of a gravestone marking Madoc's burial in the West Indies, but this appears to have been written later and is probably fallacious.

The Welsh and the Druids before them were well acquainted with astronomy and Madoc knew the lodestone, which he could use as a compass.

---

142. Deacon, Richard, Madoc and the Discovery of America, George Braziller, New York, 1966.

Despite Madoc's prowess as a seaman, it seems likely that he failed to locate Mobile Bay on his last trip and landed at the mouth of the Mississippi River. Indian legends and the availability of the ships for journeying upstream support that hypothesis. There is little doubt that Madoc was able to accurately identify his ship's latitude, but ascertaining longitude was much more difficult and a place where he could easily have erred. Five centuries later, the French explorer La Salle missed the mouth of the Mississippi and landed in Texas, a mistake that cost him his life when his men mutinied.

There are several accounts of White Indians in the west claiming that their ancestors landed at the mouth of the Mississippi and sailed up that river. Such an event suggests that the two groups of Madoc's followers remained separated and their paths may never have crossed.

The ancient maritime log of Missing Ships of Britain of A.D. 1172 listed two ships from the Madoc expeditions. They were the *Gwenan Gorn (Stag's Horn)*, commanded by Madoc, and the *Pedr Sant (St. Peter)*, commanded by Riryd.

BOOK III

THE WELSH INDIANS

CHAPTER IX

UP THE COOSA RIVER

The anthropologist was distraught attempting to thwart the effort by the combined forces of Indians and Government to prevent him from investigating his ancient find.

"I'm doing this alone and have no political connections or institutional backing. But I don't want to see this incredible discovery lost forever. But if I fight, the tribes will turn on me. I have a good relationship with most of them now..."

"Jim," she interrupted, "Don't be ashamed of standing up for science."

James Chatters, Ancient Encounters

One landing place for Madoc and his compatriots is thought to have been the shores of Mobile Bay. In 1519, Diego Ribeiro, a Portuguese cartographer, drew a map with a line pointing to Mobile Bay called *Tierra do los Gales*, meaning, "Land of the Welsh." From there, another line pointed north.

Mobile Bay was located by the Frenchman Pierre le Moyne d'Iberville in 1701. As he and his companions explored the bay, they ran across some ancient buildings that they could not explain twenty miles south of what is now the city of Mobile.

The best evidence for Mobile Bay being a landing site comes from a Cherokee chief named Oconostota. In 1782 Oconostota was interviewed by U.S. Army Colonel John Sevier, who later became Governor of Tennessee. Oconostota told Sevier that white people calling themselves Welsh had come over a great water and landed at the Bay of Mobile. Sevier's recount of the interview states that the Welsh *first* landed near Mobile, the word "first" possibly implying that Oconostota was aware of another landing.

Oconostota further stated that the Welsh had been driven away from the Mobile area by the Indians. They traveled up river to the north and eventually to the Hiwassee River in Tennessee. (Fig. 12)

Oconostota could not have known about the story of the Welsh except through his forebears, and indeed, he does credit his father and grandfathers with relating it to him. Oconostota also described a revered skin-wrapped book that the Welsh had possessed that is thought to have been a Bible or a psalter. An elderly Cherokee woman named Peg had been given the book by a White Indian who is said to have lived far up the Missouri River. Oconostota told Sevier that the book was destroyed when the Peg's house burned.[143]

Oconostota is well known to historians, and Oconostota is known to have been acquainted with Mobile. In 1736 he visited Mobile and met with emissaries from France and Britain who resided there in the 18th century, and who were friends of the Cherokee tribe.

In the estuary surrounding Mobile Bay, one tributary is called the Dog River. In 1550 The Spanish called the river by that name but the Mobile Indians are thought to have called it that before then. According to Cherokee historian Penelope Allen, the Dog River was formerly known as the Mad Dog River. Since Madoc is frequently referred to as Madog, it is compelling to associate Madoc with the naming of the Dog River.[144]

After having been driven out of the Mobile area, the Welsh trekked north, traveling up the Alabama River and its tributary, the Coosa. The first solid remains of their presence are located just below De Soto Falls on top of Lookout Mountain in Alabama.

In 1782 the Cherokee expedition of John Sevier and his company took them through the Hiwassee country of Tennessee to Chattanooga, then to the Coosa River in Alabama. During his life Sevier fought thirty-five battles with the Indians and was victorious in every one. His Indian campaigns made him more acquainted with the territory than any other white man of the period. He was Tennessee's first governor and served for twelve years. He is known as the founder of that state. The Cherokees loved and feared him. He "never acted in

---

143. Olson, Dana, The Legend of Prince Madoc and the White Indians, Jeffersonville, Indiana, 1987, p.37.

144. Armstrong, Zella, Who Discovered America? Lookout Publishing Company, Chattanooga, 1950, p.82.

cruelty and was never accused of inhumanity and had a friendly demeanor."[145] In one campaign he captured thirty Cherokees. As he had no other place to take them, he took them to his own plantation where they remained as his guests for years. They taught Sevier's daughter Ruth the Cherokee language, and she served as interpreter for her father. She was adopted as a princess or chief's daughter in the Cherokee tribe.

Sevier's account of his interview with Oconostota in 1782 is recorded in correspondence with Amos Stoddard in 1810. Upon inquiring of Oconostota about the stone fortifications near the Hiwassee River, Sevier quoted Oconostota as saying:

> It has been handed down by the Forefathers that the works had been made by the White people who had formerly inhabited the country now *called Carolina.* (Tennessee had not yet become a state).

Oconostota's granddaughter Elizabeth married Joseph Sevier, the son of the governor. She recounted that Oconostota had seen a coracle at Fort Serof, on Mobile Bay. (A coracle is a small round boat that was unique to Ireland and Wales, but any coracle left at Mobile Bay by the settlers with Madoc would have thoroughly deteriorated long before Oconostota's time.) Elizabeth stated that the whole tradition of the Welsh Indians was passed down in the Cherokee tribe from one generation to another. She stated that her grandfather Oconostota, after visiting Mobile in 1736, was quite certain that his father and grandfathers had accurately described their landing place, for they gave Oconostota details of the bay, Dauphin Island, and the three rivers emptying into the bay. They also mentioned the Mobilia tribe as native to the area. According to Elizabeth, her grandfather said that the White Indians were Welsh based on their saying that they came from a land called Gwynet far across the seas. James Stuart (a friend of the Cherokee living in Mobile) told Oconostota that this must be Wales.[146]

In 1942, young Gene Andress, age fourteen, visited relatives near Gadsden, Alabama. Nearby lived his friend, Doug Davis. The two boys met with a talkative old Muskogee Indian Chief named Tappawingow who told them ancient legends about White men sailing up the nearby Coosa River, trading in wood, furs and metals. He told them of a nearby cave at a place named *Tulla* where relics

---

145. Haywood, John, Civil and Political History of the State of Tennessee, Heiskell and Brown, Knoxville, p.183 and p.189.

146. Deacon, Richard, Madoc and the Discovery of America, George Braziller, New York, 1966 p.191.

could by found. They located the cave and began to dig, discovering six vases and enough broken pieces of pottery to fill a box. Roman coins that had been minted in Britain were also found. These coins were in circulation in Wales long after the departure of the Romans. Madoc is purported to have visited the capital city of the Toltecs in central Mexico. It was named *Tula*. This suggests that Madoc's group traveled up the Coosa and occupied the site. It is also suggestive that Madoc had been in central Mexico.[147]

North of Gadsden on Little River, a tributary of the Coosa on Lookout Mountain, is De Soto Falls. About five miles downstream from the falls are stone walls which were built in ancient times. The view from these walls presents a commanding view down the river and they appear to have been constructed so as to protect from assault.

Just below the falls and two hundred feet above the river a stone wall was constructed across a peninsula made by a bend in the river. This wall was sixty-nine feet in length. At the edge of the cliff enclosed by the wall is a narrow path thirty feet in length. The path leads to five 10'x10' cave chambers inside the cliff at the apex of the peninsula. These chambers are partly natural formations and partly chiseled out by metal tools. They interconnect and open onto the face of the cliff where a slight misstep or push could make one topple 150 feet over the edge. The fortifications were first described by Josiah Priest in 1833 and later by Albert Pickett in his *History of Alabama*, which was published in 1845.[148] The site was visited by the author in 2001. Unfortunately the wall no longer exists as several houses and a nearby dam have been built from the stones. An ancient metal axe was reported as having been found in one of the chambers, but its present whereabouts is unknown. (Figs. 13, 14)[149]

Pickett described ditches in front of an inner and an outer stone wall enclosing the cliff site. He stated that Indians had told early settlers that White people had built the walls and fashioned the chambers. The Indians said that these people wore clothes, and had fair skin and beards. The settlers presumed it was De Soto, but De Soto was in the locality much too briefly to have built these fortifications and his meticulous journals never mention the site.[150] From the notes of John Sevier it is almost certain that he came across the fort during his Cherokee campaign in 1782.

---

147. Olson, p.39.
148. Armstrong, p.67.
149. Hendon, Carolyn, personal communication, 2001.
150. Armstrong, p.67.

Arthur F. Griffiths, a Kentucky surveyor, compared the remains at De Soto Falls with a plan of Dolwydden castle, Modoc's birthplace, and found that the mode of design was almost identical.[151]

Fifty miles east of De Soto Falls and two miles east of the town of Chatsworth, Georgia, is Fort Mountain. On top of its 2832 foot summit are the most impressive of the Welsh Indian fortifications. The site now has a degree of protection by being a state park. (Figs. 15, 16) On the north peak of the saddle back mountain, a stone wall extends 885 feet across the summit from the east precipice to the west precipice. Within the wall are pits or foxholes. An easily identifiable entrance is protected by these foxholes. There is a spring within the protected area. The climb up the mountain is exhausting. The defenders were known to have cut down all of the trees from the bottom of the mountain to the top, thereby thwarting any surprise attack. Studies by Knight, Haywood and Pickett are in agreement that the De Soto Falls and Fort Mountain Forts were built a few hundred years before the arrival of Columbus and that they are quite unlike any known Indian construction.

The Cherokee tradition states that the builders of the Fort Mountain site had pale faces and that the Indians had later chased them out of the country. The Cherokee said that they called them the "Moon-eyed People" and considered them to be able to see better at night so as to watch their enemies. The Welsh, being miners, were commonly visually dark adapted and had a reputation as being vigilant in the dark hours so as to observe and attack their enemies. In 1834, gold miners in the Nacoochee Valley of Georgia discovered a subterranean village consisting of thirty-four log houses. Perhaps this was the origin of the Cherokee tale describing "Moon-eyed People" and an abode for Welsh miners. The word "Welsh" continues in the Cherokee language, and is associated with forges and furnaces.[152]

The people who built the forts at Fort Mountain and De Soto Falls were not mound builders. There are impressive remains of Indian mounds representing the Mississippian Culture at Etowah, near the city of Cartersville, Georgia, and not very far from either of the above forts. (Fig. 17) The mounds at Etowah were built of earth. The Indians north of central Mexico were not stonemasons and it is not reasonable to attribute to them the building of stone forts. The Welsh were accomplished stonemasons. They passed this way and

---

151. Deacon, p.203.
152. Armstrong, p.85 and p.189.

were in deadly peril of being assaulted by the Indians. It is logical that the Welsh built these fortifications for defensive purposes.

Two other mountain top stone fortifications have been identified in north Georgia that echo the presence of the Welsh. These are on Ladd Mountain in Bartow County, twenty-five miles southwest of Fort Mountain and on Alec Mountain in Habersham County, seventy miles east of Fort Mountain and near the Nacoochee Valley subterranean village. The stone walls at the Ladd Mountain site have been removed to build a road. This site is not far from the Mississippian Indian village at Etowah. The Alec Mountain site was "tested" by Phillip Smith in 1956, "but no cultural material was found."[153] Not finding cultural material at mountain top fortresses should not be surprising because these forts would have been occupied only when danger threatened, that danger being personified in the form of the invading Cherokee.

After being driven from Fort Mountain, the route of the retreating Welsh enters Tennessee. On the banks of the Hiwassee River in Polk County was Savannah Fort. Judge Haywood names four additional sites of fortifications in the vicinity of nearby Chattanooga, including one on Sand Mountain in Catoosa County, Georgia. With the possible exception of the Sand Mountain site, all of these fortifications have been destroyed.[154] (Fig. 18)

The Cherokee have said that when they arrived in East Tennessee they found white people, who were living in conjunction with forts in several places. They identified the sites as: (1) the Hiwassee River area (Savannah Fort), (2) along the Tennessee River near the Little Tennessee River, (3) at Pumpkintown (now Athens), (3) across from Dallas Island, and (5) at "*Big Chicamauga (Creek) where they entered into a treaty, by which they* (the white people) *agreed to depart the country if the Cherokees would permit them to do so in peace, which they did.*"[155]

A Scotsman named Brown entered the land of the Cherokee in 1761 and settled on the bank of the Hiwassee River. He found,

> ...remains of old forts on the Hiwassee and Tennessee Rivers about which were hoes, axes, guns and other metallic utensils. The Indians of 1761 told him the French had been there and built those forts. [In Brown's view] ... the former inhabitants appear to have lived in houses made by setting up

---

153. Faulkner, Charles H., The Old Stone Fort, Exploring an Archaeological Mystery, University of Tennessee Press, Knoxville, p.15-16.

154. Deacon, p.205; and Faulkner, p.15-16.

155. Haywood, John, The Natural and Aboriginal History of Tennessee, F. M. Brooks, Kingsport Tennessee, 1973, p.219.

poles and then digging out the dirt and covering poles with it. The houses were round and generally ten feet in diameter.[156]

At that time the French had established Fort Toulouse on the Tallapoosa River in Alabama and explored East Tennessee to an extent. They were drawn away to the northeast by the French and Indian conflicts and did not build any forts in East Tennessee.[157]

In 1898, the Bureau of Ethnology reported on the extensive remains in Polk County, Tennessee (Savannah Fort). The remains included an ancient settlement, a cemetery and a fort of undressed stone that enclosed a square area.[158] At another site in East Tennessee a stone was found in a previously undisturbed burial mound with an inscription. The interpretation from the ancient Coelbren as used in twelfth century Wales read, "Madoc ruler thou art." It has been suggested that this may be the tomb of Madoc; but that is not reasonable as it would mean that the Welsh built the fortresses in Alabama and Georgia and moved to Tennessee within one generation.[159]

When the Welsh arrived on the banks of the Hiwassee and Tennessee Rivers, they found themselves in an area that had been inhabited for centuries, as far back as 15,000 B.C. when the Paleo-Americans inhabited the area. These people were subsequently replaced by the Archaic and Woodland Cultures who left their artifacts, shells and potsherds in caves and middens about the area. In about A.D. 1000, the Woodland Culture suddenly gave way to the Mississippian, which was first centered on Hiwassee Island at the mouth of the Hiwassee River. These people spoke a Muskogean dialect. About A.D. 1300, Creek Indians arrived and built Mississippian Culture mounds on Dallas Island in the Tennessee River downstream from Hiwassee Island, and they later built on other islands and on the river banks. The Dallas Island site was the Indian town of Chiaha described by scribes journeying with Hernando De Soto's expedition in 1540. The Mississippian Culture began to decline at Cahokia in about A.D. 1150. Its decline at Dallas and Hiwassee Islands was considerably later and they were still building sites in 1450.[160]

156. Haywood, p.219.

157. Benthal, Joe, personal communication, Madisonville, Tennessee, 14 September, 2003.

158. Gibson, Frances M., The Seafarers: Pre-Columbian Voyages to America Dorrance and Company, Philadelphia, p.203.

159. The Brandenburg Stone Exhibit, Meade County, Kentucky Public Library, on loan to the Charlestown, Indiana Public Library, 2001.

The Cherokee entered the valleys of north Georgia in the thirteenth century and later built villages on the Little Tennessee, Hiwassee and Tellico Rivers in Tennessee. Around 1500, this powerful tribe expelled the Welsh, and in 1715 they expelled all the other Indian tribes from the area. The Yuchi fled to the Savannah River and to Florida, the Shawnees escaped north to Kentucky and Ohio, and the Creeks migrated to the south and west as a result of their conflicts with the Cherokee.

Another Cherokee tradition as told by Chief Oconostota is that a great battle between his people and the White Indians was fought on the Tennessee River at Muscle Shoals, Alabama. He is quoted as saying:

> "...that a war had existed between the two nations for several years. At length it was discovered that the Whites were making a large number of boats which induced the Cherokee to suppose they were about to descend the Tennessee River. They (the Cherokee) then assembled their whole band of warriors and took the shortest and most convenient route to the Muscle Shoals in order to intercept them on their passage down the river. In a few days the boats hove into sight. A warm combat ensued with various success for several days."

Both sides suffered no small amount of losses. At length, the Welsh agreed by treaty to leave the area, prisoners were exchanged and the two warring parties parted "on a friendly basis." The hasty departure of the Welsh explains why axes, hoes and other metal utensils were found at the abandoned forts on the Hiwassee and Tennessee Rivers.[161]

Judge John Haywood, the author of a compilation of early Tennessee history, elaborates on Oconostota's account by saying that the Cherokees waged war on the Welsh and drove them to their fort at the mouth of Chickamauga Creek in present day Chattanooga. At that point, the two warring parties entered a treaty with the Welsh agreeing to leave the area. The Muscle Shoals treaty was a bit later than the Chickamauga treaty and included Welsh living beyond the Chickamauga area.

In the attempt to establish an estimated date that the Welsh were driven out of Tennessee several historical factors need to be considered. There was another place that a great battle was fought between the Welsh and the Indians,

---

160. Gilbert, Martin, *The Dent Atlas of American History*, J.M.Dent, London, p.6; and, Livingood, James W., *A History of Hamilton County*, Tennessee, Memphis State University Press, 1981.
161. Deacon, p.186.

that being at the Falls of the Ohio River at Louisville, Kentucky. The Great Battle at the Falls of the Ohio involved the Welsh who had originally landed at the mouth of the Mississippi and a coalition of Indian tribes led by the Shawnee and Iroquois. Kerr, in his *History of Kentucky*, states that this battle occurred between 1660 and 1670, and coincided with the rampage of the Iroquois through the Ohio Valley.

Oconostota stated that the date of the battle at Muscle Shoals was unknown but is "probably closer to the 17th century than to the 13th century."[162] That description would place the battle at Muscle Shoals as occurring sometime after 1450. Haywood interpreted Oconostota as saying that both the Muscle Shoals and the Falls of the Ohio battles were fought at about the same time, and Armstrong repeated that according to Oconostota, the treaties of these two battles occurred at about the same time.[163] This is inaccurate. There was no treaty after the Battle at the Falls of the Ohio because there was no Welsh tribe remaining to negotiate. I suggest the treaties of which Oconostota spoke were the treaties at Chickamauga and at Muscle Shoals. Since the Cherokee were the instigators of both the Chickamauga and the Muscle Shoals battles, Oconostota's forefathers would have been familiar with both of these treaties. The Cherokee were not involved in the battle at the Falls of the Ohio. Kerr's date for the battle at the Falls of the Ohio is based on knowledge of movements by the Iroquois, who were involved in that battle, and the date given by Kerr appears to be accurate.[164]

The Spanish had long been concerned about the Welsh Colonists. The Spanish Archives of Seville show that several expeditions were sent to find the "Gente Blanca." De Soto and the other Spanish explorers were searching for gold, but another goal was to search for descendants of Madoc's colony. The Spanish sent additional expeditions to the southeast in search of the Welsh in 1557, 1566, 1624, 1628, and 1661, but found no trace. Oconostota relates that the Welsh were gone long before the Spanish expeditions began. As mentioned, it has been claimed that Oconostota said the battle at the Falls of the Ohio occurred at about the same time as the battle at Muscle Shoals. This creates a problem with the De Soto expedition, which began in 1539. De Soto encountered the Yuchi Indians in East Tennessee, and was at the present site of Chattanooga (Chiaha)

---

162. Deacon, p.209.

163. Armstrong, p.90-93.

164. Clift, G. Glenn, History of Maysville and Mason County, Kentucky, Transylvania Printing Company, Lexington, 1936, p.13; and, Deacon, p.115 illustration.

on June 4-5, 1540, where he passed by Welsh built forts. That he failed to locate the Welsh at that time indicates that they indeed had already departed. It also means that the battle at Muscle Shoals took place well before 1540 and must have predated the Great Battle at the Falls of the Ohio by a century and a half or more.[165]

In 1566-1567 Spanish explorer Juan Pardo followed De Soto to the Tennessee Valley. He departed from the Spanish Colony of Santa Elena, which was located on Parris Island, South Carolina. On his return, he visited the Indian village of Chiaha, which he called Olamico. This site was the Dallas Island village of the Creek Indians, and also the old site of a Welsh fort on the Tennessee River across from Dallas Island. It is also the site of the first Hamilton County Court House. Pardo found himself in jeopardy from Indian attacks, and on October 20, 1567, he laid out a fort at Chiaha. He left corporal Marcos Jimenez and twenty-five soldiers there "that they should be there and guard the fort." He also built a fort five days later further south. These forts were built in three to four days and are presumed to have been wooden palisaded enclosures. Pardo returned to Santa Elena in 1567; twenty years later the British overran the Spanish colony.[166]

Several sites in southern Tennessee have been found that reflect the presence of the Welsh. Skeletons of extremely tall individuals and Roman coins were found in a cave near Fayetteville, and the design of the entrance to Old Stone Fort, near Manchester, suggests the presence of the Welsh. Old Stone Fort is located on a peninsula, the apex of which is the junction of the Duck and Little Duck Rivers. Carbon datings from sparse samples of charcoal taken from trenches dug in the walls of the fort have given dates of A.D. 30, 220, 305, and 430. These dates precede the Welsh and even precede the advent of the bow and arrow to America, but conical stone mounds that flank the entrance appear to have been built later. The entrance is rather complex and contains a cul-de-sac which makes it more easily defendable. The pattern of the entrance has been compared to the entrance at Carn Fadrun in Wales.[167]

Almost no artifacts have been found at Old Stone Fort indicating that the ancient builders and any more recent inhabitants were either exceptionally careful to avoid leaving their belongings, or the fort was occupied for such short periods that almost no artifacts were left at the site. Only seven projectile points

---

165. Armstrong, p.94-95, and p.187.
166. http://appalachiansummit.tripod.com/chapt2.htm.
167.

have been found at the site. These were found on the cliffs leading up from the river.

Old Stone Fort was built on the top of a steep embankment leading up from the rivers and a moat had been dug connecting the rivers in the lowland near their junction. The walls have been estimated to have been over ten feet high and twenty feet thick, and the artificial moat between the rivers was twenty feet deep at one time.[168]

The walls of Old Stone Fort are not stone. There are two parallel rows of rock rubble at the base, but the mass of the walls is earthen. This is unlike the Welsh construction at Fort Mountain or Savannah Fort. Charles Faulkner of the University of Tennessee has concluded that Old Stone Fort was built in stages by Indians of the Hopewellian Culture. He bases his opinion on the disparity of the various radioactive carbon dates and structural similarities with Hopewell sites in Ohio. Because of the lack of artifacts at the site he believes that it served a ceremonial function. However the design of the fort, the diligent effort required in the construction of the walls, which were atop cliffs leading up from the rivers, the moat at the rivers' confluence, and the complex entrance with its cul de sac all point to a defensive purpose.

A large tree growing in a wall of Old Stone Fort was cut down in 1819 and 357 (var. 337) annular rings could be counted. That tells us that the walls were built before, possibly long before, 1462 (var. 1482). It also means that the walls ceased being cared for and the fort was abandoned shortly after that date.[169]

The North American explorations of René Robert Cavelier Sieur de La Salle began in Montreal in 1669. In the summer of that year, he employed fourteen men and outfitted an expedition with five canoes and provisions intending to search for the Ohio River, which he had heard about from the Iroquois. He was persuaded to join an expedition of seven Sulpician priests whose intent was to establish a mission among the western tribes. A party of Seneca Indians who had wintered at La Salle's settlement acted as guides to Lake Ontario.

On the southern shore of Lake Ontario La Salle and the Sulpicians were led to a village of the Seneca (Tsonnontouan) tribe. This tribe was a member of the New York Confederation of Iroquois, and while generally friendly to the French, were known to be touchy and unpredictable. While with the Seneca, the Sulpician priest Galinée related that one day they:

---

168. Armstrong, p.59.
169. Armstrong, p.82, Deacon, p.186; and, Faulkner, p.23.

...heard that a party of Tsonnontouan warriors was returning from a distant expedition with a war prisoner; the captive belonged to a western tribe and seemed just the man they needed (to use as a guide). They decided upon an attempt to purchase him. The following morning Galinée went to see the prisoner, a handsome and sturdy youth of eighteen or twenty years of age, already bound to the stake. He sent the Hollander (a Dutchman who was the expedition's interpreter) to the chief with offers of presents in exchange for the prisoner, but met with stern refusal; the youth was assigned to an aged woman whose son had been killed in the war. While the instruments of torture were being prepared in his very presence, Galinée exhorted the victim to confide in God. Presently the captive was approached by an Indian holding the barrel of a gun that had been held in the fire until it glowed red hot. This was applied first to his insteps and slowly raised until the flesh along his legs was burned. For six endless hours, his body was thus seared, amid a jeering mob. Eventually his tormentors released him from the stake and chased him across the public place, prodding him with red hot brands. In the throes of agony, the unfortunate youth fell. Immediately they heaped hot coals and ashes upon him. When this diabolical treatment began to pall, they pelted him with stones and, rushing upon his quivering body, tore it to pieces; one seized his head, another his arms, a third his legs; these pitiful remains to be cooked and gorged upon. Attracted to the scene of torture, La Salle's first impulse was to thrust himself upon the relentless persecutors, but he soon realized the futility of an action which would bring certain death upon himself and his companions. Sick at heart and helpless, he fled from this inhuman scene... Filled with horror and disgust, the explorers hastened away from this fiendish tribe. [170]

Later in the autumn of 1669, La Salle was given a Shawnee brave who was a captive of an Iroquois tribe living west of Niagara. This Shawnee was named Nika and he proved to be La Salle's faithful companion for the next eighteen years.

After reaching Lake Erie La Salle and the Sulpicians parted. La Salle is believed to have located a tributary of the Ohio, which he descended to the Falls of the Ohio at Louisville. At that time all fourteen of his men abandoned him. With incredible fortitude he eventually made his way back to Montreal accompanied only by Nika, his Shawnee guide and companion.

---

170. Chesnel, Paul, *History of Cavelier de La Salle*, translated by Andrée Chesnel Meany, G.P. Putnam's Sons, New York and London, 1932, p.27-28.

Before returning to Montreal, La Salle turned west and discovered the Illinois River and there is a possibility that he may have discovered the Mississippi River in 1671, a year before Joliet. In 1681-2 La Salle returned to Illinois and explored the Mississippi to the Gulf of Mexico. On April 9, 1682 he stood on the shore of the Gulf, dressed in a gold-laced red cloak; he planted a cross, buried a plaque and made a speech officially claiming possession of the Louisiana Territory for the King of France. On his return journey he fell ill and had to spend the winter in a fort he had established at Chickasaw Bluffs (Memphis). [171]

Olson states that in a report of this journey, La Salle said that the Old Stone Fort was occupied by the Yuchi Indians at that time (1682), but it is highly unlikely that La Salle ever saw the Old Stone Fort.[172] The question as to who built Old Stone Fort may never be answered. Faulkner's opinion that it was connected to the Hopewell Culture may be correct, but there seem to be few clues beyond the archaeological similarities.

I would conclude that the fortifications at Old Stone Fort were built in ancient times, and any Welsh presence there would have been extremely brief. If the Welsh ever did inhabit the fort, they played no consequential part in its history and vice versa.[173]

In those days Middle Tennessee was the land of the Yuchi, one branch of which was known as the Chisca tribe. It is likely that the Welsh, who were enemies of the Cherokee, badly needed allies. Oconostota stated that the White Indians were their enemies, but makes no similar aspersions about the Yuchi. In turn the Yuchi were apparently friendly to the Welsh, with whom they may have traded and from whom they could have learned skills in return for allowing the Welsh to live in their territory.

Sometime before the 18th century the Yuchi spread to East Tennessee and the Hiwassee River area. There they occupied the deserted forts of the Welsh and were found to be in possession of the metal tools which were left behind when the Welsh deserted the area in haste.

---

171. Parkman, Francis, La Salle and the Discovery of the Great West, Signet Classics, published by The New American Library of World Literature, Inc., New York, 1963, (originally published in 1869), p.46,229,231.

172. Olson, p.49.

173. Bureau of American Ethnology, Bulletin 145, 'Indian Tribes of North America,' p.116-120; and, Olson, p.56; and, Faulkner, p.53-55.

The Yuchi and their language have uncertain origins and relations. Pritzker states that Yuchean is "a linguistic isolate, possibly related to the Siouan language family," and Van West reports that it "bears a resemblance to the Muskogean as well as the Siouan linguistic families." They are reported to have cultural similarities to the Catawba Indians, a Siouan speaking tribe that lived in North Carolina.[174]

An association between the Yuchi and the Welsh tribes is suggested by the similar Shawnee names for the two, the Shawnees calling the Welsh, *Talegewi*, meaning stranger or foreigner, and the Yuchi, *Tahogalewi*.[175]

The Welsh also were probably on friendly terms with the Creek Indians of the Mississippian Culture on the Tennessee River. Haywood describes five Welsh fortifications in the Chattanooga area very near the Mississippian mounds on Dallas Island and Hiwassee Island. The location of these fortifications does not appear to be a defensive posture against the Creek, but rather against the Cherokee. There is no evidence of conflict between the Welsh and the mound builders on Hiwassee and Dallas Islands, rather a close relationship is suggested by a description of the Creek Indians of the Tennessee-Alabama region being lighter in complexion than their Muskogi brothers. The Creeks of this region called themselves "white" people and the other Muskogi "red" people. Some of the Yuchi were also referred to as "white Indians".[176] Thus the Welsh, Yuchi, and Creeks are thought to have been on friendly terms and may have interbred.

When White settlers began streaming into Middle Tennessee in the late eighteenth century, they found the land free of human inhabitants. Although the settlers were frequently under attack by the Creek, Cherokee, Chickasaw and Shawnee, those tribes only used the area as a hunting ground and did not live there. Haywood stated:

> The country from French Lick (Nashville, south to) as far as the Elk River, and beyond it, had not a single permanent inhabitant except for the wild beasts of the forest; but it had been inhabited many centuries before by a numerous population. At every lasting spring is a large collection of graves made in a particular way, with the heads inclined on the sides and

---

174. Pritzker, Barry M., Native American Encyclopedia, Oxford University Press, New York, 2000, p.396; and, Van West, Carroll, Editor in Chief, The Tennessee Encyclopedia of History and Culture, Tennessee Historical Society, Rutledge Hill Press, Nashville, p.1093-4.

175. Pritzker, p.396; and, Van West, p.1093-4.

176. McMahan, Basil, The Mystery of Old Stone Fort, Nashville, 1965, p.66.

feet stones; the whole of which is covered with a stratum of mould and dirt about eight or ten inches deep. At many springs is the appearance of walls enclosing ancient habitations, the foundations of which were visible whenever the earth was cleared and cultivated; to which walls, entrenchments were sometimes added. These walls sometimes enclose six, eight, or ten acres of land, and sometimes they are more extensive. Judging from the number and frequency of these appearances, it cannot be estimated, but that the former inhabitants were ten times, if not twenty times, more numerous than those who at present occupy the country.[177]

The Haywood description of the stone graves sounds very much like other graves credited to the Welsh, as does the description of six to ten acre agricultural plots surrounded by stone walls. The presence of these sites in Middle Tennessee suggests that small groups of Welsh may have had scattered habitations throughout the area. However the remains that have been found in the stone lined graves have been identified as Indian, although archaeologists have not been able to identify the tribe.[178] Perhaps it was the Arikara tribe or their progenitors, the Skidi-Pawnee, who built the walls and dug the graves in Middle Tennessee. The Arikara later were found to bury their dead facing the east in stone lined graves. The Skidi-Pawnee are reported to have been in the Ohio Valley before migrating west in the sixteenth century.[179] Another possibility is that some of the graves were occupied by a mixed breed of Welsh and Yuchi (or Creek) and the remains could therefore resemble the Indian.

In northeast Tennessee, a peculiar race of dark skinned people of unknown origin called Melungeons has existed for centuries. The most accepted provenance of these people identifies them as either the remnant of a group of Portuguese sailors who were shipwrecked in 1665 off the coast of the southeastern U.S., or a group of survivors from the Spanish Colony of Santa Elena in South Carolina, which was overrun by the British in 1587.[180] It has been theorized that either group interbred with the Indians to produce the Melungeons, who were then driven westward into Tennessee by the English settlers. Now a third possibility has been purported: that the Melungeons are descendants of the Welsh Indians and the Yuchi. All of the prominent surnames

177. Haywood, p.95.

178. Faulkner, Charles H., personal communication, Knoxville, Tennessee, 2003.

179. Faulkner, personal communication; and, Pritzker, Barry M., Native American Encyclopedia, Oxford University Press, New York, 2000, p.350.

180. Burkindine, Katelyn, 'Evidence That Muslim Populations Throve in Pre-Columbian America,' The Barnes Review, 7, no.5, 2001, p.33.

of the Melungeons have been claimed to be British or Welsh and the Melungeons spoke an English dialect. They were never enslaved and claim to be European.[181]

The Yuchi did intensive hoe agriculture, planting corn, beans and squash. De Soto and Pardo knew them in East Tennessee as the Chisca. Following attacks by the Cherokee, most of the Yuchi fled to the Savannah River area, but some, called *Tomahittans*, moved up the Tennessee Valley to the Holston River in Virginia. There they were found by the English explorers James Needham and Gabriel Arthur in 1673. The Tomahittans told these men that,

> ...eight dayes jorney down this river lives a white people which have long beardes and whiskers and weares clothing, and on some of ye other rivers lives a hairey people, not many years since ye Tomahittans sent twenty men laden with beaver to ye white people, they killed tenn of them and put ye other tenn in irons, two of which tenn escaped..., ye prisoner relates that ye white people have a bell which is six foot over which they ring morning and evening and att that time a great number of people congregate togather and talkes he knowes not what, they have many blacks among them, oysters and many other shell-fish, many swine and cattle. Theire bulding is brick,...(sic)[182]

The escaped prisoner's description of a large bell that summons people to congregate and chant, and the presence of many Blacks (slaves) indicate that these people were the Spanish Catholics, North Africans and slaves who were refugees from Santa Elena.

Oconostota concluded by saying after their defeat at Muscle Shoals, the White Indians "then descended the Tennessee down to the Ohio, thence down to the Big River (the Mississippi), then they ascended it up to the Muddy River (the Missouri) and thence up that river for a great distance. They were then on some of its branches, but they are no more White People; they are now all become Indians, and look like other Red People of the country."[183]

Further corroboration of Oconostota's testimony comes from B. F. Owen who interviewed an old Indian prophet in 1854. Owen was told that "Long ago

---

181. Olson, p.51.

182. Abraham Wood, letter to John Richards, August 22, 1674, 'The Journeys of James Needham and Gabriel Arthur in 1673 and 1674 Through the Piedmont and Mountains of North Carolina to Establish Trade with the Cherokee,' http://rla.unc.edu/Archives/accounts/Needham/Needham-Text.html.

183. Deacon, p.187.

White people lived on Conestoga (Conasauga) Creek" (a tributary of the Hiwassee River in Polk County, Tennessee) "and plowed and raised grain. Indians called them *Welegens* and in time made war on them and drove them away."[184] In the twelfth century, the Welsh on the island of Lundy were known as Welegens.[185]

---

184. Armstrong, p.45.
185. Gibson, p.203.

Chapter X

To the Falls of the Ohio

The philosophy professor was dramatically making an analogy about an individual's life, using a bucket of water.

"My hand is your life," he said. "When I put it into the bucket, it raises the level of the water. When I remove my hand, the level goes back to where it was before,... as if my hand had never been there."

A hush fell over the classroom; then students slowly began nodding. I dropped the class.[186]

There is a wealth of information from early White settlers in Indiana and Kentucky that describes the area around the Falls of the Ohio at Louisville as a stronghold for the Welsh, however, the continental landing site and the route they took to the Falls is debatable.

When Madoc returned to Wales after his second expedition, he reported that most of the men of the first expedition had perished. Whether this was a result of natural forces or at the hands of the Indians is unknown. This indicates that he found Mobile Bay on his second expedition. It is not disputed that Madoc was an experienced and skilled seaman, and it is doubtful that he would not have been able to locate a site he had found before; but such an event happened to La Salle five centuries later when he failed to find the mouth of the Mississippi and landed in Texas. In Madoc's case, natural events may have

---

186. Orsey, Robert R., oral communication of a classroom experience at Northwestern University, ca. 1960.

89

intervened, such as a hurricane that drove his ships off course, or a request or demand by the people on board to be put ashore. Such an event may have necessitated landing at an alternate site. It has been stated that Columbus discovered remains of a ship's mast and an iron pot on the island of Guadeloupe in 1502. If these were from Madoc's third expedition, they would be evidence that he ran into bad weather. In the 1172 Log of Missing Ships of Britain a cross was drawn next to the *Pedr Sant*, commanded by Riryd. This indicates that the *Pedr Sant* was lost at sea at sometime in the second expedition and not the third, because the fate of the ships of the third expedition would not have been known in Wales.

There are documented encounters of Colonists with White Indians in the eighteenth century that allege that the ancestors of the Welsh landed at the mouth of the Mississippi River. If we follow that assumption, once on the mighty Mississippi, they probably stayed in their ocean going ships rowing upstream, as Madoc and his sailors did not use the ships to return to Wales.

On the other hand, if they found Mobile Bay on the third voyage, they could have taken the Tombigbee River north and portaged to the Tennessee River and then continued downstream to the Ohio. Or they could have taken the Tombigbee to the Natchez Trace, an old buffalo and Indian trail that led to Nashville and the Cumberland River, and then gone downstream to the Ohio. They would not have encountered the Welsh who preceded them by a year by either of these routes. (Fig. 19)

It can be discounted that the Coosa group of the Welsh would have been able to become a mighty tribe with strong fortresses that had command of the desirable and strategic area around the Falls of the Ohio after their defeat at Muscle Shoals around 1500. The base for the Cherokee tribe was in the southern Appalachians, but they were a large tribe who had spread into eastern Kentucky and they would have been aware if the Welsh they defeated had settled at the Falls of the Ohio. Also the time interval between the Muscle Shoals Battle and the Falls of the Ohio Battle does not appear to have been great enough for them to build the numerous forts and towers that formed the strong defensive network that was in the central Ohio Valley.

There have been several findings near the Cumberland River in northern Middle Tennessee that have been interpreted as an indication of passage by the Welsh. Northeast of Nashville on Rock Creek near Castalian Springs, a peculiar stone was found in a creek bed. It was presented to the Tennessee Historical Society in 1878. It was described by Gates P. Thruston in 1890 and has been named the Thruston Tablet.[187] (Fig. 20) It contains a pictoglyph of a Viking ship and an altercation and conciliation involving round-eyed warriors and almond-eyed Indians. The depiction of the Viking ship (a type that was used by the Welsh) on the tablet has been taken as an argument that Madoc sailed up the Mississippi and nearby Cumberland Rivers to the site. If it is a depiction of a ship of Madoc, it indicates that the Welsh did land at the mouth of the Mississippi and proceeded north via that route in their ocean-going craft. That journey would have been long and difficult, but predictably much quicker and much easier than if they had gone overland. It could also be argued that the drawings on the Thruston Tablet were drawn from the memory of their transoceanic voyage and the conflict and conciliation with the Indians occurred later.[188]

In the early nineteenth century Captain David Williams reported that workmen collecting saltpetre in a cave near the Cumberland River five or six miles above Carthage, Tennessee, found "many human skeletons." One of bodies was female with shrivelled flesh and yellow hair. Around her wrist was a silver clasp with letters resembling those of the "Greek alphabet."[189] In another nearby cave three more bodies with visible fair white skin, auburn hair and blue eyes were found.[190]

A cogent argument can be made that the Thruston Tablet is of Viking origin and not Welsh. The findings of rune stones along the Arkansas River in Oklahoma indicate that the Vikings were in the Mississippi River Basin. Only one ship is engraved on the Thruston Tablet, whereas Madoc had ten. The incipient Welsh settlers included women and children but the round-eyed figures carved on the Thruston Tablet were all warriors. The Vikings had a propensity for altercations wherever they went; the Welsh would have wanted to avoid conflict.

On the other hand, there is no record of such a journey by Vikings in the Sagas. The ancient mummified body of the white woman found near the site

187. Pohl, Frederick, J., The Viking Settlements of North America, Clarkson N. Potter, New York, 1972, p.318.

188. Deacon, Richard, Madoc and the Discovery of America, George Braziller, New York, 1966, p.209; and, Armstrong, Zella, Who Discovered America? Lookout Publishing Company, Chattanooga, 1950; and, Olson, Dana, The Legend of Prince Madoc and the White Indians, Jeffersonville, Indiana, 1987, p.54.

189. Haywood, John, The Natural and Aboriginal History of Tennessee, F. M. Brooks, Kingsport, 1973, p.149.

190. Armstrong, p.52; and, Haywood, John, A Civil and Political History of Tennessee, Heiskell and Brown, Knoxville, 1823.

where the tablet was found reveals that women had been present, and records in stone done by Vikings were typically Rune stones, not pictoglyphs. The Thruston Tablet remains a fascinating find; the uncertainty of its origins make it even more so.

Madoc and his people would have traveled up the Mississippi and Ohio Rivers as far as their ships would take them. That was to the Falls of the Ohio. Until they reached the Falls they found the river to be wide and serene. Above the mouth of the Wabash the hills of Kentucky and Indiana began crowding the flood plain, coming closer to the banks of the river and enhancing the scenic beauty. Their idyllic journey was suddenly interrupted when they approached the Falls of the Ohio. They first encountered the Falls at Sand Island. Above this island near the Indiana shore is a giant swirling vortex that nineteenth century boatmen named the "Big Eddy." It comprises several acres and is 150 feet deep. It was formed eight to ten thousand years ago when the Falls was thirty-five feet high and six hundred feet wide.[191] The Big Eddy sucked in many steamships and lesser vessels before locks and dams were built around the Falls.

The leading ships of Madoc may have become caught in the Big Eddy; later ships would have been alerted and beached downstream from the treacherous whirlpool. In 1825 construction on the first canal around the Falls began at Louisville. The locks of the canal and the subsequent McAlpine Dam led commercial traffic to Louisville and made it the dominant city at the Falls. The Welsh built their villages near the center of the Falls on the Indiana side of the river and near the swirling waters of the Big Eddy. They were not interested in commerce but in protection from attack that the dangerous currents provided. They soon recognized other benefits of the Falls. The shallow waters contained abundant mussels, and fishing was excellent as was hunting, because large animals used the shallow waters near Sand Island as a river crossing. Agriculture could be practiced in the fertile land of the flood plain. The climate was pleasant and no Indians lived there, although Indians did use the area for hunting and fishing. The Indians considered the Falls area unhealthy because of the moist cool air and a malady they called "lung fever."[192] (Fig. 21)

The Falls of the Ohio is a cataract made by the largest exposed Devonian coral reef in the world. Prior to the last great Ice Age the waters from the Kentucky River flowed north into the Great Miami River; The Licking River

---

191. Olson, p.61.
192. Baird, Clay, A Journey to the Falls, 1994.

flowed north into Mill Creek in Cincinnati and beyond; Kinniconick and Salt Lick Creeks flowed east as they do now, and then north into the Scioto River. The Scioto, Mill Creek and the Great Miami River all flowed north, the reverse of their present direction of flow. Divides near Madison, Indiana; Manchester, Ohio; Portsmouth, Ohio; and several places farther upstream, separated the watersheds. Downstream, only a comparative trickle of water from a creek or two flowed over uneroded land where the Falls is now located. When the ice began melting, water inundated the valleys of the rivers and creeks. The previous outlets to the north for these streams remained blocked by ice. As a result floodwaters eventually broke through the divides and created the current channel of the Ohio River. When the natural dams at these divides broke, the torrent rushed to the Falls and over its coral reef. The bedrock that the rushing waters exposed is over 350 million years old. The Falls is much tamer now but the river still drops twenty-five feet in the two to three miles that the water crosses the exposed rock.[193]

In his booklet, *A Journey to the Falls*, Baird asserts that the Welsh arrived at the Falls 300 years before Columbus.[194] If true, this not only dates their arrival to the Falls, but it also means that the trip from the Gulf to the Falls took less than twenty-two years. This negates any possibility that it was the Coosa branch of the tribe that originally settled the area after their defeat at Muscle Shoals. It also means that the Mississippi group wasted little time traversing from the Gulf to the Ohio River Valley. For this reason the possible Welsh occupancy of Old Stone Fort, the cave findings near Fayetteville, Tennessee, and the connection with the Yuchi would have involved the Coosa branch of the Welsh rather than those who sailed up the Mississippi and Ohio Rivers to the Falls.

Colonel Reuben Durrett, a Kentucky historian, reported that in 1799 six skeletons had been found in Jeffersonville, Indiana, across the Ohio River from Louisville. Each of the six skeletons was wearing a breast plate bearing a mermaid and a harp, the Welsh coat of arms. The harp was the Welsh national musical instrument and the mermaid indicated the person wearing the shield was a mariner of Prince Madoc. The inscriptions on the shields has been translated as "Virtuous deeds meet their just reward."[195] (Fig.22)

---

193. Fowke, Gerard, The Evolution of the Ohio River, Hollenbeck Press, Indianapolis, 1933.
194. Baird.
195. Olson, p.62; and, Durrett, Reuben, Traditions of the Earliest Visits of Foreigners, Filson Club Number 23, 1908.

Another account by Durrett was of a gravestone found near the Falls with the inscribed date of 1186. The name on the stone was illegible.[196]

In 1898, John Brady discovered a helmet, a shield of armour, and an arm shield on a vacant lot in Louisville. They were inspected by archaeological experts who identified them as Persian. The date of their manufacture predated the Madoc voyages as they have been traced to the eleventh century. They could have been taken to Wales by Vikings or Crusaders.[197]

In 1819 McMurtrie wrote that in 1808 a huge sycamore tree with more than 200 annular rings had been felled in Louisville in order to build the foundation for a flour mill. An iron axe was found lying under the bottom of the roots a few feet from the surface. The axe had been present far too long for English settlers to have lost it there. The Indians did not possess ferrous metallurgy and were restricted from the Falls area by the Welsh. La Salle's visit to the Falls took place around 1670, when the sycamore tree would have been sixty-two years old and already a large tree.[198]

In 1809 workmen were sinking a well near a branch of the Little Miami River in southwestern Ohio when they came across a wall made of hewn limestone at a depth of eighteen to twenty feet. An examination of a retrieved stone revealed that it had apparently been cut with an iron tool.[199]

Just below the Falls in Indiana, a graveyard exists that contains hundreds of prehistoric remains of people of medium stature, all buried with heads inclined, facing the rising sun. To the west of this graveyard and separated from it by a spring is another cemetery containing fifty tombs presumed to be of kings of the Welsh colony. These tombs were made of rough hewn stone and all of the remains are of males, none of whom were less than 6'6" tall. They were buried in a sitting position with weapons in their laps and facing the rising sun. The left temple of each had been crushed by a blunt instrument. Skeletons from ancient Britain show skulls that had been trephined.[200]

Madoc's father, Owain Gwynedd, had been a huge man, a trait shared by his ancestors and his descendants. One of Owain's wives was Chrisiant, his first cousin. One must suspect that after arriving in the New World, the descendants

---

196. Olson, p.62; and, Durrett, Traditions...

197. Olson, p.62.

198. Durrett, Reuben, T. 'Who Buried the Hatchet Under the Sycamore Tree?,' Centenary of Louisville, Filson Club, 1893.

199. Olson, p.62.

200. Olson, p.74.

of Owain continued as the kings of the Welsh colony and continued the practices of polygamy and incest. This is evidenced by Indian legends of giants among the White Indians, and by skeletal findings in the Indiana cemetery and elsewhere of apparent Welsh Indian chiefs who were over seven feet tall. The height of these men is in sharp contrast to the average height of the majority of the Welsh skeletal remains.[201]

Early settlers found disheveled piles of human skeletons at Corn Island near the head of the Falls and at Sand Island at its base. These were taken as evidence that a great battle had taken place and that one tribe had been annihilated. All of those found were of medium stature except for one man who had been seven feet tall. Thousands of arrowheads, spearheads and an occasional battle axe can still be found on the banks of the river near the Falls.[202]

In 1912, Craig Crecelius found an inscribed stone near Brandenburg, Kentucky, on the Ohio River thirty miles downstream from the Falls. The inscription is in true alphabetic lettering and not the pictographic art of the Red Indians. (Fig. 23) The inscription could not be deciphered, and for a time the stone appeared as an exhibit in such places as county fairs. It was given to the Meade County Public Library in the 1960s. Eventually pictures of the Brandenburg Stone were sent to an ancient history society which included Alan Wilson and Brian Blackett. These men were able to identify the inscription as being in Coelbren as it was written in ancient Wales. The inscription was translated as "*Toward strength* (meaning to promote unity) *divide the land we are spread over, purely* (meaning justly) *between offspring in wisdom.*" This translation identifies the stone as a boundary marker between heirs. The usage of Coelbren dates back to before A.D. 490. It was listed on charts as the alphabet for Welsh children as late as 1920. By 2001, Wilson and Blackett had deciphered fifty-five inscriptions from ancient Coelbren. As of October 2002, the Brandenburg Stone Exhibit was on lease from the Meade County Library to the Charlestown, Indiana, Public Library, where it has been on display.[203]

Several stone forts have been identified in the Falls area. (Fig. 24) Three of these are on Harrod's Creek, Kentucky, a mile upstream from Corn Island. These three forts were built on man made earthen mounds and commanded an

---

201. Olson, p.74.

202. Funkhouser, W.D. and Webb, W.S., Ancient Life in Kentucky, Berea College Publications, Berea, Ky. 1928.

203. The Brandenburg Stone Exhibit, Meade County, Ky. Public Library, on loan to the Charlestown, Ind. Public Library, 2001.

excellent view of the Ohio River. One of these forts has been described as having a land area to the rear, which was the only place the fort was vulnerable because it was built on a narrow bend of the creek. The landed facet of the fort was protected by a stone wall along the top of a ridge. The wall contained circular pits or foxholes.[204]

One mile upstream from Harrod's Creek and across the river on the Indiana side is Battle Creek. The name of this creek is curious because no Revolutionary or Civil War battle was ever fought there. The battle that was fought there was centuries ago. About a quarter of a mile from the mouth of the creek early settlers found the bones of forty-five individuals scattered in such random disorder that they believed the victims had been slain in battle. This battle probably occurred on the same day as the Great Battle at the Falls.

Three miles upstream from Battle Creek on the Indiana shore is a peninsula of land known as Rose Island. Rose Island is located at the mouth of Fourteen Mile Creek and lies between the creek and the Ohio River. Ancient stone walls were previously present at Rose Island but have been taken down. The stones were placed on barges and hauled downstream to be used to build the foundations for the Big Four Railroad Bridge and other structures. The Big Four Bridge was completed in 1895. In the 1930s more destruction to the site occurred with the construction of an amusement park named Rose Island. (Fig. 25)

The original stone structure at Rose Island was described in awe by nineteenth-century observers. In 1927, after visiting Wales, Herman Rave wrote that the Rose Island site was nearly identical to the Welsh Fortress of Pen Man Mawr. Rave (quoted by Olson) described Rose Island as he had seen it previously in the early 1880s:

> "...It had, almost undisturbed, the walls of a great fortress..., Rose Island is really a pear shaped hill, towering 250 feet above the Ohio, dropping to a wide area of level land at the (mouth of Fourteen Mile Creek). The great hill, containing about 10 acres is partly flanked at the narrower place where it joins the uplands by precipitous cliffs, both toward the river and toward the creek. The wide front... was protected by a great rubble-built stone wall...It was at least 12 feet high. Just inside this wall was a shallow ditch and in this ditch at intervals were some seven mounds cast up apparently as places from which lookout could be kept. (Rose Island was called the "Great Stone Fort" by neighboring farmers. It)...was evidently designed to accommodate a large number of defenders. It was the central place of

---

204. Olson, p.78.

defense for an area covering about thirty miles in circumference. (Stone pits or foxholes were also found at the site. The various walls at Rose Island, both natural and artificial, totalled an amazing 3600 feet in length.)[205]

In 1873, state geologist William W. Borden described the Great Stone Fort: "The summit of the ridge is pear shaped with a very narrow neck at the north. This part of the ridge is but 50 yards in width and a stone wall some 12 to 14 feet in height separates the pear shaped enclosure from the country to the north."[206]

Gerard Fowke, an archaeologist for the American Museum of Natural History, Archaeological Institute of America, and Smithsonian Institute, firmly disagreed with the accounts of Rose Island by Rave, Borden and Professor E.T. Cox. Fowke declared that the stone walls were of natural origin. It must be noted that Fowke wrote in 1933, fifty-nine years after Cox, and by 1933 the Rose Island site had been completely altered from what it had been in 1874.[207] (The earlier describers of the fort had concluded that *some* of the walls were of natural origin). (Fig. 48)

Rose Island was purchased by the U.S. Government for use as the Jefferson Proving Grounds and Ammunitions Arsenal in 1940. It is now a state park. No organized archaeological digs have taken place there since the 1880s and reports of those digs have been lost.

Forts similar to the Great Stone Fort at Rose Island have been found near the Ohio River at Marble Hill, Indiana, and at Wiggins (Wiggam's) Point. Wiggins Point is on Big Creek near the hamlet of Deputy, Indiana, and about thirty miles directly north of Rose Island. This hilltop fortress was protected by a wall 425 feet long. A smaller fort has been located just one half mile west of Wiggins Point. In 1939 the fort at Wiggins Point was mapped by Dr. Carl Bogardus, a physician and historian now living in Warsaw, Kentucky. Dana Olson has located the sites of these two forts. He found that stones from the larger fort at Wiggins Point have been used to build an antebellum house across the creek and the smaller fort has been dismantled to build a nearby smokehouse.[208]

In 1874, a geologic report by Indiana State Geologist Professor E. T. Cox and his assistant W. W. Borden stated that from:

---

205. Olson, p.78.
206. Olson, p.83.
207. Fowke; and, Funkhouser.
208. Olson, p.83-87.

...Fourteen Mile Creek to Wiggins Point, a distance of about 30 miles, there appears to be a line of antiquities that mark the dwelling places of intermediate colonies and these, when pushed to extreme by an invading foe, may have sought protection in the strongholds at either end of the line. At this place [Wiggins Point], I have frequently found human bones protruding from the bank [of Big Creek]. They are buried in a sitting posture and are covered with shells and fragments of pottery.[209]

In addition to the forts, stone towers were built on artificial earthen mounds at strategic sites on both sides of the Ohio River from the Falls to the mouth of the Great Miami River. Dr. J. W. Baxter of Vevay, Indiana, has described seven of these towers between Carrollton, Kentucky, and Rising Sun, Indiana, and a total of nine towers have been identified. Each tower occupied a site on a high hill from which smoke signals could be seen at the next site. Their purpose was communication to the next tower in case of attack. Dr. Bogardus remembers two of these stone towers just below Warsaw, Kentucky.[210]

Another site of a stone fort was at the mouth of the Great Miami River. William Henry Harrison, then the Governor of Indiana, gave a detailed description of this fort:

> The works at the mouth of the Great Miami was a citadel, more elevated than the Acropolis of Athens, although easier of access, as it is not like the latter, a solid rock, but on three sides as nearly perpendicular as could be, composed of earth. A large space of lower ground was, however, enclosed by walls uniting it with the Ohio. The foundations of that being of stone, as well as those of the citadel that forms the western defense, is still very visible where it crosses the Miami, which, at the period of its erection, must have discharged itself into the Ohio much lower down than it now does.[211]

Remains of a village and burial ground of suspected Welsh origin have been discovered in the Ohio River town of Augusta, Kentucky, upstream from the other Welsh villages. Twenty miles southeast of Augusta is Fox Field, an old Indian village of the Fort Ancient Culture, where stone fortifications were later built by a different people. Other stone fortifications found in Kentucky were on the banks of the Ohio at Petersburg and at Carrollton. The Carrollton site was described as a formidable quadrangular fortification on an artificial

---

209. Olson, p.83; and, Funkhouser.
210. Olson, p.85-87.
211. Olson, p.85-87.

embankment. Paths to the fort could still be made out when the fort was described in the early nineteenth century.[212]

Fortifications believed to be of Red Indian origin were also described by early Kentucky historians including those found at Ruddles Mill and on Hinkston Creek in Bourbon County; at Falmouth in Pendleton County; and on South Elkhorn Creek in Woodford County. Collins described the Ruddles Mill site as circular and including a quarter of an acre of ground with openings at the four cardinal points. He considered this fort to be subject to erosion when the creek flooded, indicating that it was an earthen structure and not built of stone. He estimated its age at no more than 150 years. (Collins published in 1847). At Falmouth he found numerous graves which he considered evidence of a "warfare of bloody and desolating character." Numerous artifacts were discovered at the Bourbon County sites including stone axes, stone chisels, and flint spear and arrow points. At Hinkston Creek a rusted iron hatchet was found. At these sites ashes of human bones revealed that funeral pyres or torture stakes had been in use.[213]

In his *History of Dearborn County, Indiana*, General, Governor, and later President William Henry Harrison wrote,

> Interesting archaeological remains are found throughout southeast Indiana. They are the traces of a people who inhabited the basins of the Mississippi and the Ohio in the distant past. Their elaborate and extensive earthworks prove they were not nomadic tribes, but a numerous people, dwelling in fixed communities, probably devoted to agriculture, and having certain fixed laws, customs and religious rites. Some of these works required an immense amount of labor and considerable engineering skill... By whom built... History is silent concerning them and their very name is lost to tradition itself.[214]

Kentucky, Ohio and Indiana abound with remains of the Fort Ancient, Hopewell and Adena Indian Cultures and some of the earthworks described by Harrison were probably of Indian origin; however the Indians did not have ferrous metallurgy and did not build with stone.

---

212. Collins, Lewis, Historical Sketches of Kentucky, Lewis Collins, J.A. and U.P. James, Maysville, Kentucky and Cincinnati, 1847, Reprinted by Henry Clay Press, Lexington, 1968, p.209, 229, and 180.
213. Collins, p.194 and p.494.
214. Olson, p.85-87.

Chapter XI

The Red Indians

"...if the two continents of Asia and America be separated at all, it is by only a narrow strait... and the resemblance between the Indians of America and the Eastern inhabitants of Asia, would induce us to conjecture, that the former are the descendants of the latter, or the latter of the former..."
                    Thomas Jefferson, *Notes on the State of Virginia*, 1787

It is difficult to trace the movements and conflicts involving the Indians of pre-colonial North America because there are great gaps of knowledge. One primary source for information is Indian legends, but legends are sometimes abstract embellishments of true historical events, or they may even be fables. But by combining stories originating from both Indians and White men with linguistic, anthropological and archaeological evidence, a picture begins to emerge.

The North American Indians were a diverse group with different origins, different languages and dialects, different cultures, different religions, and to an extent a different genetic heritage. The last Ice Age ended about 8000 B.C. and after that the peoples that became known as "Indians" began to cross the Bering Strait. At that time the ice was melting rather quickly resulting in a rise in sea levels and the elimination of the land bridge between Siberia and Alaska. Therefore, the Indians could not simply walk to America as the Paleo-Americans had done, but must have paddled small craft, probably a canoe type vessel, from island to island across the strait. Once in Alaska they slowly headed south via the coastline and the river valleys.[215]

Their migration was pushed forward when subsequent immigrants arrived.Through warfare and competition for food, wave after wave of immigrants exerted pressure on those who came before them. Their hunter-gatherer life style severely limited the number of people an area could support. Less successful tribes were either absorbed by a larger group or faced extinction. How many different waves of immigrants crossed the Bering Strait can never be determined. The first waves of Indians forced the Paleo-Americans to migrate farther south. In North America, subsequent waves moved the earlier arrivals into Mexico or east to the Great Plains, Mississippi Valley and East Coast. Some of the immigrant tribes thrived and multiplied, conquering their enemies and increasing their territory until they divided, the parent tribe spawning splinter tribes. This resulted in a group of tribes that all spoke a common language, which in time became separate dialects. Eventually they learned farming and practiced agriculture and remained settled in an area until the land became less fertile. They started fires to burn the landscape in order to establish farming plots and enlarge the grazing area for the buffalo and other large animals that they hunted.[216]

The main tribal groups of pre-Columbian Indians in eastern and central North America can be identified linguistically. The largest of these language groups is Algonquian. The Algonquian speakers were numerous tribes, who resided mostly in the north and east in pre-Columbian times, but they also inhabited the western U.S. and Canada, each tribe speaking its own individual dialect of the basic Algonquian language. The Algonquians were one of the later arrivals to North America and arrived on at least two separate occasions. In a remarkably preserved account, the Lenni Lenape, a large Algonquian tribe, recorded their history in what they call the *Wallum Olum*, which is a pictographic account of their history dating from about 1600 B.C., when the tribe was still in Siberia. The *Wallum Olum* depicts the tribe crossing the Bering Strait to America in about 1000 B.C. The *Wallum Olum* tells the story of the Lenape tribe, their good times and bad times, their splits and their mergers, their battles and their

---

215. Clift, G. Glenn, History of Maysville and Mason County, Kentucky, v.1, Transylvania Printing Company, Lexington, 1936, p.13.

216. Diaz-Granados, Carol, and Duncan, James R., Petroglyphs and Pictographs of Missouri, University of Alabama Press, Tuscaloosa, 2000; and, McCutcheon, David, The Red Record-The Wallum Olum, Avery Press, Garden City, New York, 1993.

migrations over many centuries. The main body of the tribe reached the East Coast in A.D. 1396 and became known as the Delaware Indians to the Colonists, but by then there were scores of tribes that had broken off from the original.[217]

In 1820 the *Wallum Olum* was given to Dr. John Russell of Carlisle, Kentucky, by Olympus, a Delaware Indian living in Indiana, in appreciation to Dr. Russell for healing him. In 1822, Russell passed the book on to Constantine Samuel Rafinesque, a Transylvania College professor. Rafinesque translated the work in 1833. It has since been translated by a contemporary Delaware woman and David McCutcheon has published her interpretation.

The Iroquois tribes were centered in upper New York State when the Colonists arrived. Before that, they are known to have lived in the south central area of the U. S. including Texas and Louisiana. From their south central base the Iroquois split, the northern branch moving north up the Mississippi Valley and then east into New York, which they reached by A.D. 800. Another branch, the Cherokee, went east into Georgia and eventually settled in the southern Appalachians, where they made war with the tribes that had preceded them to that area, including the Welsh.[218] Nearly all Indian tribes, and especially the New York Iroquois, were rather constantly at war, trying to occupy the territory of other tribes, even though the territory of a given tribe was evanescent and generally when attacked and defeated a tribe would simply move on. Tribes who were decimated in battle would often join another tribe, which would welcome the newcomers since the additions would strengthen their own tribe. The New York Iroquois created a confederation of five tribes for aggressive warfare. The tribes of the New York Confederation were the Mohawk, Seneca, Cayuga, Onondaga and Oneida. The Tuscarora joined them in 1722 or 1723. The Iroquois were not averse to internecine conflict and made war and annihilated the Erie, even though the Erie were their cousins and spoke the Iroquois language. They drove the Huron tribe, which was also Iroquois, west into Michigan. A branch of the Huron later became the Wyandotte.[219]

In the southeast, Muskogean speaking peoples predominated in Mississippi, Alabama and Georgia. These peoples included the Creek, Choctaw, Chickasaw and Seminole tribes. These four tribes plus the Cherokee comprised what were known as the "Five Civilized Tribes" in the nineteenth century.

---

217. McCutcheon.

218. Jennings, Francis, The Founders of America From the Earliest Migrations to the Present, Norton Press, New York, 1994, p.72.

219. Pritzker, Barry, Native American Encyclopedia, Oxford University Press, 2000.

Despite the successful enculturation and subsidence of warfare by these tribes, the U.S. Government of Andrew Jackson removed them from their homes and forced them to migrate to Oklahoma. They were packed into railroad cars and onto flat boats and wagons. A large segment of the Cherokee tribe walked on the infamous "Trail of Tears" march where many of them perished. The cruelty of the Government action is surpassed only by its irony, the Cherokee having previously committed the same atrocity in the same locale to the Welsh and the three Red Indian tribes that had lived in the area.

The traditional reason given for the forced expulsion is "White greed" for farms owned by Cherokees. That this was a factor is evidenced by the wretched behavior of some of the Whites in seizing Cherokee property with avarice, but it ignores the fact that the countryside was sparsely populated and the Cherokees were active participants in the area's commerce. Schools had been established by and for the Cherokee where they were taught to read and write in Cherokee and in English. Many of the Cherokees and Whites had intermarried. John Ross was a Scotsman and a successful Chattanooga developer and businessman. Although his lineage was only one-eighth Cherokee, he served as the chief of the Cherokee tribe, and made the march to Oklahoma with the rest of the tribe.[220]

Andrew Jackson was a U.S. Army General who won an overwhelming victory against the British in the Battle of New Orleans in 1815. In 1814 he led a campaign against marauding Creek Indians, wiping out an entire Creek force of eight hundred braves, and in 1817 he led a campaign against the Seminole. Unlike John Sevier, Jackson was known as a partisan and vindictive man. Jackson had served as Sevier's associate for a period and these two giants of Tennessee history knew each other well. It would be strange if Jackson had not heard the stories that Sevier had been told by Chief Oconostota about the Cherokee expulsion of the White Indians. Perhaps to Jackson, the old Indian fighter, it was pay back time for the Cherokee.

The Sioux were a populous group of tribes who occupied an extensive area in the central and northern Great Plains in pioneer times. Their migrations had led them from the eastern U. S. to the Great Lakes area, where they were located when the Colonists first arrived. A large group of Sioux tribes who spoke different but similar dialects of the same Siouan language is the Lakota-Nakota-Dakota. These tribes are often spoken of simply as the "Sioux." The Lakota were

---

220. Livingood, James W. A History of Hamilton County, Tennessee, Memphis State University Press, Memphis, 1981.

also known as the Teton Sioux and were the more westerly of the three. They began entering the Missouri Valley around 1650 from Wisconsin and Minnesota. They were a large, combative and inhospitable tribe whose intrusion severely affected the well being of the tribes who lived in the Missouri Valley. The Lakota-Nakota-Dakota had previously been in continuous warfare with several Algonquian tribes in the Great Lakes area including the Objibwa (Chippewa) and Anishinabe. When the Algonquians began trading for French rifles, the balance was turned against the Sioux and they began migrating west. In the upper Missouri Valley the Sioux threatened the Arikara, Mandan, Hidatsa and Cheyenne tribes, but they were successfully rebuffed until 1781, when a smallpox epidemic decimated the tribes of the Missouri Valley. By that time Siouan speaking tribes lived in the area from Lake Michigan to the Rocky Mountains of Montana and south to Arkansas. The Catawba and Tutelo tribes were isolated Siouan speaking peoples who inhabited Virginia and the Carolinas when the English arrived in the seventeenth century.[221]

Caddo speaking tribes inhabited areas of the Great Plains and included the Caddo, Wichita, Pawnee and the Arikara who will be discussed later. An examination of the Caddo, Sioux and Iroquois languages indicates a common, but distant origin.[222]

This is by no means a complete list of the linguistic groups and tribes of the eastern U.S. as more than 250 dialects have been identified north of Mexico. Some of these languages, including that of the Yuchi, are linguistic isolates or have uncertain origins.[223]

Indian events prior to 1492 cannot be positively identified in time. To come to a reasonable estimate one must extrapolate from known events such as the number of chiefs that reigned over a tribe between the events. Calendar beads were employed in compiling the *Wallum Olum*, each bead delineating a year's passing. It is recorded that nineteen chiefs presided between 1360 and 1620, giving an average tenure of 13.68 years per chief. Knowing the number of Lenape chiefs who presided over the tribe between two events can then give an estimate as to the time frame between the events. From the *Wallum Olum* it has been shown that the Delaware Indians first arrived at the East Coast in A.D. 1396. They recorded Verrazano's visit in 1524 and the arrival of English Colonists in the 17th

221. Coe, Michael; Snow, Dean; and Benson, Elizabeth, Atlas of Ancient America, Equinox, Oxford, England, 1986; and, Pritzker, p.328-329.

222. Jennings, Francis, p.72; and, Livingood.

223. Pritzker.

century. The Lenape crossed the Rockies and entered the Great Plains in A.D. 808.[224]

Like the Bible, the *Wallum Olum* begins with the creation of life. It then speaks of the Great Flood, making one suspect that the outpouring of people from the deluge affected the ancestors of the Lenape. It is not until near the end of the Third Book of the *Wallum Olum* that they crossed the Bering Strait to Alaska. Their migration paths led up the Yukon River and along the coast to eastern Alaska. Many of their sachems (chiefs) are mentioned in conjunction with the doings of the tribe.[225]

After the bow and arrow was introduced to America around A.D. 500, the Indian tribes could more effectively hunt buffalo and other large game. This allowed a tribe to increase its food supply and population. With increased numbers, the Lenape spun off splinter tribes, some of which remained on the Plains. These tribes included the Cheyenne, Arapahoe, Blackfeet and Cree. On the Plains the Lenape and their splinter tribes fought with various tribes including the Sioux, Shoshone (Uto-Aztecan speaking), and Apache (Athapaskan speaking). Some Lenape tribes moved north to Canada and the Great Lakes and became the Menominee, Potowatomi, Ottawa, Sauk, Fox, and Ojibwa.

In Book Five of the *Wallum Olum*, the Lenape arrived at a great river and found the site inhabited by a tribe of mound builders that they called the Tallegewi (Tallega, Talega, Talegewi, Allegewi). When the Tallegewi saw how large and powerful the Lenape tribe was, they denied them passage. A protracted war then raged between the Lenape and the Tallegewi which lasted through the reign of four Lenape Sachems. A great battle was eventually fought while Long Bread was Chief of the Lenape. After the battle the defeated Tallegewi escaped down the river. Most historians accept Cahokia as the site of this battle between the Lenape and the Tallegewi.[226]

The Cahokia community was a large and complex center of the Mississippian Culture located near St. Louis. This culture is known for building huge truncated mounds. At Cahokia it began about A.D. 800 and climaxed between 1050 and 1150. (Fig. 26)

The Mississippian Culture represented a decided advancement from all other cultures preceding it. These people lived in communities of thousands of

---

224. McCutcheon.
225. McCutcheon.
226. McCutcheon.

people and were more sophisticated than their predecessors. They practiced agriculture on a larger scale and planted pumpkins, squash, corn, beans, and sweet potatoes. Their pottery was superior and more varied than that of previous cultures. They built huge earthen mounds for ceremonial purposes and large community buildings of wood and thatch, which could hold up to three hundred people. Cahokia and its surrounding Mississippian Culture sites began to decline by 1150, and by 1350 people of the Oneota Culture of Wisconsin and Iowa occupied the area, as shown by the difference in the artifacts found. The Oneota artifacts showed smaller, triangular projectile points, incised, shell-tempered pottery and other differences from the Mississippian. The Oneota people became the Siouan speaking tribes Missouri, Iowa and Oto.[227] The tribe which later became known as the "Cahokia" tribe was part of the Illinois group of tribes, an Algonquian speaking people that moved into the area in the late seventeenth century from northeastern Illinois.[228]

The cause for the demise of Cahokia is uncertain. Warfare has been suggested, and there is reason for believing that they suffered a crushing defeat at the hands of the Lenape near the time they began to decline. Another factor that may have been involved in their demise is that the Cahokia Culture may have been unsustainable due to the cruelty of some of the customs, which invoked fear among the people. At Cahokia, skeletons have been unearthed having had their hands and feet cut off.

The Natchez Indians either originated in Cahokia or were an extension of that culture. The Natchez had a hereditary monarch. In contrast, the Lenape had a democratic system. The Natchez practiced human sacrifice. Medicine Men or soothsayers could be put to death if they failed to accurately predict the weather. The extraordinary amount of human labor required to build the mounds is almost unimaginable. Women generally did not marry until age twenty-five, limiting their childbearing years. They practiced infant head flattening.[229]

Bernal Diaz accompanied Hernando Cortez on his expedition and conquest of Mexico in 1519-1521 and wrote of his experiences. He witnessed a macabre religious ceremony by Aztec priests which horrified and disgusted him. During the gruesome spectacle, the priests situated themselves on top of a pyramid where they performed the bloody extraction of a human heart from an alive and

---

227. Diaz-Granados and Duncan.
228. Pritzker.
229. Pritzker.

awake victim. As the heart was still pulsating and gushing blood, they held it up in front of the multitude.[230]

I have no doubt that the huge truncated pyramids at Cahokia and other Mississippian Culture sites are an extension of MesoAmerican Cultures (Olmec, Maya, Toltec, Aztec), whose cultures in turn suggest an Egyptian influence. In North America, the fear, cruelty, superstition and inequality created by such a culture would make it unsustainable. The people did not have to go far to escape from despots to an area where the land was fertile and game was plentiful.[231]

An example of the lack of altruism involving the successor of a mound building culture is the Tunica tribe, who were linguistic cousins of the Natchez. The Tunica were descendants of the Hopewell Culture, a mound building culture generally predating the Mississippian. They lived adjacent to the Natchez until driven further south by the Chickasaw. The Tunica moved in with the Houma tribe in Louisiana and despite being given a friendly reception, after several years they killed most of their hosts and forced the others to move away.[232]

In about 1660 a great battle was fought at the Falls of the Ohio. It involved the Shawnee, a large tribe with roots in the Lenape and in the Fort Ancient Culture of Ohio.[233] At the battle at the Falls a coalition of tribes, led by the Shawnee and the ferocious Iroquois, defeated the Welsh Indians. It seems likely that the great battle mentioned in Book Five of the *Wallum Olum*, which was fought against the Tallegewi, took place at Cahokia and not at the Falls of the Ohio as Olson has claimed.[234] In the Algonquian language "Tallega" means foreigner or stranger. The Shawnee referred to the Allegheny mountains as the "Tallega Mountains," and the Delaware Indians called the Iroquois speaking Cherokee "Tallegwi."[235] The Ohio River was referred to as the "Alliwegisipi" by some Indian tribes.[236] At present, *Tallega* is not a recognized name for any specific Indian tribe. I suggest it referred to any tribe that had a culture and language different from Algonquian. That would include the Cahokians, the

230. Diaz.

231. Pritzker; and, Pauketat, Timothy R., 'A Guide to the Prehistoric and Native Cultures of Southwestern Illinois and the Greater St. Louis Area,' Illinois Archaeological Educational Series No.2, Illinois Historical Preservation Agency, 1993.

232. Pritzker.

233. Howard, James H., Shawnee - The Ceremonialism of a Native American Tribe and Its Cultural Background, Ohio University Press, Athens, 1981, p.4-5.

234. Olson, p.71.

235. Woodward, Grace Steele, The Cherokees, University of Oklahoma Press, 1982, p.19.

236. Eckert, Allan W., That Dark and Bloody River, Bantam Books, New York, 1995, p.xvii.

Cherokee, and also the Welsh. Perhaps the captive Tallega woman who recorded the *Wallum Olum* for the Lenape for a period was Welsh.

The date of any battle between the Lenape and the Cahokians would have occurred before any theoretical conflict between the Lenape and the Welsh at the Falls, because Cahokia was farther to the west, and the Lenape would have to cross the Mississippi before they came to the Ohio. The culture at Cahokia was in decline after 1150 AD and had disappeared by 1350 AD. If one accepts 1150 as the date of the decisive Lenape-Cahokia battle and 1396 as the date the Lenape arrived at the Delaware River, the Lenape must have traversed the Ohio Valley about 1250, when the Welsh colony would have been very young and weak.

After the Great Battle at the Falls the carnage was so complete that very few of the Welsh could have escaped down the Ohio River. The Shawnee history states that "what Talegwa that were left...were with us."[237]

A Mohawk (Iroquois) Indian tradition involves the Welsh who had "not allowed us to pass" (on the river), and respects the Welsh with whom they had battle.

At the Falls, it appears that the Great Battle probably occurred in the seventeenth century. In his *History of Kentucky*, Kerr places a date between 1660 and 1670 on the battle, basing his estimate on the Iroquois' sweep into the Ohio Valley, the Iroquois being among the major combatants.[238]

An attempt by the Red Indians to establish an advanced society is represented by the Hopewell Culture, a mound building culture centered in southern Ohio and surrounding areas. This culture disappeared about A.D. 1000, a date that corresponds to the earlier Iroquois migration from the Mississippi Valley to the northeast. The mound builders of the Hopewell Culture were followed by mound builders of the Fort Ancient type, but that culture also disappeared no later than the sixteenth century. As with the Cahokians and Hopewellians, the Fort Ancient Culture may have disappeared largely as a result of invasion by hostile Indians including the Shawnee, Lenape, and Iroquois.

The New York Iroquois confederation officially began in 1579, but it was loosely associated for warfare by 1390 due to encroaching pressure from the Lenape. In their rampage in the middle of the seventeenth century the Iroquois pushed westward, wiping out their cousins the Erie. They entered Ohio and

---

237. Shawnee United Remnant Band, article, Montgomery County, Ohio newsletter, p.91.

238. Kerr, Judge Charles, editor, HIstory of Kentucky, by William Elsey Connelley and E. M. Coulter, The American Historical Society, Chicago and New York, 1922, Volume I, p.31-32; and, Clift, p.13.

attacked the Miami, a large Algonquian tribe that included several subtribes, among them the Piankashaws and the Weas. The Miami had lived in Ohio for a considerable period of time and their culture was at least partly descended from the Ohio mound builders.

In addition to battling the invading Iroquois, the Miami were also being crowded by the Shawnee, who had been living near Lake Winnipeg but began moving south and east about A.D. 1240. They reached Ohio by the seventeenth century. The Shawnee were a large Algonquian speaking tribe who were known to fight just as ferociously as the Iroquois. The Miami, fearing the Iroquois, allied with the Shawnee and gave the Shawnee land for settlement in southern Ohio.[239] This temporarily stopped the Iroquois advance, although they later pushed westward to the Illinois River where they attacked the Illinois tribes and their French allies as early as 1684.

Meanwhile the Welsh, centered at the Falls, had successfully defended and enlarged their territory and refused the Indians the use of their lands for hunting and the waters at the Falls and environs for fishing. This infuriated the Indian tribes who repeatedly attacked the Welsh, but the Welsh were able to repulse them and continued their control over the central Ohio Valley.

The Algonquians then conspired with their enemies the Iroquois to help them defeat the Welsh. The Shawnee have passed down a description of the great battle that their ancestors fought at the Falls. It states that a large war party of Indians came from the north, down the Ohio, massacring the Welsh inhabitants along the way. Fires on the stone towers built by the Welsh alerted the downstream defenders of the impending arrival of the large war party. The Welsh were led by a "Tall Chief named Yellow Hair who had held the Indians at bay, denying them the fisheries of the place for ages."[240] The Welsh gathered at Corn Island at the head of the Falls, where they anticipated that treacherous eddies and currents would protect them. But the Shawnee were not ignorant of the waters at the Falls, and Hawk Wing, the Shawnee chief, led his canoes safely to the shores of Corn Island. The Indians surprised and attacked at dawn and found the Welsh asleep or bowing to the rising sun, having just awakened. Yellow Hair slew a score of Red men; then he was confronted by Hawk Wing. What followed was a terrible encounter between the two combating chiefs with both fighting ferociously and to the death. In a lengthy battle for survival each

---

239. Eckert, Allan W., p.xiv.
240. Olson, p.75.

chief used all of his cunning, strength, and endurance. When they were both covered with wounds and blood, Yellow Hair sank exhausted, and Hawk Wing buried his hatchet into the brain of Yellow Hair. Yellow Hair was defeated, and as the blood gushed from his pierced skull, the end of the colony that had been in existence for nearly five hundred years became imminent. The Indians proceeded to slaughter kneeling women and children until not one of the White race remained.

Some of the Welsh were driven down the river to Sand Island at the base of the Falls where another finding of thousands of bones showed that the massacre continued. The Shawnee and their allies then destroyed the habitations of the Welsh, leaving only dead bodies at the site. Such is the description of the battle given by Mrs. Mary Louise Kelly, a Shawnee and a descendant of Hawk Wing. Her mother had told her the story. Chief Tobacco of the Piankashaws gave a similar account. From this battle and the warfare preceding it, Kentucky became known as the "Dark and Bloody Ground" to the Indians, and no longer would they make their homes there as they considered Kentucky haunted by the spirits of the Welsh.[241]

The recollection of the battle at the Falls is so overwhelming that it is difficult to overstate. I am not aware of any battle in America that compares to it in the vicious ferocity of the attack or the carnage suffered. The conflicts at Gettysburg, Little Bighorn, Wounded Knee, and the Alamo are more publicized, but pale in comparison to the slaughter in the Great Battle at the Falls. The number of casualties suffered in the siege at Vicksburg may have been as great or greater than at the Falls, but at Vicksburg the life of the community was gradually squeezed out over a six week period and the attackers did not have the degree of savagery exhibited two centuries earlier by the Indians at the Falls. The Iroquois and Shawnee led the attack and the Iroquois were particularly vicious. The other tribes, having committed to the battle and not wanting to appear less ferocious, adopted Iroquois methods. Thus when Hawk Wing slew Yellow Hair with his battle axe, the wanton indiscriminate slaughter rose to a rage induced frenzy made more terrifying by the yelps of the attackers and the screams of the victims. Words appear to be inadequate to describe the full horror of the spectacle as the men, women and children of the Welsh were hacked and

---

241. Olson, p.75; and, Clift, p.14; and, Funkhouser, W.D., and Webb, W.S., Ancient Life in Kentucky, Berea College Publications, Berea, Ky. 1928.

bludgeoned. In a matter of hours, all that was left of the vibrant Welsh colony was a massive litter of human corpses and the stench of death.

In 1922, Kerr described the aftermath of the battle:

> The particulars of the sanguinary conflict are lost, but that it was so bloody that both memory and horror of it remained in the Indian mind until long after the white settlers began to arrive. No Indian ever again dared set foot on Kentucky soil with the design of establishing a tribal home. He might cross over it in his wanderings or by stealth skulk in its forests and brakes to hunt game, but for a home – nevermore.[242]

It was not unheard of for Indian tribes to be brutal in their wars. The Iroquois had just annihilated the Erie tribe, even though the Erie were their cousins and spoke the same language. At about the same time, the Cherokee were raiding and extinguishing the Xualae tribe, a small peaceful tribe living in West Virginia. But at the Falls, the Indians attacked with an unparalleled vengeance. In contemplating the Great Battle, I have concluded that it was more than simply a conflict between tribes over territory. It was an all out racial and cultural clash between two disparate civilizations, and as such it was a prelude to the two centuries of Indian Wars the nation would soon fight. To the Welsh the attack was unprovoked. They had attempted to live in peace with the Indians, but only by remaining distant and semi-isolated. The boundaries of their territory were well drawn and defended as boundaries were in Europe. They did not attack the Indians except perhaps in retaliation, but the Indians were unwelcome in their territory and in their society. It may be significant that after nearly five centuries, the Welsh continued to bury their dead in a sitting position facing the rising sun, which is the direction from which they came. Also, the kings were buried with armor and weapons in their laps. The Indian attacks came from upriver. Since the Ohio River at the Falls flows from east to west, the kings would be facing their enemies. The spirits of the dead kings were maintaining vigilance.

To the Indians, the Welsh were the *Tallega*, the foreigners, who were not following an unwritten code of customary and accepted Indian behavior. The Iroquois had already had bloody conflicts with White Colonists in the St. Lawrence Valley and along the eastern seaboard. It was evident to them that the Welsh tribe was growing in power and numbers as it developed colonies in

---

242. Kerr, p. 31-32.

Indiana, Kentucky and the Ohio Valley. The boundaries of the Welsh were slowly being pushed outward, enlarging their territory, a territory into which the Indians were restricted from entering. In this scenario war was inevitable and the goal of the Indians was more than victory; it was the total extinction of the Welsh tribe.

In the nineteenth century, settlers came across numerous locations that evidenced the growth and power of the Welsh colony. Artifacts proving their previous existence were found not only on the Ohio River banks, but inland as well. The stone grave burials found in parts of Kentucky are generally unlike Indian burial customs. Stone graves have been found in northeastern (Mason and Nicholas Counties) as well as southwestern (Christian County) parts of the state, but nowhere are they numerous. Funkhouser called the people who did these burials the "Stone-Grave People," and he believed them to be Welsh as ancient graves are to be found in Wales of the same type.[243]

The stone graves found in Mason County were adjacent to a Fort Ancient Culture site north of May's Lick called Fox Field. Clift writes that in 1827 there were found

> ...distinct traces of ancient fortifications (at this site). The principal fort contained about one acre of ground; the others were not more than half so large. The walls of these entrenchments were quite plain as were the marks of trenches or subterranean passages leading to Lee's Creek, three hundred yards distant-apparently tunneled to provide a supply of water, secure from danger to a blockading enemy. On about one hundred acres of land around, the soil to a depth of one to three feet was mixed with shells, flints, potter's ware, and bones of various description-among the latter several entire human skeletons, besides fragments of others, lying without regularity as if they had fallen in battle and had been hastily and carelessly buried. The potter's ware, in shape somewhat resembling articles now in common use, was made of muscle shells and stones, pulverized and thoroughly mixed; the vessels were carved on the outside, and remarkably strong, notwithstanding the exposure to the elements for centuries. All is conjecture as to the age of these fortifications – the trees in the several forts and upon the walls being quite as large as in the surrounding forests.[244]

---

243. Funkhouser and Webb.

244. Clift, p.14; and, Glass, Sherman, Return to Fox Fields, The Manchester, Ohio Signal, 1984; and, Taylor, Robert, 1874 letter, 'Prehistoric Race Left Many Mounds Throughout Ohio River Valley,' The Kentucky Explorer, February, 1995, p.69.

The Fort Ancient Culture existed in southern Ohio, northern Kentucky and western West Virginia. In this area it followed the Adena and Hopewell Cultures and was contemporaneous with the Mississippian. (800-1500 AD). The numerous artifacts found at Fox Field in Mason County are from the Fort Ancient Culture and numerous mounds from that culture existed in the area. (Fig. 27) The stone graves and fortifications are thought to have been built at a later time by a different people who moved to the site. These people could not have been numerous and their time at the site could not have been long for they left relatively few artifacts. One well known and fascinating find at Fox Field was a bear's tooth containing a distinct etching of a Maltese Cross.[245]

Southwestern Kentucky sites with a possible Welsh connection include the stone-graves identified by Funkhouser and the mummified skeleton of a white woman with short red hair and pale skin, who was found at Short Cave, which is near Mammoth Cave. She was clothed in deer skin with a fawn hoof necklace, beads made of seeds, and a feathered umbrella headdress.[246]

Evidence of a protracted war before the Great Battle at the Falls exists in the form of battlefield sites in Bracken, Pendleton and Bourbon Counties, all in Kentucky. The town of Augusta has been built on the Bracken County battlefield site. In 1775 ten exploring pioneers found there:

> ...evidence of a great struggle between a race of men said to be almost of giant size, traditionally called the White Indians (Welch), and the American Red Indians. The Red Indians, by superior numbers, had exterminated their foes, and the site of what was to be Augusta had been probably one of its most decisive battles.[247]

General John Payne settled in Augusta and discovered a burial ground while digging his cellar. He claimed to have dug up 110 skeletons, counted by the skulls. The skeletons were of all sizes, from infants to men seven feet tall. Several older Indian chiefs of different tribes in the area were queried about the site. All denied that an Indian village had ever been located there.[248]

---

245. Clift, p.14; and, Funkhouser and Webb; and, Glass.

246. Durrett, Reuben, Traditions of the Earliest Visits of Foreigners, Filson Club, No.23, 1908, p.81.

247. Rankins, Walter, Historic Augusta and Augusta College, 1949, p.1-2.

248. Collins, Lewis, and Richard H., History of Kentucky, Morton Publishing, Louisville, 1924, p.209-210; Rankins, p.1-2; and, Funkhouser and Webb.

In 1910, Col. Bennett H. Young published his *Prehistoric Men In Kentucky*. In his book he described:

> ...a remarkable stone fortification... situated in Madison County, about three miles east of Berea. The fort occupies what is known as Indian Fort Mountain. For the military skill displayed in the selection of this mountain as a stronghold, and for patience and labor expended in building the necessary walls to render it impregnable, too much cannot be said in praise of both the genius and the skills of the men who constructed the fortifications. The old forts in Kentucky were not built by Indians, but by a past people greatly skilled in arts.[249]
> (Figs. 28, 29, 30)

In 1923 W. G. Burroughs explored, surveyed and mapped the walls of Indian Fort Mountain for the Kentucky Geological Survey. The mountain is a steep-sloped knob jutting 1500 feet into the sky at the edge of the Bluegrass basin. From atop this mountain a commanding view is seen which could alert one of an attack. Carbon dating of residue found at the walls by David Moore of the University of North Carolina gave dates of A.D. 40 and a questionable date of 580 B.C., indicating that fires were present at those times. In November of 1987 another fire burned 657 acres of forest on top of this mountain. Burroughs wrote that the stone fortifications at Indian Fort Mountain were apparently for ceremonial purposes. This is curious because the commanding views afforded by the high overlooks, the steep and in many places unclimbable slopes of the mountain, and the stone walls themselves appear obviously for defense against an attacking enemy. Unfortunately the stone walls on Indian Fort Mountain have not been preserved, and on warm autumn days the hiking trails on the mountain are filled with college students and area residents.[250]

Thirty-five miles east of Indian Fort Mountain on the Middle Fork of the Kentucky River in eastern Lee County sits the village of Tallega (pronounced Ta-LEE-ga). When the author visited Tallega, he was unable to find anyone who knew the origin of the name of the village although it was said that Tallega was a Shawnee name and the Louisville and Atlantic Railroad used the name for its

---

249. Pugh, Ellen, Brave His Soul, Dodd, Mead and Company, New York, 1970, p.119.

250. Perry, John, Berea College., personal communication, 2000; Burroughs, W.G., Kentucky Geological Survey, Series VI, Plate 34, 1923; Armstrong, Zella Who Discovered America? Lookout Publishing Company, Chattanooga, 1950, p.75; and, Funkhouser and Webb.

railroad stop when it built the line in 1902. The Post Office originally named the village "Zold", but later changed the name to match that of the railroad stop.[251]

In western Lee County a mountainous area known as the Pinnacles surrounds the Kentucky River. (Fig. 31) In county folk lore this area, with its peaks rising 1000 feet above the river, served as an Indian look out. The area contains many caves and Shackleford quotes a legend that the "territory was once the haunt, if not the actual dwelling place of a tribe of people of unknown origin and descent." The caves revealed "unusual artifacts, defying identification and an ancient human skull has been found in one of the caves." The skull showed marks indicating the person had died from a sharp blow of an instrument like a hatchet.[252]

The Rockcastle River is a tributary of the Cumberland. It was named in 1767 by explorer Isaac Lindsay who fancied he saw castles among rock formations that towered over the river. Narrow valleys, huge boulders, steep hillsides, and swift winding creeks make the area difficult to traverse. In 1861 Confederate General Felix Zollicoffer referred to the Union's position on the Rockcastle Hills as an "intrenched camp, a natural fortification, almost inaccessible."[253] From the headwaters of the Rockcastle River it is only a twenty mile portage northwest to Indian Fort Mountain or northeast to the Pinnacles. Carbon dating of the skull found at the Pinnacles gave a date of A.D. 1000, too early to have been associated with the Welsh of Madoc but within the time frame for Viking explorations to North America. The six Rune stones found along the Arkansas River in Oklahoma included dates between 1012 and 1024. These Rune stones show that Vikings explored the basin of the Mississippi River early in the eleventh century. The Vikings are known to have been assiduous record keepers of their voyages. This especially involved the carving of Rune stones, but Viking pictoglyphs have been found in New England. The Thruston Tablet is a pictoglyph found near the Cumberland River. The literacy rate among the Vikings could not have been high. It is understandable that if the stonemason were illiterate, he would have carved a pictoglyph to tell his story.

The interpretation of the Thruston Tablet by Gates Thruston is that there was a battle between almond-eyed Indians and round-eyed warriors who had

---

251. Palmer, Olga, personal communication, Tallega, Ky., 2003; and, McGuire, Helen, personal communication, Beattyville, Ky., 2003.

252. Shackleford, Nevyl, article appearing in The Lexington Leader, 14 November, 1957.

253. KCOJ-Rockcastle County, Kentucky, http://www.kycourts.net/Counties/Rockcastle_text.asp.

arrived in a Viking ship. On the left side of the pictoglyph the Indian and Viking figures appear to be in battle. On the right a female Indian and a round-eyed warrior clasp hands. She is holding what appears to be a wampum belt that indicates marriage. The figures at the bottom and at the far right are dead round-eyed warriors. The figure on the right has been dismembered and is holding his heart. The figure at the bottom holds a bent spear implying that it was made of metal. At the bottom of the tablet is a square hut containing a warrior smoking a peace pipe. The battle depicted on the Thruston Tablet appears to have been a major conflict and not a minor skirmish.

One possibility for the identity of the Indian tribe involved on the tablet is the Tuscarora. The Tuscarora tribe was part of the northern branch of the Iroquois, which migrated north along the Mississippi River and then headed east. The Tuscarora were the most southern of these tribes and when the Colonists arrived in the seventeenth century, they found them living in Virginia and North Carolina. The Tuscarora later moved to New York and joined the New York Iroquois Federation in 1722 or 1723.

If the Tuscarora and the Vikings did encounter each other, a battle would seem to be inevitable given their belligerent natures. The Thruston Tablet shows that a conciliation occurred. This means neither was victorious for if one had defeated the other there would have been no conciliation. The small Viking force would have been followed and harrassed by the more numerous Tuscarora. The Vikings would have sought safety; the Rockcastle Hills, Indian Fort Mountain, and the Pinnacles could have become their refuge. Their end was not long in coming and would have been the result of annihilation or capture by the Tuscarora.

The Vikings are known to have frequently included a few females on their explorations. Therefore the fact that one of the bodies found in caves along the Cumberland River upstream from Carthage, Tennessee, was female, is not inconsistent with a Viking source. However the number of Viking women in the group would have been far too few to sustain their existence as a people.

One of the walls found by W. G. Burroughs on Indian Fort Mountain was described as a gently curving row of scattered rocks. The ruins of this particular stone structure were located on a relatively level site removed from any approaches to the mountain and do not appear to have served any defensive purpose. I suspect they may be the remains of a foundation of a Viking longhouse.

There is no mention of such a Viking adventure in the Icelandic Sagas. It is likely that they did not sail directly from Iceland and they certainly did not return there. Norwegian raiders were cruising the Irish Sea in the ninth century. Danes began raiding the Atlantic coast of France in 834. Early campaigns to Spain, Morocco, and the Mediterranean took place in 844, which involved one hundred ships, and in 859, which involved sixty-two vessels. Other expeditions to the south occurred in 968, 966, 971 and 1013 and included Icelanders.[254] In Spain and North Africa the Vikings would have been exposed to ancient Phoenician legends about wealthy exotic lands to the west. Those legends corresponded to others that were told in Ireland about St. Brendon and St. Finbarr. Could not a few bold Viking sea captains have sailed southwest to the Southern Isles and then followed the Phoenicians across the waters to the New World as Madoc and Christopher Columbus would later do?

In the New World these Vikings would have become the blond-haired, blue-eyed, Norse speaking San Blas Indians of Darien, the composers of the Arkansas River Rune stones and the Thruston Tablet, the builders of the walls and longhouse on Indian Fort Mountain, and the people of unknown origin and descent that kept lookout at the Pinnacles. The last of these Vikings predictably ended his life as a hermetic troglodyte, the unwritten saga of his incredible adventures appearing only in county legends about the mysterious tribe that roamed the Pinnacles.[255]

After the Battle at the Falls, the Iroquois resumed their belligerence and forced the Shawnee out of Ohio. Some of the Shawnee went east into Pennsylvania and some (called Shawanoe) south into Tennessee and to the Savannah River area. Others retreated westward into northern Illinois or down the Ohio River into Southern Illinois. The Miami also were forced out of Ohio and moved west into Illinois and Wisconsin. The Iroquois then went back to their homeland in New York and did battle against the British in the French and Indian Conflicts.

Clift described the situation in Kentucky at the time:

> The Iroquois left the land they had conquered in the Ohio Valley to be guarded by their kinsmen, the Wyandots, who were to see that no harm came to their kingdom, Kentucky, and that no enemy camped within its

---

254. Brondsted, Johannes, The Vikings, Penguin Books, Baltimore, 1960, 1965, p.58; and, Logan, F. Donald, The Vikings in History, Routledge, London, 1992, p.126-128.
255. Bronsted, p.58.

borders. They were to protect it and that they did, with a fierceness that left future white settlers shaken and awed. Only as a hunting ground could they know Kentucky's fertile grounds and but for game could they send their canoes along its rivers. Kentucky was thrust into a stillness and deep solitude punctured only by the sounds of wild life and the occasional stealthy stalk of the Indian hunter.[256]

---

256. Clift, p.14.

CHAPTER XII

Soon after the first English colonists arrived in America, tales of White Indians who spoke Welsh began to circulate. Captain John Smith of Jamestown believed the stories and is quoted:

> The Chronicle of Wales reports that Madoc, sonne of Owen Gwyneth, Prince of Wales, seeing his brothers at debate as to who should inherit, prepared certain ships with men and ammunition and left his country to seek adventure by sea. Leaving Ireland to the North he sayled West till he came to a land unknown. Returning home and relating what pleasant and fruitful countries he had seen and for what barren ground his brethern and kindred did murder one another, he provided a number of ships and got with him such men and women as were desirous to live in quietness that arrived with him in this new land in 1170. (He) left many of his people and returned for more.

Although these words appear to be taken from Powell's book (Caradoc), they are evidence that Captain Smith believed the story.[257]

Durrett reported that "Around every fireside (in Kentucky) where pioneers gathered, stories of the Welsh colonists were repeated."[258]

---

257. Armstrong, Zella, Who Discovered America? Lookout Publishing Company, Chattanooga, 1950, p.161.
258. Armstrong, p.90.

One of the earliest accounts by a Welshman about the existence of Welsh Indians was contained in a remarkable letter written on March 10, 1686, by the Reverend Morgan Jones, the minister of a church near New York, to Dr. Thomas Lloyd, of New York. This letter was eventually presented by Dr. Lloyd to Edward Llwyd, Keeper of the Ashmolean Museum at Oxford, England.

In the letter, Morgan Jones described how in the year 1666, when he was chaplain to Major General Bennett, the Governor of Virginia, he was sent by ship to South Carolina. Having landed at a place named Oyster Point, he and his party suffered great hardships until lack of provisions induced them to travel back to Virginia overland:

> I and five more travelled through the wilderness till we came to Tuscora [sic] Country. There the Tuscora Indians took us prisoners... That night they took us to their town and shut us close to our no small dread.
>
> The next day they entered into consultation about us, which after it was over the interpreter told us that we must prepare to die the next morning. Thereupon, being much dejected, and speaking to this effect in British [Welsh] tongue "Have I escaped so many dangers and must I now be knocked on the head like a Dog?" Presently an Indian came to me which afterwards appeared to be a War Captain belonging to the Sachem of Doegs, whose origin I find is from the old British, and took me and told me in the British tongue that I should not die, and thereupon went to the Emperor and agreed for my ransom.
>
> They then welcomed mé to their town where they entertained us for four months during which time I had the opportunity of conversing with them familiarly, and did preach to them three times a week in the same language and they would confer with me about anything that was difficult therein; and at our departure they supplied us with what was necessary to our support and well being.
>
> This is in brief a recital of my travels among the Doeg Indians.
>
> They are settled upon the Pontiago [Pamlico] River, not far from Camp Atros. I am ready to conduct any Welshman, or others, to the country.
>
> Morgan Jones, sonne of John Jones of Messaleg,
>
> Newport, in the County of Monmouth.[259]

Several points deserve scrutiny about Morgan Jones's story, one being that he waited twenty years after the event to write the letter and also he gave no corroboration by his companions. The "Dog" Indians were referred to by Paul

---

259. Deacon, Richard, *Madoc and the Discovery of America*, George Braziller, New York, 1966, p.110.

Marana, an Italian living in Paris, who in 1673 referred to the Doeg Indians as descendants of the Welsh. His source of information is obscure but could not have come from Morgan Jones, because Jones's letter was not written until 1686. The Pamlico River is in coastal North Carolina, which is not an area where the Welsh Indians of Madoc are thought to have inhabited. When Keltic people invaded the British Isles around 400 B.C., they brought their language with them. Welsh (Cymric), Old British, Cornish and Breton are similar and related languages of the P-Keltic division of the original Keltic tongue. Gaelic, Irish, Scottish and Manx are a little less similar to Welsh, being part of the Q-Keltic division. The "British tongue" alluded to by Morgan Jones could have been any of these dialects.[260]

Sometime between 1660 and 1665, a Welsh sailor from Brecon (in southern Wales) named Stedman was shipwrecked in the Atlantic and washed ashore somewhere between Florida and Virginia. (Early Spaniards used the term "Florida" to pertain to the entire southeast coast). Stedman was found by Indians and claimed to recognize the language they spoke as being similar to Welsh. When he replied to them in that language they expressed astonishment, were extremely friendly and supplied him with the best things they had. They told Stedman that their ancestors came from a country named *Gwynedd in Prydain Fawr* (Great Britain).

The account of this episode was related in a letter from a Charles Lloyd to Reverend N. Owen in 1777. Also included in Lloyd's account is an experience of Oliver Humphreys, a merchant of Surinam who related that the master of an English ship, while repairing his vessel in a remote part of the Florida coast became acquainted with the Indian tongue spoken there and afterwards found it to be similar to Welsh.[261] (Again, any of the Keltic dialects of Great Britain would satisfy the description given).

Although it is not impossible that distant isolated groups of Welsh Indians of Madoc were encountered in the above instances, it seems unlikely; the Welsh Indians are not known to have inhabited the South Atlantic coastal area. But perhaps there is truth to the stories as they could be involving the Lumbee Indians, who were living in the coastal Carolinas and are thought to include descendants of the lost colony of Roanoke Island (1587). At least twenty Lumbee surnames match those of the Roanoke Island colonists. The Lumbee Indians are

260. Duncan, John, 'The Origin of the Picts,' www.scotshistoryonline.co.uk/ origin1.html.
261. Deacon, p.113.

recorded as always having spoken English, but it is plausible that there were speakers of the Keltic languages among them.[262]

A report by a Lieutenant Joseph Roberts appeared in *The Palladium*, a Frankfort, Kentucky weekly and was later printed in *The Public Advertiser*, a Louisville paper, on May 15, 1819. Lt. Roberts is quoted:

In the year 1801, being at the city of Washington in America, I happened to be at a hotel, smoking a cigar according to the custom of the country and there was a young lad, a native of Wales, a waiter in the house, and because he had displeased me by bringing me a glass of brandy and water, warm instead of cold, I said to him jocosely in Welsh, 'I'll give thee a good beating'.

There happened to be at the time in the room one of the secondary Indian Chiefs who on my pronouncing these words, rose in a great hurry stretching forth his hand, at the same time asking me in the ancient British tongue — 'Is that thy language?' I answered him in the affirmative shaking hands at the same time, and the Chief said that was likewise his language and the language of his father and mother and of his nation. I said to him "so it is the language of my father and mother and also my country."

Upon this the Indian began to inquire from whence I came and I replied from Wales, but he had never heard of such place. I explained that Wales was a principality in the kingdom called England. He had heard of England and of the English, but never of such a place as Wales.

I asked him if there were any traditions amongst them whence their ancestors had come. He said there were and that they had come from a far distant country, very far in the east and from over the great water. I conversed with him in Welsh and English; he knew better Welsh than I did and I asked him how they had come to retain their language so well from living with other Indians. He answered that they had a law of established custom in their nation forbidding any to teach their children another language until they had attained the age of twelve years and after that they were at liberty to learn any language they pleased. I asked him if he would like to go to England and Wales; he replied that he had not the least inclination to leave his native country and that he would sooner live in a wigwam than a palace. He had ornamented his naked arms with bracelets, on his head were placed ostrich feathers.

I was astonished and greatly amazed when I heard such a man who had painted his face of yellowish-red and of such an appearance speaking the ancient British language as fluently as if he had been born and brought up in the vicinity of Snowden. (Mount Snowden is in Gwynedd). His head was shaved excepting around the crown of the head and there it was very

---

262. Pritzker, Barry M., Native American Encyclopedia, Oxford University Press, 2000.

long and plaited and it was on the crown of his head he had placed the ostrich feather which I mentioned before to ornament himself. The situation of those Indians is about 800 miles southwest of Philadelphia, according to his statement and they are called Asguawa or The Asguaw Nation.

The Chief courted my society astonishing(ly), seeing that we were descended from the same people. He used to call upon me almost every day and take me to the woods to show me the virtues of the various herbs which grew there; for neither he nor his kindred were acquainted with compound medicine.[263]

About eight hundred miles southwest of Philadelphia is not a precise location and depends upon how the distance is measured. It could be pertaining to the following: the Falls of the Ohio; Lee County, Kentucky, (the village of Tallega); Hancock County, Tennessee, (the Melungeons); or Robeson County, North Carolina, (the Lumbee Indians). But if the distance is measured as a straight line on maps available around 1800, one finds that it accurately measures the distance from Philadelphia to Kaskaskia, Illinois, where Welsh Indians and their fortifications were reported to have been seen by General George Rogers Clark and Captain Abraham Chaplain of Kentucky, ("whose veracity may be entirely depended upon,"). Names of others who gave reports of meeting Welsh Indians near the Mississippi River include Captain Davies, Captain Lewis, Lewis Hicks, and Joseph Peepy, an interpreter.[264] Captain Chaplain had been stationed at Kaskaskia between 1770 and 1775, when the British were in command. He met some Indians, who spoke in Welsh with two men under Chaplain's command, who were of Welsh descent.

A clue as to the identity of the *Asguaw* is contained in a report by Thomas Bullitt. In May of 1773 Bullitt met with Shawnee Chief Black Fish on behalf of Virginia's "Great White Father," Lord Dunmore, in hopes that a treaty of peace might be negotiated over settlements in Kentucky. Black Fish stated that he did not have the power to negotiate or grant permission to settle Kentucky as it did not belong to him, but to the ghosts of the murdered *Asgens*, a white people from the Eastern Sea. He claimed that the forefathers of the Shawnee had long ago killed off the Asgens but were now in fear of their spirits."[265]

---

263. Armstrong, p.176.

264. Durrett, Reuben, Traditions of the Earliest Visits of Foreigners, Filson Club Number 23, 1908, p.45-52; and Deacon, p.118-119 and p.160.

265. Slaymaker, J.S., 'Rediscovering the Forgotten White Ancestors of Many American Indians,' The Barnes Review, 2000, v.7 no.5 p.7; and, Eckert, Allan W., The Frontiersmen, Little Brown and Company, 1967, p.65.

Durrett mentions that a small group of Welsh escaped from the Great Battle at the Falls and made their way to the Missouri River. This could be in reference to the stories in circulation about the Mandans, a tribe of White Indians living far up the Missouri River who were reported to speak Welsh, or it could mean that Durrett was aware that some of the Welsh had truly escaped and survived for over a century after the Great Battle at the Falls.[266]

An account that Funkhouser describes as "absolutely reliable" involves a notarized letter from Mrs. W.T. Lafferty, Chairman of History, Kentucky Federation of Women's Clubs and Head of the Woman's Division, University Extension. She is quoted:

> "My father, A.H. Ward, was born in Harrison County (Ky.) in 1815 and died in 1904. A lawyer, a member of Congress, a scholar when men had time to be scholars, he was always interested in history, and his unpublished reminiscences are among my treasures.
>
> "His father, Andrew Ward, was of Welsh descent. He was an Indian fighter serving under various enlistments from young manhood until wounded at Fort Meigs while serving in the army of the North West Territory under General Harrison.
>
> "He told my father that he had met and talked with Welsh Indians, that they understood him and he understood them."[267]

Francis Lewis was a signer of the Declaration of Independence who was born in Wales. His father was an Episcopal clergyman and his mother the daughter of a clergyman. After his captivity in the French and Indian War he became an elected delegate to the General Congress from New York and in 1776 a delegate by the Provincial Assembly and a member of Congress until 1778. His story, which appeared in his biography, was recapped by the *Saturday Evening Post*, July 9, 1947:

> There was the case of signer Francis Lewis, a rich, weather-beaten New York City merchant in his sixties who had seen quite a bit of the world. He was born in Wales, shipwrecked a couple of times and once captured by the Lake Ontario Indians during the colonial wars with France. According to his story, he escaped being tied to a stake and burned alive because he "began talking to the Indians in Welsh — and they understood him!"[268]

266. Durrett, p.1-6.

267. Funkhouser, W.D., and Webb, W.S., Ancient Life in Kentucky, Berea College Publications, Berea, Ky., 1928.

268. Armstrong, p.125.

The Indians of the Lake Ontario area were Iroquois and Algonquian. These tribes took part in the Great Battle at the Falls and may have taken captives as most Indian tribes frequently did. The captives were sometimes sold or traded to other tribes and would sometimes marry into and become part of the tribe of their captors. Thus it is quite possible that this account by an esteemed American is true.

John Filson, the eminent historian, visited Louisville in 1782. He held a meeting to which he invited prominent men of the area to discuss the stories circulating about Madoc and the Welsh Indians. In attendance were such notables as General George Rogers Clark, Colonel James Moore, Major John Harrison, John Sanders, Dr. Alexander Skinner and James Harrison, who recorded the meeting. Some of their discussion follows:

> General Clark learned from an Indian Chief at Kaskaskia, who was of light complexion, of a large earthwork near the Kaskaskia River, which the Chief said was the house of his ancestors.
>
> Colonel Moore was told by an old Indian of the long war between the Red and White Indians with the final battle at the Falls of the Ohio where nearly all of the White Indians were slaughtered. This statement was confirmed by General Clark who heard it from the son of Chief Tobacco of the Piankashaws.
>
> Major Harrison told of a graveyard on the north side of the Ohio River where thousands were buried in confusion indicating a battle. The skeletons were later covered with silt from the river.
>
> John Sanders told that he had met several Indians with different tribes who had light complexions, gray eyes and sandy hair.
>
> Dr. Skinner described two mounds in Louisville, unlike those made by the Red Indians.
>
> In 1784, Filson wrote the first *History of Kentucky* in which he included these statements. He thoroughly believed in the existence of Madoc and the White Indians.[269]

---

269. Durrett, p.45-52.

BOOK IV

THE MANDANS

CHAPTER XIII

WESTERN ENCOUNTERS

There is not a truth existing which I fear or would wish unknown to the
whole world.

Thomas Jefferson

The first people of the European colonies in the New World to venture into
the northwest were the French explorers and traders. By the early eighteenth
century many of them had wandered the Missouri and other western rivers and
had brought back tales of encountering White Indians with beards.

In Governor Sevier's letter to Amos Stoddard, he mentions a Frenchman
who was taken prisoner by the Cherokees in 1730-1735 near the Mississippi
River. Before he was captured he "lived high up the Missouri River where he said
he traded with a Welsh tribe who spoke much of the Welsh dialect and were fair
and white and told him that they came from a nation of white people. They had
scraps of old books with them but they were too tattered to interpret."[270]

Pierre Gaultier de Varennes, the Sieur de la Verendrye, was a French
nobleman who heard about the Welsh Indians in the west. In 1735 he decided to
explore the territory and search for them. He took a French expedition, which
included his two sons, inland from the Great Lakes to the Missouri River. In 1738
he came upon the Mandan tribe living in eight separate villages on the upper

---

270. Armstrong, Zella, Who Discovered America? Lookout Publishing, Chattanooga, 1950,
p.170.

131

Missouri River in what is now North Dakota. He received an invitation from the chief to stay with the tribe.

La Verendrye was fascinated by what he saw. In his journal he recorded that the Mandans were:

> ...mixed white and (dark). The women are fairly good looking, especially the light colored ones; many of them have blond or fair hair. Both the men and the women are very industrious. The men are of good size and tall, very alert and for the most part, good looking. Most of the women do not have the Indian features. The towns and permanent villages were laid out in streets and squares.

He found the eight villages to be kept extremely clean and well defended with palisaded walls and ditches.

He described dome-shaped houses in which the Mandans lived. These houses were built to a regular plan and were made of a framework of logs and covered with willow branches. The houses were partially excavated. Several feet of earth were then piled on top of the willow. (Fig. 32) Deacon compared the description of the Mandan earth house to the "motte and bailey castles" built by Robert of Rhuddlan in 1073 in North Wales.[271] The Mandans claimed to be the first human inhabitants of that part of the world. They lived well, had totally different customs from other tribes, and practiced agriculture more than hunting. Neatly laid out fields of Indian corn, beans, melons and pumpkins (all crops which were much more at home farther to the south), testified to their agricultural skill.

La Verendrye mentioned the remarkable fact that whereas all other Indians he had encountered were beardless, some of the Mandans grew beards. Verendrye also spoke of the frequency of gray hair among the tribe. (Pure Indians do not have beards, nor do they develop gray hair). Deacon has uncovered fourteen references to the "bearded Indians".[272]

Although their villages were peaceful, they were surrounded by defensive works in the form of ramparts and trenches. Bougainville, another French traveler, mentions earthworks and moats surrounding the villages.[273] It has been

---

271. Deacon, Richard, *Madoc and the Discovery of America*, George Braziller, New York, 1966, p.208.

272. Deacon, p.114; and, Olson, Dana, *The Legend of Prince Madoc and the White Indians*, Jeffersonville, Indiana 1987, p.94-95.

273. Olson, Dana, *The Legend of Prince Madoc and the White Indians*, Jeffersonville, Indiana 1987, p.94-95.

estimated that the Mandan nation had a population of fifteen thousand at the time of the La Verendrye and Bougainville visits.[274]

La Verendrye's meticulous narratives were corroborated by other French travelers, and Reuben Thwaite recorded that a tradition of white, bearded Indians was rife among the French traders and explorers in the eighteenth century. The skin color of these Indians was said to vary from almost white to a copper color and there were whole families among them with gray hair.

Prince Maximilian of Wied, a German traveler, visited the Mandan villages in 1833 and gave a more detailed account of their physical characteristics. Maximilian extolled about the "ethereal beauty of the women... the men were rather above medium stature, many of them robust, broad-shouldered and muscular, with noses not so long and arched as those of the Sioux... sometimes aquiline or slightly curved, sometimes quite straight, never broad, nor had they the high cheek bones of the Sioux."[275] Maximilian was accompanied by a twenty-three year old Swiss painter named Karl Bodmer. Bodmer documented the land, people and animals and painted. He was an outstanding painter as reflected by the quality and popularity of his paintings. While visiting the Mandans he instructed Four Bears, who was the chief of the lower village at that time, and a warrior named Yellow Feather in painting. Bodmer described them both as talented and excellent students.

According to Maximilian's description, the Mandan lodges resembled beehives. They were made of timber plastered thick with earth and placed close together. The huts were slightly vaulted and were provided with porticos. In the center of the roof was a square opening for smoke to exit, over which there was a circular screen made of twigs. The interior was spacious. Several crossbeams were attached to four strong central pillars and supported the roof. The dwellings were covered on the outside with matting made of osier (willow) over which was laid hay or grass, and then a covering of earth. The beds were placed against the walls and consisted of skins and blankets. The huts were grouped into large villages defended by palisades, ramparts and ditches, and each village was surrounded by a regular pattern of fields of growing crops.

Stories of the Welsh Indians in America were popular in England. *The Gentlemen's Magazine*, a London publication, carried several articles on the topic in

---

274. Pugh, Ellen, Brave His Soul, Dodd, Mead and Company, New York, 1970, p.83.
275. Deacon, p.115; and, Olson, p.96.

the eighteenth century.[276] Among them was an article by a Mr. Edward Williams, reporting that:

> ...about twenty years ago I became acquainted with a Mr. Binion of Coyty in the County of Galmorgan, who had been absent from his native country about thirty years...Mr. Binion said that he had been an Indian trader from Philadelphia for several years; that about the year 1750 he and five or six more penetrated much further than usual to the westward of the Mississippi and found a nation of Indians who spoke the Welsh tongue.
>
> They had iron among them, lived in stone built villages, and were better clothed than the other tribes. There were ruined buildings, one among them appeared like an old Welsh castle, another like a ruined church.
>
> They showed Mr. Binion a book, in Manuscript, which they carefully kept, believing it to contain the mystery of Religion. They told Mr. Binion that it was not very long since a man had come among them who understood it. This man, whom they esteemed a prophet, told them a people would some time visit them, and explain to them the mysteries in their book, which would make them completely happy.
>
> A Gentleman in company with Messrs. Binion and Williams at that time, in a letter to me confirms the above statement. He says that Mr. Binion declared that these Indians worshipped their book as God but could not read it. When Mr. Binion said that he came from Wales, they replied,
>
> "It was from thence that our Ancestors came, but we do not know in what part of the World Wales is."[277]

This article is a secondhand account, which I would deem unreliable. Apparently the writer is mixing accounts from various sources. The Mandans, who lived in North Dakota in 1750, probably had never heard of Wales, and the stone houses and castles appear to describe the ruins on the Ohio River, not the Missouri River.

A letter written by George Chrochan to Governor Dinwiddie of Virginia in 1753 gave information concerning the Welsh Indians. In the letter he stated that he was acquainted with French traders who related the story that some Indians who were trading with the Spanish happened to get lost on their way home:

> They had come upon a large settlement of people on a river that ran to the Sun's setting whom they took to be the French. They were not Indians, although they lived as Indians. The Governor of Canada sent three young

---

276. Deacon, p.131.
277. Deacon, p.131.

priests, dressed as Indians with Indian guides to the place where these people were settled and found them to be Welsh.

The priests brought back some old Welsh "Bibles" to satisfy the Governor that they had been there....[278]

This is a third-hand account that describes a tribe of White people with Welsh "Bibles" who lived as Indians on a river that fits the description of the upper Missouri.

The Reverend John Williams of Wales was the author of two books on the subject of Madoc. He tells of a Mr. Charles Beatty,

> ...a missionary from New York, who being accompanied by a Mr. Duffield, visited some inland parts of North America in the year 1755. If I rightly understood his journal, he travelled about 400 miles to the southwest of New York. During his tour he met with several persons who had been among the Indians from their youth, or who had been taken captive by them and had lived among them for several years, among others, one Benjamin Sutton, who had visited different (Indian) nations and had lived many years with them.

Williams quotes Mr. Beatty:

> "He [Benjamin Sutton] informed us that he was with the Choctaw Nation, or tribe of Indians at the Mississippi; he went to an Indian town a very considerable distance from New Orleans, whose inhabitants were of a different complexion; not so tawny as those of other Indians, and who spoke Welsh. He said he saw a book among them, which he supposes was a Welsh Bible which they kept carefully wrapped up in an otter skin, but they could not read it; and that he heard some of the Indians afterwards in the lower Shawnaugh (Shawnee) Town speak Welsh with one Lewis, a Welshman, a captive there. This Welsh tribe now live on the West side of the Mississippi River, a great way above New Orleans." [The lower Shawnee Town is on the Ohio River, less than one hundred miles from Kaskaskia, which is on the Mississippi River.]

In the Tuscarora Valley Mr. Beatty met another man, named Levi Hicks, who told us he had been:

> "...among the Indians from his youth, and told us he had been, when attending the Embassy (Treaty Meetings) in a town of Indians on the west

---

278. Deacon. p.128.

side of the Mississippi River who talked Welsh, as he was told, for he did not understand them, and our interpreter (an Indian named Joseph Peepy) once saw some Indians whom he supposed to be of the same Tribe, who talked Welsh, for he told us some of the words they said, which he knew to be Welsh, as he had been acquainted with some Welsh people."[279]

This lengthy sentence describes an Indian town on the west side of the Mississippi River whose people spoke Welsh.

An article published in 1804 in the *Palladium*, a Frankfort, Kentucky, newspaper, reports the story of Maurice Griffith. Griffith was a Welshman who came to America when he was young. He was captured in Virginia by Shawnee Indians in 1764. In 1766 or 1767 he was taken on a hunting expedition up the Missouri River with five Shawnee braves where they encountered:

> ...three white men in Indian dress. After proceeding with them four or five days' journey, they came to the village of these white men, where they found the whole Nation of the same color, all having the European complexion... A council lasted three days and Griffith was present; he had not admitted that he knew their language. It was finally decided that the six strangers should be put to death and Griffith thought the time had arrived for him to speak. He addressed the council in the Welsh language, said they had not been sent by any warlike nation and that they were actuated by curiosity and had no hostile intentions; that they merely wished to trace the Missouri to its source and they would return to their country satisfied with the discovery they had made without any wish to disturb the repose of their new acquaintances.
>
> Astonishment glowed in the countenances not only of the council but of his Shawnee companions, who clearly saw that he was understood. Confidence was given to his declarations. The King advanced and gave him his hand and from that moment they were treated with the utmost friendship. Griffith and his five Shawnee companions remained with the Nation eight months.
>
> As to the history of these people Griffith could learn nothing satisfactory. All they knew was that their ancestors had come up the river from a very distant country. They had intermixed with no other people by marriage and there was not a dark skinned man in the nation.[280]

Griffith and his five Shawnee companions stayed with the nation of White Indians (presumably Mandan) for eight months. His estimated that they were a

---

279. Armstrong, p.187.
280. Armstrong, p.186; and, Deacon, p.116.

tribe of fifty thousand people ranging for fifty miles along the Missouri.[281] This is surely an exaggeration. He may have included the nearby villages of the Arikara and Hidatsa in his total. The story is otherwise credible. Some interesting points in Griffith's report are that he claims this tribe of Welsh Indians did not interbreed with other tribes before his visit in 1766, and he alluded to the Chief as "King."

By the late eighteenth century, articles in *The Gentlemen's Magazine* and *The Public Advertiser* of London had led to a modest but influential cult among a few Welsh literary figures. In 1791, a charlatan named "Chief" or "General" William Bowles entered the Madoc controversy. Bowles had no Indian blood, but he had made himself a member of the Creek tribe and called himself "Commander in Chief" of the tribe. In his Indian headgear he was a picturesque figure in London, as colorful as he was glib. He was an instant success in the taverns and also the literary salons, where his talent as a raconteur made him welcome. Even the royal family entertained him. When Bowles arrived in London he gave newspaper interviews and held a conference proclaiming that he had come from the Creek Indians. He declared that the Welsh Indians were an established fact in America, and he identified the Welsh Indians as being the *Padouca* tribe. William Owen, a writer for the *Gentleman's Magazine* was taken in by Bowles and published an account of his adventures with the Welsh Indians. Bowles was an inveterate liar and far from lending any long term support to the Madoc legend, which was his aim, in the end he managed only to discredit it.[282]

The reports of John Evans stand in stark contrast to those of all others who visited the Mandans. Evans' adventures were reviewed in 1949 by David Williams in the *American Historical Review*. Williams' article was titled "John Evans Strange Journey."

In 1791 John Evans departed his homeland of Wales at the age of twenty-one with the high purpose of finding the Welsh Indians. He was sponsored by a consortium of benefactors who raised money for the expedition for which he was chosen, and he was told to expect financial help from the Welsh community living in Philadelphia. Evans was the son of a poor Methodist preacher. In his youth he was known to be honest and pious, but when he arrived in London, acquaintances spoke of him as an opportunist and an adventurer who was more fond of money than the gospel. At this young age, he already showed a liking for

---

281. Deacon, p.116.
282. Pugh, p.44-52.

hard liquor and had sought out General Bowles in the taverns. Late in the summer of 1792 he sailed to America. He visited with Welsh contacts in Philadelphia and Baltimore whom he befriended. They discouraged him, gave him no money, and advised him to abandon his quest because Indian tribes were savage and dangerous. One of his contacts in Philadelphia was Dr. Sam Jones, a pastor who founded Rhode Island College, which became Brown University.

Mr. Arthur T. Halliday of Baltimore later discovered notes in the attic of his great grandfather, Jabez Halliday. Jabez had known Evans and had written:

> John Evans had little help or encouragement from Welsh settlers in Philadelphia and Baltimore. He had been promised assistance, but it was never forthcoming. I think the reason he didn't find the Welsh Indians was that he didn't intend to help them (his fellow countrymen) any more when funds were not forthcoming. His whole idea seemed to me to be to keep what he found to himself and, for some mysterious reason, to capitalize his findings by selling his discovery to somebody else.

After finding out all that he could about the Welsh Indians, Evans decided that if they existed they were probably either the Padoucas or the Mandans. He decided they lived somewhere far up the Missouri River. To get there he had to go through either Spanish Louisiana or British Canada. Fatefully, he chose the former.

In March of 1793 he crossed the Allegheny Mountains to the Ohio River. He then sailed down the Ohio to the Mississippi, and then up the Mississippi to St. Louis.

At that time Spain, France, Britain, and the young American nation were all competing for the North American continent. The Spanish, who then controlled the Louisiana Territory, differentiated the Scots, Irish, and Welsh from the British, considering the three former nationalities to be potential espionage agents that they could use against the British. It was definitely not in the best interests of Spain to have Britain claim that Madoc preceded Columbus in the discovery and colonization of America.

In 1793 St. Louis was an open frontier town on the border of civilization. Its population consisted of 1000 Whites and 300 Negro slaves. Evans arrived in St. Louis as an inquisitive stranger and was promptly arrested as a British spy by the suspicious Spanish. Evans spent two years in prison before he was released, the Spanish having come to accept his mission to find the Welsh Indians. By this time Evans had focused on the Mandans, discarding the idea that the Padoucas could be Welsh. (The Padoucas were a Plains-Apache tribe that spoke an Athapaskan dialect. The French called them Comanches). Evans was then cajoled, coaxed, bullied and flattered into being a Spanish agent.

In 1795, Evans set off up the Missouri River with James Mackay, a Scotsman who was employed by the Spanish Government as an explorer. The expedition had two goals: to dislodge the British, and to explore and survey the territory for the King of Spain. Mackay drew up a manifesto which warned all foreigners away from the territory, which was claimed by Spain. Evans was to describe all of the Indian tribes that he encountered. After traveling three hundred miles, the party reached the lands of the Omaha tribe where they built Fort Charles and spent the winter. When they attempted to continue their journey up river the following spring, they met a party of Sioux on the warpath and were forced to turn back to Fort Charles.

Later in 1796 they set off again. This time they reached the Cheyenne tribe with whom they traded, and after nine weeks and seven hundred miles they reached the Arikaras, who demanded that Evans turn over his supplies to them. This was the farthest any Spanish exploration team had ventured up the Missouri River. In September they crossed the boundary into the territory of the Mandans and entered their village.

Evans gave out medals, flags and other presents to the Mandans and even gave a speech extolling Spain, his new master. He tore down the Union Jack and hoisted the flag of Spain at the fort that had been established by René Jessaume, a Frenchman in the employ of the British North West Company.[283] The date was September 27, 1796. Two weeks later Spain declared war on Britain. This meant that Evans had become guilty of treason against Britain and he could not return to his native land.

Evans spent the following winter with the Mandans, whom he found to be courteous, hospitable, humorous and high spirited and well supplied by the crops they grew. They must have had an affinity for the Welshman because he was able to do about anything he liked, and once they saved his life when Jessaume threatened to kill him.

The Mandan tribe that Evans saw was considerably smaller than the one that hosted the early French traders. A smallpox epidemic in 1781-2 had greatly

---

283. Shane, Ralph M., A Short History of Fort Berthold, TAT Museum edition, New Town, North Dakota, 1997, p.2-3.

weakened the tribe and they had been forced by the Sioux to move their villages up the river farther to the north and west.

When located by La Verendrye in 1738, the Mandan villages were at sites near the mouth of the Heart River in the vicinity of present day Bismarck, North Dakota. They are believed to have settled there around 1575. In 1790, D'Eglise described them as living in eight villages on the upper Missouri, but by the time of Evans' visit in 1796 they had moved farther upstream to a location that was only a few miles south of the villages of the Hidatsa tribe on the Knife River.[284]

When Evans returned to St. Louis, he was given a payment of two thousand dollars, a huge sum in those days. He was also given a post as a surveyor for the Spanish and an assurance of security for life. In 1797, Evans wrote this to Dr. Samuel Jones of Philadelphia: "In respect of the Welsh Indians, I have only to inform you that I could not meet with such a people, and from intercourse I have had with Indians from latitude 35 to 49, I think you may with safety inform our friends that they have no existence."[285]

Evans' account of his quest put an end to the matter of the Welsh Indians in the eyes of many, but the perspicacious Jabez Halliday wrote that he was convinced that Evans never returned to Philadelphia because he had lied to his friends. Jabez Halliday personally inspected and described in detail a Mandan *bull boat*, which was identical to the Welsh coracle. (Fig. 33) John Evans denied ever seeing such a boat in connection with the Mandans. The boat seen by Mr. Halliday had been found in an abandoned Mandan village on a tributary of the Missouri. Mr. Halliday later met a Mandan who told him that the bull boat enabled his tribe to fish more effectively than other tribes, but that his tribe also used the canoe, which was larger and faster.

James Mackay's notes on the journey describe a tribe (whom he deceivingly calls the "Paducas"), who lived south of the Cheyenne River, that

> ...does not seem to be of the same race with the other Indian nations around them and from whom they differ in almost everything. They are honest, peaceable and sincere in all their transactions, friendly to each other and courteous to strangers. Their manners more approaching civilization, their skin more fair, their countenance more open and agreeable in their features in a Great Degree, resembling that of White people...[286]

---

284. Shane, Ralph M., p.2-3.
285. Deacon, p.137-150.
286. Deacon, p.146.

Mackay was being purposefully duplicitous in his account. First he knew that the tribe he was describing accurately was not the Padoucas, who lived much farther to the south and were fully Red Indians, and secondly the Mandans were no longer living south of the Cheyenne River but by the time of Mackay's visit had long ago moved much farther north.

It seems likely that the generous treatment that Evans received from Spain was due to his refuting the Welsh Indian story and not for any other service. Evans was already an alcoholic, and by 1797 his efficiency had long been impaired by growing cravings for strong liquor and a fondness for the bordellos, so that by then his only use to the Spanish was in denying the existence of the Welsh Indians. They sent Evans to New Orleans where he stayed with the Spanish Governor who declared in writing:

> It is in the interests of His Catholic Majesty that the reports of British Indians in Mandan country be denied once and for all. If, however, as seems possible, the subject of associations with the Mandans is not mentioned by the British, it might be more expedient to refrain from referring to this tribe, but to relate the denial only to the Padoucas who have already been said by the British to have an association with the Welsh.[287]

This explains Mackay's mistake in identifying the Mandan tribe as the Padoucas; he intentionally was attempting to mislead the British.

Evans' life continued in a downward spiral. He became not only a drunkard but a cheat in land deals that he controlled involving French landowners in Cape Girardeau. His only contribution appears to have been an accurate map that he drew of the Missouri River as far as the Mandan villages. This map was sent by President Thomas Jefferson to Meriwether Lewis on January 13, 1804. The map was probably the last service that Evans performed for the Spanish because in May of 1799, Don Manuel, the Spanish Governor wrote "Poor Evans is ill. I perceived that he deranged himself when out of my sight. The strength of the liquor has deranged his head; he has been out of his senses for several days."[288]

Evans died in New Orleans later that same month at the age of twenty-nine. It is possible that in addition to his drinking, illness may have contributed to his demise; his family had suffered from tuberculosis, which can reactivate. Or perhaps he was overtaken by remorse. At any rate his life, so full of bright

---

287. Deacon, p.149-150.
288. Deacon, p.146.

promise and sturdy patriotic dreams in his youth, ended sadly in perfidy and squalor.

The map that Evans drew survives and accurately describes the Mandans living on the Missouri River between the 47th and 48th parallels. (Fig. 47) Curiously the map is not written in Spanish as would be expected, but in English and French. His map shows the lower, main village of the Mandans on the west bank and the little village on the east bank. He also accurately placed the villages of the Gros Ventres (Hidatsa) on the Knife River just above those of the Mandans, and he placed old abandoned villages of the Mandans about twenty miles downstream. (The latter were probably old Hidatsa villages, but even today archaeologists cannot tell the difference between old village sites of the Mandans and those of the Hidatsa).

Of particular interest on the map are references to the "*Dog* River" and an "old village of the *Dog* Indians."[289] The Dog River corresponds to the Cheyenne River, named for the Cheyenne Indians, an Algonquian speaking tribe. On the banks of the Cheyenne River was an old village that is thought to have been the site of a Mandan and later an Arikara village. In the eighteenth century the Cheyenne tribe was migrating west and for a period associated with the Mandans, Hidatsa, and Arikara in the upper Missouri area. They were named *Chien* (meaning "dog") by the French and the tribe became generally known by the name *Cheyenne* as did the Cheyenne River in South Dakota and the Sheyenne River in North Dakota. The English translation "*Dog*" was not in general usage and I have found no other reference to the Cheyenne as the "Dog" Indians. The French trappers and traders that Evans encountered would have referred to this tribe as the *Chien*. Large game constituted most of the food supply for the Cheyenne and they were known to eat dog meat, which may have given them their name, but that practice was by no means limited to the Cheyenne.

The Hidatsa and Arikara and probably the Mandans as well were known to have a Society that went by the name of the "Dogs". The letter from Morgan Jones mentions a "Doeg Society," which he associated with the Welsh, and the term "Dog Indians" was used by Paul Marana pertaining to the Welsh Indians of Madog. Evans had fully researched the Welsh Indians and was surely aware of these papers. He designates a site on the west bank of the Missouri between the Cannonball and Grand Rivers as the "old village of the Dog Indians." This is near the present village of Fort Yates, North Dakota, which has been the site of a

---

289. Deacon, p.114.

village of the Hidatsa (Awaxawi) and Arikara (Ricarrees). The Cheyenne and the Sioux later built villages of buffalo-hide tipis near this site. The Arikara are the tribe most likely to have been living nearest to this site when Evans visited. There is no record that the Arikara were ever called by the name "Dog Indians," and Evans was well acquainted with the Arikara tribe.

Did Evans have a motive in conspicuously using the term "Dog Indians" on his map? Could he have been sending a concealed message to his friends in Philadelphia that the (Ma)-Dog Indians did exist and were living on the upper Missouri? Or did he found it humorous that more of his chicanery might lead his friends to put their efforts into investigating yet another tribe (the Cheyenne)? Other names that he used on his map in the upper Missouri area seem to reflect a flippant, condescending and contemptuous attitude. Examples of this are: *Rum Island, Island of the Sucker five,* and the reference to the Hidatsa as the *Big Bellies* rather than *Hidatsa,* which they called themselves, or *Minatarees,* the Mandan name for the tribe. My guess is that Evans fully recognized the double meaning of "Dog Indians," but he didn't really care whether his Philadelphia friends did or not. His only concern was being paid by an unsuspecting Spanish governor.

The handwriting on Evans' map reveals more about this enigmatic man. A graphological analysis agrees with several aspects of his personality that his actions reflect, including those related by Jabez Halliday. These include: an adventurousness and eagerness for new experiences; generosity, but with a catch, he wanted something back; he was protecting himself; and he was resentful and did not want to worry about being acceptable to others.[290] For an in-depth understanding and fair judgment of his behavior one needs to consider that Evans was a complicated man in a complicated situation. In the end his death was self induced; he could see no way to extricate himself from the control and protection by the Spanish.

Captains William Clark and Meriwether Lewis, of the Lewis and Clark Expedition of 1804-1806 wintered with the Mandans en route to the Pacific. With their party of soldiers and explorers, they spent six months at Fort Mandan, which they built across the river from the lower Mandan village. (Fig. 34) According to Ambrose, the Lewis and Clark Expedition owed its survival to the Mandans during the exceptionally cold winter season of 1804-1805. The Mandans supplied them with corn, beans and squash and donated horses so fifteen of Clark's men could accompany Mandan hunters when a herd of buffalo

---

290. Martin, Renee C., Your Script Is Showing, Golden Press, New York, 1969.

appeared on the plains near their village. The thermometer dipped to -45 degrees F. in December of 1804. The average temperature at Fort Mandan in January of 1805 was -3.4 degrees F.[291]

During their stay with the Mandans, Lewis and Clark were told of their perpetual war with the Sioux.

At that time Shahaka (Sheheke, or White Coyote, more commonly called Gros Blanc and Big White in the Lewis and Clark journals) was the principal Chief of Metntahanke, the lower village of the Mandans. He was given a medal by Lewis and Clark in recognition of the friendly service he gave them during the winter of 1804-1805. When the expedition returned to the Missouri River from the Pacific, Lewis and Clark persuaded Shahaka to return with them to visit Philadelphia and Washington with a view of visiting President Jefferson. Clark had first invited Black Cat, the upper Mandan Village Chief. Black Cat indicated that he wished to go to see the Great Father (President Jefferson), but declined because he feared a Sioux attack on the Mandan villages. After much pleading from Jessaume, Big White agreed to go if he could be accompanied by Jessaume, Jessaume's Mandan wife, and their son. While in Philadelphia, the Chief was painted by Charles Balthasar Julien Fevre de Saint Memin. The original portrait belongs to the American Philosophical Society of Philadelphia.

President Jefferson later invited Lewis and Shahaka (Big White) to his home, Monticello, for the purpose of showing the latter his collection of Indian objects from the Northwest. Shahaka remained in the East for a year. He left for his home in the Mandan village in May, 1807. On the first attempt by the army to return Big White to his village, they were attacked by the Arikara and had to turn back to St. Louis. Three were killed and seven injured in the attack. Later Big White was returned safely to the delight of the Mandan nation, who had despaired of ever seeing him again.[292]

A man on the Lewis and Clark expedition named Starnes wrote in later years: "When the seventy year old General Clark spoke of the daughters of the Mandans his eyes beamed with youthful fire and he answered me that they were the handsomest women in the world."[293]

Clark's high regard for the beauty of the Mandan women was shared by many other explorers, who mentioned their blue eyes, fair skins and often fair or ruddy locks. George Catlin visited the Mandans in 1832 and wrote that the

---

291. Ambrose, Stephen E., *Undaunted Courage*, Simon and Schuster, New York, 1996, p.180.
292. Deacon, p.213; and, Ambrose, p.461-468.
293. Armstrong, p.123-124.

women had a "mildness and sweetness of expression, and excessive modesty of demeanor" rendering them "exceedingly pleasing and beautiful."

La Chapelle, a cohort of the Sieur de la Verendrye, was left behind to study the Mandan language. Unashamedly he confessed that he never mastered the language, but had learned a great deal about their amorous customs which were, he declared, "a remarkable combination of primitive, lascivious ceremonies and a romantic code of behavior that had a flavor of the troubadour." He commented that the erotic rites they practiced attracted many visitors among the European traders and that they were accompanied by the music of an instrument resembling a primitive harp. (The harp was the Welsh national instrument). Their love songs were plaintive and melodious.[294]

In 1811, Henry M. Brackenridge and John Bradbury visited the tribe. Each published a report of his journey. Brackenridge, speaking of the Mandan chief, Big White Man, who was six feet ten inches tall, described him as "a fine looking Indian, and very intelligent - his complexion fair, very little different from that of a white man much exposed to the sun."[295]

Meriwether Lewis said of Black Cat, the Mandan chief of the upper village, "This man possesses more integrity, firmness, intelligence and perspicacity of mind than any Indian I have met with in this quarter."

George Catlin considered Ma-To-Toh-Pa (Four Bears), the Mandan chief of the lower village in 1832, to be "the most extraordinary Indian on the continent for his generosity, good manners, bravery and good looks".

Two tribes and their subgroups have lived in close association with the Mandans: those were the Arikara and the Hidatsa. The Arikara (Riccarees or Ree) were a Caddoan speaking tribe who were closely related to the Pawnee. They followed the Mandans up the Missouri River and were known to take over old Mandan villages and live in their deserted houses, those houses being better constructed than their own. The Pawnee, Omaha (Siouan speaking), and Cheyenne (Algonquian speaking), were also known to build earthen houses at one time, and so it is not certain which tribe first designed them. By the eighteenth century the Cheyenne had begun living in buffalo hide tipis.[296]

The Hidatsa were called Minatarees, or *Minitaris* by the Mandans, and *Gros Ventres* or "Big Bellies" by the French. Both the Hidatsa and the Arikara sought

294. Pugh, p.88; and, Olson, p.95; and, Deacon, p.217.
295. Pugh, p.88; and, Olson, p.95.
296. Pritzker, Barry M., A Native American Encyclopedia, Oxford University Press, New York, 2000, p.307.

protection from the Sioux by allying themselves with the Mandans. Both tribes built the round earthen structures that were characteristic of the Mandan villages.

The Hidatsa and Arikara are covered more fully in Chapter Sixteen.

CHAPTER XIV

FOLLOW YOUR DREAM

I love the people who have always made me welcome to the best they had.

I love a people who are honest without laws, who have no jails and no poorhouses.

I love a people who keep the commandments without ever having read them or heard them preached from the pulpit.

I love a people who never swear, who never take the name of God in vain.

I love a people "who love their neighbors as they loved themselves."

I love a people who worship God without a Bible, for I believe that God loves them also.

I love the people whose religion is all the same, and who are free from religious animosities.

I love the people who have never raised a hand against me, or stolen my property, where there was no law to punish either.

I love the people who have never fought a battle with white men, except on their own ground.

I love and don't fear mankind where God has made and left them, for there they are children.

I love a people who live and keep what is their own without locks and keys.

I love all people who do the best they can.

And oh, how I love a people who don't live for the love of money.

George Catlin

George Catlin was one of the last White men to have close contact with the Mandan tribe. Catlin was born in Wilkes Barre, Pennsylvania, the fifth child of fourteen. His mother had been a captive of the Indians as a child and his family had often talked about the Indians. Catlin attended law school in Connecticut then moved to Philadelphia, not to practice law, but to study painting. One day an Indian delegation came to town and reawakened an old fascination which became an obsession with him, that is to go to the lands of the Indian, not only to paint, but to study their customs and write their history before, as he said, "it was too late." In 1832 he left his career, his parents and his wife and set out on his dream. Later that year, he boarded the steamboat *Yellowstone* at St. Louis and headed upstream on the Missouri River. He disembarked at Fort Union near the mouth of the Yellowstone River on the North Dakota-Montana border. There he painted the Blackfeet, Crow, Assiniboine, and Cree Indians. Catlin had a great deal of sympathy and understanding for the Indians in general. He realized that although an Indian in Washington may seem mute, dumb and embarrassed, so would a White man in an Indian village, and for the same reason; "he has nobody to talk to."[297] He looked upon the Indians in their native state as "the most honest and honourable race of people" that he "ever lived amongst" and credited them with being "the last of all the human family to ever pilfer or steal."[298]

From Fort Union, Catlin paddled downriver in a canoe with two experienced, ribald, and hard drinking trappers as guides: Jean Baptiste and Abraham Bogard. On his return trip to St. Louis, Catlin stopped for lengthy periods to paint ten more tribes, his favorite subjects being the Mandans whom he painted profusely. He spent much of the next eight years with various Indian tribes, much of that time with the Mandans. He compiled copious notes for a two volume work about the history and cultures of the North American Indians that he published in 1842. He devoted sixteen of fifty-eight chapters of his *Letters* to the Mandans. This was followed by a successful lecture tour in America and in Britain that included the presentation of an Indian Chief to Queen Victoria. (Fig. 45)

Before Catlin left St. Louis on his way up the Missouri River, the elderly General William Clark told him that the Mandans were a strange people, "half white..."[299] In his book, Catlin stressed their physical differences with other tribes, their hair being fine instead of coarse, and some had light colored or gray hair, and their eyes were often gray, hazel or blue. In his words:

---

297. Catlin, George, North American Indians, Penguin Books, 1989, p.79.
298. Catlin, p.47.
299. Catlin, p.89.

A stranger in a Mandan village is first struck with the different shades of complexion, and various colours of hair which he sees in a crowd about him; and is at once almost disposed to exclaim that "These are not Indians." I am full convinced that they have sprung from some other origin than that of the other North American tribes, or that they are an amalgam of natives with some civilized race...

While visiting the Mandan villages, Catlin made friends with Mah-to-toh-pa (Four Bears), the Mandan chief of the lower village whom he greatly admired. He described Four Bears as the most popular man in the nation; he was free, generous, elegant, gentlemanly in his deportment, handsome, brave, and valiant, a high minded and gallant warrior. Four Bears hosted Catlin to a feast of roasted buffalo ribs and a pudding made from the flour of prairie turnips and flavored with berries. It was the custom in all the tribes that Catlin visited for the chiefs and other tribal leaders to have multiple wives, and Ma-to-toh-pa had six. Catlin found that the polygamy in the Mandan tribe was confined to the chiefs and medicine-men, although there was no regulation prohibiting others from marrying several wives if they could afford to do so.[300]

Catlin described their fishing craft as unlike any used by other Indian tribes, the Mandan craft having a frame shaped like a round tub under which buffalo skins were stretched. The craft was exactly like the coracle used in Wales and was operated in the same manner.

By the time of Catlin's visit in 1832 the Mandans had interbred with other Indian tribes, including the Hidatsa, and by this time the Mandans were half breeds, but still many of the women had blond or reddish hair. Catlin estimated that eight to ten percent of the tribe had gray hair.

In 1738, La Verendrye had come across one male Mandan who wore a cross and spoke the names of Jesus and Mary, and other French traders described Welsh Bibles that they had seen and even brought back with them. Nearly a century later Catlin found no visible traces of Christianity among them, but there were traces in their legends and in the elaborate and lengthy ceremonies that he witnessed. Various ceremonies involved the *Great Flood* and the *First Man*, who was a White man from whom the Mandans descended. A ceremony that amazed, excited and appalled Catlin was known as the *Okipa*. It began with the bull dance. It involved a "big canoe," which reflects the Great Flood. The bulk of

---

300. Catlin, George, Letters and Notes on the North American Indians, Michael M. Mooney, editor, Clarkson N. Potter, New York, p.148,165.

the ceremony was a test for young men to prove themselves as warriors and involved the most egregious of tortures including days of starvation and dehydration followed by the skewering of skin and muscles and hanging of the youths until they lost consciousness. (Fig. 46) Upon awakening, each man then typically offered a finger to the Great Spirit and the finger was promptly hacked off. Next, buffalo skulls and other weights were attached to the skewers and they ran in circles around the big canoe until they dropped. This was aptly named the Last Race. Visitors to the Mandans who were unaware of this ceremony expressed astonishment at the finding of so many Mandan warriors with missing fingers.[301]

The most amazing fact about the Okipa ceremony is that it was voluntary, and some young men elected to go through the tortures repeatedly. What the warriors gained by going through the ordeal was status as a leader in battle and the respect and admiration of the tribe. Those who never participated were held in low esteem. The barbarity of the ceremony and its continuation as a special annual event reflects an element of masochism in the men of the Mandan nation. The origin of the Okipa ceremony is obscure; Catlin was not aware of a similar rite in any other tribe. He considered the tortures to be "ignorant, barbarous and disgusting," and saw them as incongruous in a tribe that he otherwise described as "the polite and friendly Mandans,... kind and hospitable".[302] The Mandans held their last Okipa ceremony in 1889.[303]

Catlin witnessed another Mandan ceremony that was based on a legend that reflects a strong resistance against procreation and marriage outside the tribe. Previous Mandan chiefs must have promulgated a strict taboo against such behavior. In the legend "at a very ancient period", an evil spirit, who is painted black, faces the "First Man," the spiritual founder of the Mandans from whom they descended. First Man was a White man who was painted white. The Mandans considered him to be the first White man in their country. In the ceremony the "Evil One" approaches the lower village of the Mandans from atop a nearby hill. He takes a serpentine path while slowly descending to the village. He approaches a pretty Mandan girl and entices her to eat and walk with him. Although "nothing happens," she becomes pregnant and is disgraced. She secretly leaves the village, going to the upper village where she gives birth. First

301. Catlin, Letters, p.189-206.

302. Catlin, Letters..., p.189-206; and, Catlin, North American..., p.151-181.

303. Baker, Linda, et al, The History and Culture of the Mandan, Hidatsa, Sahnish, North Dakota Department of Public Instruction, Bismarck, 2002, p.42.

Man discovers her whereabouts and kills the child by throwing him into the river.[304]

After leaving the Mandans, Catlin descended the Missouri River looking for evidence of earlier Mandan habitations. He was successful in finding traces of previous village sites that he thought were Mandan. He believed the Mandans had been compelled to abandon those sites because of their perpetual war with the Sioux who endeavored to extinguish them. It became obvious to him that the tribe was weakening under the constant attacks, for as they moved north, their fortifications had become less formidable and their defenses less adequate. He claimed to have identified six or seven sites of Mandan fortifications between the Cheyenne River in South Dakota and the mouth of the Ohio. (Fig. 33) At the earlier, downstream sites, Catlin found that the village palisades had been twenty to thirty feet high and covered walkways had led to the river. He found the site of a village near the Cheyenne River that he believed they had previously abandoned. He estimated that their numbers then were three times what they were in 1832. He later wrote:

> I have descended the Missouri River from the Mandan village to St. Louis, a distance of 1800 miles [actually less than 1200 miles] and taken pains to examine its shores. On the banks of that river I saw repeated remains of old Mandan villages. I am fully convinced that I have traced them down nearly to the mouth of the Ohio. Their ancient fortifications are numerous. Some of them enclose a great many acres. Built on the banks of the river, with walls in some places twenty or thirty feet in height, and covered ways to the water, they evince a knowledge of the science of fortifications not a century behind that of the present day. I submit they were never built by any nation of Indians in America, and present to us incontestable proof of the former existence of *a people far advanced in the arts of civilization.* (The remains of some of the old villages are still identifiable by depressions in the ground left where the circular wood and earthen houses once stood.)[305]

I am convinced that most of the abandoned village sites that Catlin identified along the Missouri and Mississippi Rivers were never occupied by the Mandans. The Hidatsa and the Arikara and their cousins the Pawnee lived in similar round earthen houses as did the Omaha and Cheyenne. The Arikara were known to move into abandoned Mandan villages and the Pawnee may have done

---

304. Catlin, North American..., p.151-181.
305. Catlin, Letters..., p.224-229.

the same. If so, they may have enlarged the villages, giving Catlin an exaggerated impression of the previous size of the Mandan nation. Catlin also credited the Mandans with building sites "along the Ohio and Muskingum Rivers." The structures seen by Catlin at these sites were probably mounds built by the Fort Ancient, Adena and Hopewell Cultures, and had no archaeological connection with the Mandans.

Catlin made other observations regarding the Mandans that he compared to other Indian tribes that he saw. He noted that the Mandans differed from the others in that they seldom took male prisoners of war and never tortured their captives. They kept no slaves although they were surrounded by tribes who did, including the Arikara and the Crow, cousins of the Hidatsa. Every White visitor who left a journal on the Mandans commented on their hospitality. They had an impressive aesthetic sense in painting and music and were fine orators and liked to talk. They had an extraordinary art of making a "beautiful and lasting kind of blue glass beads, like those used in trade by seamen from the island of Lundy, and which they wear on themselves in quantities, and decided value above all others that are brought to them." (Indian tribes obtained blue glass beads of Venetian origin from traders. The Mandans remanufactured these beads into a different form).[306]

Such a flattering stance in the description of the Mandans is not limited to Catlin. The early French traders and practically all visitors extolled their pleasing appearance, industry, aesthetics and technological methods. But these visitors also saw in the Mandans a race similar to their own and with a demeanor more resembling their own. This is in stark contrast to the way they viewed the Red Indians who, as described to John Evans, were deemed "savage and dangerous." Meriwether Lewis described the Mandans, "These are the most friendly, well disposed Indians inhabiting the Missouri. They are brave, humane and hospitable." Of the Sioux, he wrote, "These are the vilest miscreants of the Savage race, and must ever remain the pirates of the Missouri, until such measures are pursued, by our Government, as will make them feel a dependence on its will for their supply of merchandise."[307]

Such glowing descriptions of the Mandan tribe versus the fear and contempt that the Colonists felt toward the Red Indians in general should

---

306. Olson, Dana, The Legend of Prince Madoc and the White Indians, Jeffersonville, Indiana, p.94-95,100; and, Fausz, J. Frederick, personal communication, St. Louis, 2003; and, Ambrose, Stephen E., Undaunted Courage, Simon and Schuster, New York, 1996, p.180Catlin, Letters... p.227.
307. Ambrose, p.206.

recognize the beholders. The contempt felt for the Red Indians was not justified, and the White settlers' comparison of the Red Indians to the White Indians was myopic; it misunderstands and fails to appreciate the culture and achievements of the Red Indians. Also, it is significant that the ancestors of the Welsh Indians had the advantage of the accomplishments of Western Civilization, at least as it existed in twelfth century Wales; an advantage that the Red Indians lacked. Today some have taken a curious turnabout by lauding the worship of a mystical natural world and ancestral spirits, which they associate with the religion of the Red Indians. Such a position can be carried to the extreme. This is exemplified by the judicial interpretation of the Native American Graves Protection and Repatriation Act of 1990 (NAGPRA). This act requires immediate burial, before scientific study can be carried out, of all ancient human remains (i.e. Kennewick Man).[308] That one of the goals of the Indians in this case is to thwart scientific verification of the origins of the Paleo-Americans is evident from a television interview in which a Umatilla Indian leader is asked "If you don't let the studies go forward, how can we find out?" His answer: "We don't want to find out."[309] It is destructive to science and truth in history when laws are passed in support of negativism such as this. The price society pays for judicial opinions based on these laws is to ensure that a group (Red Indians) retains its popular status as the recognized aborigines of America, even when such a status has been disproved. The situation is remarkably tantamount to the subterfuge played by the Spanish Governor of Louisiana and his employee John Evans two hundred years ago, when they intentionally denied the existence of the Welsh Indians.

The resemblance of the Paleo-Americans to known M-130 peoples (Polynesians, Australians, Ainu) was discussed in Chapter One. The Red Indian tribes that replaced the Paleo-Americans lack this genetic marker, although the M-130 marker is now a common finding in Northeast Asia and Mongolia. There is one North American Indian linguistic group that has the M-130 marker however, and that is the Athapaskan speaking *Na Dene* tribes. The Na Dene people therefore can be considered to be the distant cousins of the extinct Paleo-Americans with whom they presumably share the M-130 marker. Athapaskan speaking tribes include the Navajo, Apache and a half dozen or so small tribes in the Pacific northwest. Some Na Dene may have entered Alaska from Northeast Asia as early as 4000 B.C., but the Apache came much later, probably arriving

---

308. Chatters, James C., Ancient Encounters, Kennewick Man and the First Americans, 2001.
309. CBS Interview '60 Minutes' with Leslie Stahl, 25 Oct, 1998; and, Nugent, John, 'Who Were the Original Native Americans?' The Barnes Review, v.5 no.3 p.5, 1999.

around 1000 B.C. It was not until A.D. 1400 that the Apache and Navajo reached the American southwest, where the Spanish found them in the next century.[310]

The presence of the M-130 marker on the Y chromosomes of the Navajo and other Na Dene people reveals their common genetic origin with the Ainu, Australians, and Polynesians and presumably the Paleo-Americans as well. The Paleo-Americans disappeared following the invasion of the Siberian clan Red Indians. It is ironic that the Navajo, with over 200,000 eligible members of their nation, are now the largest Indian tribe in the United States.[311]

The Government's case for immediate burial of Kennewick Man might have been strengthened if any of the tribes involved in the law suit to confiscate and immediately bury the remains of Kennewick Man had been Na Dene and therefore related (however distantly) to the Paleo-Americans. In fact, none of them is Na Dene. The Y chromosome markers of the Umatilla and other tribes involved in the suit show that their Y chromosomes are no more linked genetically to the Paleo-Americans than are Europeans. It is also true that the Y chromosomes of the Siberian clan Red Indians are much closer genetically to those of Europeans than to the M-130 Na Denes and Paleo-Americans; both the Siberians and the Europeans contain the M-45 marker and lack the M-130 marker. This is not the whole story, because the Navajo and Apache of today no longer share the physical traits of the Paleo-Americans. Evolution and cross breeding have occurred and the Na Denes and Siberian clan Red Indians now share a significant amount of genetic material. But this sharing does not involve their Y chromosomes, which indicates they have had a different origin.

Political intervention into the studies of archaeology and anthropology is not limited to the United States. In the 1950s, when an archaeologist employed by the National Museum of Canada made the discovery of remains of a longhouse that "smelled of a European presence," he failed to publish his findings because, in his words, it would have "given the high priests of the profession conniptions."[312]

Catlin concluded:

---

310. Wells, Spencer, The Journey of Man: A Genetic Odyssey, Princeton University Press, Princeton, New Jersey, 2003.

311. Pritzker, Barry M., A Native American Encyclopedia, Oxford University Press, New York, 2000, p.335.

312. Mowat, Farley, The Farfarers: Before the Norse, Steerforth Press, South Royalton, Vermont, 2000, p.2,200.

I shall leave the Mandans in the morning, and with my canvas and easel and paint pots in my canoe, wend my way again on the mighty Missouri. Taking leave will be done with decided feelings of regret. The singular customs of the Mandans have raised an irresistible belief in my mind that they have had a different origin, or are of different character, from any other tribe that can be in North America... I am inclined to believe that ten ships of Madoc made their way up the Mississippi River and their brave and persevering colonists made their way through the interim to a position on the Ohio River, where they cultivated the fields and established a flourishing colony. At length they were set upon by Indians, whom perhaps they had provoked to warfare by being trespassers on their hunting grounds; they were besieged. It was necessary to erect fortifications for their defense.[313]

In the end they all perished, except those perhaps who might have formed alliance by marriage with the Indians. Their offspring would have been half-breeds. At length being despised, as all half-breeds of enemies are, they gathered themselves into a band, moved off, and increased in numbers and strength as they advanced up the Missouri River to the place where they had been known for many years past by the name of the Mandans, a corruption, or abbreviation perhaps, of Madawgwys, the name applied by the Welsh to the followers of Madawe (Madoc).[314]

Although Catlin's conclusions are not wholly accurate, they are remarkably perceptive. Catlin gave no indication that he was aware of Chief Oconostota's revelations to John Sevier regarding the landings at Mobile Bay or the ruins in Alabama, Georgia, and Tennessee.

After leaving the Plains Indians, Catlin's life continued its adventure. He exhibited his paintings and Indian artifacts in cities in North America and in Europe. After his wife died, he went to South America where he continued to paint Indians, but he considered the South American natives ugly and uninteresting in comparison to the Plains Indians of North America. He sailed from Peru to the Aleutians, painting the coastal tribes as he went. In the end, he was able to sell only relatively few of his paintings. He died penniless and was judged a failure by his peers; but I think otherwise. His book is still in print, and today his paintings hang in museums and galleries across America. Together, they "constitute the first, last and only complete record of the Plains Indians ever made at the height of their splendid culture".[315] Who would measure the life of

---

313. Catlin, Letters..., p.224-229.

314. Catlin, Letters..., p.224-229; Olson, p.100; and, Deacon, Richard, Madoc and the Discovery of America, George Braziller, New York, 1966, p.214-219.

315. Matthiessen, Peter, in the Introduction to George Catlin's North American Indians, Penguin Books, p.viii.

George Catlin to have been more successful if he had become a wealthy Philadelphia lawyer? Catlin followed his dream; not many men do.

The origin of the word Mandan has not been ascertained. It may be as Catlin suggests a corruption of Madoc, or it may be from madden, a type of red dye. That this may be the origin of their name is suggested by the Welsh word, "mandon", which is "the woodruff, a species of madder used as a red dye."[316] Pritzker has reported that Mandan is a Dakota word.[317] Edwin Benson is the tribal authority on the Mandan language and has a reputation for not stating something unless he is sure of it. He told the author that the French gave the Mandans their name, but he does not know the meaning of the French word used.[318] La Verendrye referred to them as the *Mantannes.*[319]

According to some Mandans their original name for themselves is *See-pohs-ka-nu-mah-ka-kee*, which means "People From the Land of the Pheasants", but this actually refers only to one large band within the tribe. Their self-designation was *Numakiki*, meaning simply, "people".

All of the visitors to the Mandans considered them to be Indians; none claimed that they were not. They lived as Indians, clothed themselves as Indians and painted their faces and bodies as Indians did. They hunted with bows and arrows. But all of the visitors noted that they were different from other Indians in their customs and they looked different; they were a *White* Indian tribe, but still Indian. Such is a description of a people who were a mixture containing both White and Red Indian ancestry.

---

316. Catlin, North American Indians, p.495.

317. Pritzker, p.335.

318. Benson, Edwin, personal communication, Halliday, North Dakota, 2003.

319. Shane, Ralph M., A Short History of Fort Berthold, TAT Museum New Town, North Dakota, 1997, p.2.

CHAPTER XV

LANGUAGE

Madoc Maho Paneta am byd. (Madoc, the Great Spirit of the race).
Mandan Ceremonial Prayer

By July of 1756 the Indian wars in the east had become particularly bloody. The frontier was afire with burning settlers' cabins and hundreds of people were taken captive by the Indians, among them the Girty brothers, Simon, James, and George, and their stepfather John Turner. Turner and the Girty brothers were taken to the Indian village of Kittanning on the Allegheny River in Pennsylvania where Turner was executed in a grisly manner. The British army destroyed Kittanning that September, but the Girtys were not recovered. Simon had been taken away and adopted by the Seneca, James by the Shawnee, and George by the Delaware. James was thirteen years old at the time.[320]

Several additional things are known about James Girty: He was not of Welsh descent and could not have learned the Welsh language as a child; he served as a "runner" between the British and the Indians for a considerable time; and he talked about the "Welsh Indians," which he linked to the Mandans. He met Francis Lewis, the signer of the Declaration of Independence, and spoke to him in Welsh, thus verifying Girty's knowledge of the language. Girty made a vocabulary list of 350 words, phrases and short sentences of the Welsh Indian language and compared them to the Welsh. Below is a partial list:[321]

---

320. Eckert, Allan W., That Dark and Bloody River, Chronicles of the Ohio River Valley, Bantam Books, New York, 1995, p.lxiii.

English	Welsh Indian	Welsh
I	Me	Mi
You	Nehi	Chwi
He	Efo	Efo
She	Ea-ah	Hi
We	Noo	Ni
Water	Duah	Dwr
Bread	Bara	Bara
River	Nant	Nant
Father	Taid	Tad
Cow	Buch	Buwch
Partridge	Cluga	Clugjar
Woods-men	Coedig	Coed-wig
stone	kraig	crreg
old	hen	hen
dance	dansio	dawnsio
valley	koom	cwm, koom
morning	borrah	bore, borra
night	nostogr	nos
thanks	dyawf	niolch
I am	yr-effi	yr wyfi
He is	ym-eff	y mae ef
You are	Yor-iddich-ni	yr ydychwi
in the boat	in y kook	yn
blue	glas	glas
milk	faeth	llaeth
to cross	croesi	croesi
harp	tefyn	telyni
to be born	genni	genin
bridge	pont	pont
estuary	aber	aber
high	uchaf	uchel
to belong	pertin	perthyn
great	mawr	mawrhyn
foot	troed	troed
disgusting	ake-e-Vee	Ach-y-fi
beautiful	prydfa	prydferth
sing	canu	canu

321. Deacon, Richard, Madoc and the Discovery of America, George Braziller, New York, 1966, p.220-237; and, Olson, Dana, he Legend of Prince Madoc and the White Indians, Jeffersonville, Indiana, 1987, p.99.

There is no evidence that James Girty ever visited the Mandans, but the Shawnee warrior chief Tecumseh and his brother Tenskwatawa ("The Prophet") sent runners who visited the tribes of the Missouri River. Tecumseh traveled tirelessly from Ohio to the Rocky Mountains in an attempt to recruit warriors for his battles against the United States. James Girty was a runner for the Shawnee and may have gone on this recruitment drive, but there is no record of it. It is not known how Girty learned the Welsh language, and for him to have learned it at the Mandan villages he would have had to spend a good deal of time there. It is more likely that the Shawnee had Welsh Indians and their children as captives and Girty learned the language from them. If Girty did visit the Mandans, he may have learned the Welsh language beforehand and therefore been able to identify the Mandan language as Welsh.

Thomas Jefferson had a passion for Indian languages and believed he could trace a tribe's origin through their language. Meriwether Lewis made an attempt to establish a vocabulary for the Mandan and Hidatsa languages while at Fort Mandan. Lewis employed two Frenchmen, René Jessaume and Toussaint Charbonneau, in the task. Jessaume was married to a Mandan woman and lived with the tribe. One of Charbonneau's wives was Sakakawea, who lived with the Hidatsa tribe on the Knife River and assisted the Lewis and Clark expedition as a guide. Unfortunately Jessaume and Charbonneau spent most of the time "arguing about the meaning of every word" and despite an immense amount of time spent on the project by Lewis, he accomplished very little.[322]

During his lengthy stay with the Mandans, George Catlin also made a study of their language. A small example of what he found follows:[323]

English	Mandan	Welsh	Pronunciation
I	Me	Myfi	Mifi
You	Ne	Chwi	Chwe
He	E	Efo, Hwn	Efo, Hoon
She	Ea	Hi, Hon	He, Hon
It	Ount	Hwynt	Hooynt
We	Noo	Ni	Ne
They	Eonah	Hwna	Hona

322. Ambrose, Stephen E., Undaunted Courage, Simon and Schuster, New York, 1996, p.203.
323. Catlin, George, North American Indians, Penguin Books,1989, p.497.

159

By the time Catlin met the Mandans they had closely associated with other tribes, especially the Hidatsa, and their language had been altered and supplemented with words from other languages.

When Catlin visited Britain he discussed his long list of Mandan words and sentences with Welsh scholars. They found that while the majority of Mandan words were unlike those of Welsh, there was an astonishing similarity when some whole sentences were translated into Welsh, and that a pattern of similarity existed. What convinced Catlin that the Mandan people might have been derived from Madoc was when he heard the Indians exhorting the aid of the "Great Spirit of the Race," *Madoc Maho Paneta am byd*, which in Welsh would be *Madoc Mawr Penarthur am byth* ("Madoc the Great Spirit forever"). Somehow Madoc was associated with their ancestral "Great Spirit," though the Mandans could not explain the reason for this.

After he returned from London, Catlin wrote a letter to a Mr. Lewis Edward of Washington stating:

> I must confess some disappointment that, after conferring with other Welsh scholars, I find that modern Mandan is basically different from Welsh, but at the same time there is no doubt at all that the similarities which do exist are of a pattern and so pronounced that there must be a link between the two languages. I now see Mandan as a two-tier, possibly a three-tier language. It consists of a language within a language, and it would seem that the more ancient part of that language is cherished for certain special occasions and for certain functions of everyday life. Quite often I found that where there were two or more words with one meaning, one of those words would be the equivalent of Welsh. The Mandans themselves invariably explained that some of the Welsh-sounding words had almost gone out of use. The tragedy is that someone did not make a study of their dialect a century previous to this.[324]

Catlin found that differences in syntax and grammar constituted the chief weakness of the claim that Mandan was derived from Welsh. Yet there may be an explanation for this weakness. "Secret languages" have existed for centuries, being used by special groups of people to preserve the identity of a language and to exclude outsiders from using it. For example the Romany tribes and the West African Lucami in Cuba have used such secret languages as have people in the Philippines. They used these secret languages as a systematic substitution for

---

324. Deacon, p.220-227; and, Catlin, p.497.

individual words without ever attempting to create a grammar. The substitute words often became taboo; they were remembered, but not spoken. Taboo words have been known to be guarded and recollected long after they have ceased to be spoken, whereas any attempt at grammatical construction would quickly be lost through lack of practice.[325]

The impression gained by some travelers was that Mandan-Welsh was a secret language. Both Catlin and Girty, and for that matter some of the early French explorers, were given to understand that certain words resembling Welsh were taboo; they were almost passwords to safe conduct or expressions of trust. Thus Catlin was told the Mandan legend about their origins, which stated "they descended from the first white man to come to this country." This was something they normally told no one.

Catlin also compared the bull boat of the Mandans with the coracle used in Wales and not only found them to be identical but the language surrounding the coracle to also be practically the same.

English	Mandan	Welsh
Coracle	Koorig	Corwg (pronounced corrug)
Paddle	Ree	Rhwyf (pronounced reef)
A fishing area	Burra	Bwrw

Of even greater interest were some of the words and phrases used by the Mandans in relation to the coracle. In addition to the above terms may be included *rudrat*, which in Mandan is a big fishing-net. The term has a marked similarity to the Welsh *rhwyd rhwth*, which was used to describe the wide-meshed part of a coracle-man's net. Then again the Mandans referred to fish not by name, but as "those ones" (Yrai Honah). In Wales even today coracle-fisherman hardly ever speak of salmon or any other fish by name, but always speak of "them" or "they." The Mandans said there was a name for fish, *pisg*, which they never used, as the very mention of the word was supposed to bring bad luck. The Welsh equivalent is *pysg*.

Mallory states that "languages upon the point of extinction are normally carried to the grave by the older members of the community when the younger

---

325. Deacon, p.220-227.

members have failed to learn it. This process can happen within three generations."[326] The Mandan language of today is far different from that described by Girty and Catlin. Today's tribal authority on the language is Edwin Benson, who teaches the language at the Twin Buttes School on the Fort Berthold Reservation. Mandan is Benson's native tongue, having learned the language from his paternal grandfather who was a full-blooded Mandan. Benson told the author that the Mandan language bears no similarity to the Hidatsa or Arikara language. Benson has been told that Mandan shares some words with the language of the Winnebago tribe, who speak a Chiwere Sioux dialect, but he has not verified this. The Winnebago tribe shares cultural traits with Plains Sioux tribes such as the Omaha who may have had contact with the Mandan tribe during their migration in the early sixteenth century. Pritzker is of the opinion that the Yuchi language may be part of the Siouan family, and Yuchean appears to be the most likely source for most of the Siouan characteristics identified in the modern Mandan language.[327]

Catlin's published list of 136 words compares Mandan to other Indian languages including Sioux (Dakota) and Riccaree. In reviewing this list I have found eighteen Mandan words which resemble their Sioux counterparts including the words for buffalo, elk, bear, and moccasins, for which a Welsh word could be expected to be used rarely or not be in existence. There is considerably less correspondence to the Riccaree words. The words for heavy, head, and hair are similar in all three languages indicating a common origin for these words.[328]

It is remarkable how much a language can change over the centuries. The English language spoken by Chaucer would be on the outer reaches of intelligibility to a speaker of twentieth-century English. Even more impressive is a comparison of two translations of a portion of the Twenty-third Psalm:

> The Lord is my shepherd, I shall not want.
> He maketh me to lie down in green pastures.
> He leadeth me beside the still waters.
> (Early Modern English)

---

326. Mallory, J.P., In Search of the Indo-Europeans, Thames and Hudson, London, 1989, p.259.

327. Pritzker, Barry M., A Native American Encyclopedia, Oxford University Press, New York, 2000, p.396.

328. Catlin, George, Letters and Notes on the North American Indians, edited by Michael M. Mooney, Clarkson N. Potter, New York, 1975, p.353-6.

Drihten me raet, ne byth me nanes godes wan.
And he me geset on swythe good feohiand.
And fedde me be waetera stathum.
(Old English, from AD 1000)[329]

Benson was visited by some Welsh people a few years ago. He found that they could not understand modern Mandan, and they found no resemblance between the Mandan language of the twenty-first century and the Welsh language of the twenty-first century.[330]

---

329. Mallory, J.P., p.22-23.
330. Benson, Edwin, personal communication, Halliday, North Dakota, 2003.

Chapter XVI

The Hidatsa and the Arikara

Archaeology is not a hard science, even though many mainstream academics may think it is. It's a life long dedication to study and probing with an open mind and a willingness to dare - it's a search for *the truth, and when* [what] *the truth reveals changes our thinking 180 degrees*, it's then that the truth hurts, and we must bear the pain, hopefully without a whimper.[331]

James Whittall

The Hidatsa

The Hidatsa are a Siouan speaking tribe. Their earliest known homelands were near Devil's Lake in northeastern North Dakota and near the headwaters of the Red River in southeastern North Dakota. They were a semi-nomadic people who practiced some agriculture, growing a variety of flint corn with a short maturation time and harvesting wild rice and artichokes.

At some point they divided into three subgroups named the Awatixa (a-WAH-tee-HAH), Awaxawi (A-wah-HAH-wee), and Hidatsa proper. The Awatixa (meaning scattered camps) are said to have been the first to arrive in the Missouri Valley of North Dakota, preceding the Mandan. The Awatixa left the Devil's Lake area and migrated west and north, reaching the Saskatchewan River, but were driven out by the Nahathaways and Stone Indians (Assiniboine). At some point the Awatixa split, one group going west to the Rocky Mountains

---

331. Cahill, Robert Ellis, New England's Ancient Mysteries, Old Saltbox Publishing House, Salem Massachusetts, 1993, p.15.

and becoming known as the Mountain Crow. The rest of the Awatixa remained settled in the Missouri Valley.

The Awaxawi (meaning people who live on the hill) were a smaller tribe who were known as the Souliers (Black Moccasins) to the French. In the Lewis and Clark maps and journals they are referred to as the Ahnaharways. They left the Devil's Lake homelands even earlier than the Awatixa.[332] From Devil's Lake, the Awaxawi entered the forests to the north and east where they lived for a "long, long time."[333]

The Awaxawi dialect differed significantly from that used by the Awatixa and Hidatsa proper subgroups, and misunderstandings sometimes occurred.[334] At one point, probably in the seventeenth century, the Hidatsa Proper made war on the Awaxawi and drove them from their Knife River area villages to the Fort Yates area in southern North Dakota. The Awaxawi had previously been driven to the Knife River area due to attacks from the Assiniboine, a Nakota Sioux tribe.

The Awaxawi are believed to have built the ancient village sites along the James and Sheyenne Rivers in southeastern North Dakota.[335] Their first identified settlements on the Missouri River were between the Heart River and the Knife River. In this vicinity there are numerous old village sites of Awaxawi and Awatixa origin. It is not possible to differentiate between Hidatsa villages and those of the Mandans using only traditional archaeological techniques because they are so similar in material culture and community patterning.[336] Legends and historical documentation, where available, have to be relied on for this differentiation, and legends from different sources may be contradictory.

The Hidatsa proper (HP) were the last subgroup of the Hidatsa to arrive at the Missouri River. Several Mandan and Hidatsa legends are consistent in that four HP braves discovered the Mandans as a large tribe with many villages near the mouth of the Heart River. The HP braves shouted across the river and the Mandans interpreted them as wanting to cross the river. In the Mandan language, this is stated "minatree," and the HP henceforth were known as the "Minatrees" and the Awatixa the "Minatrees of the Willows." The French called the HP and Awatixa *Gros Ventres* (Big Bellies). (This is not the same tribe as the

332. Wood, W. Raymond, and Hanson, Jeffery R., Reprints In Anthropology, Volume 32, J & L Reprint Company, Lincoln, Nebraska, 1986, p.79.

333. Wood, p.97.

334. Wood, p.31; and, Baker, Linda et al, The History and Culture of the Mandan, Hidatsa, Sahnish, North Dakota Department of Public Instruction, Bismarck, 2002, p.9.

335. Wood, p.64.

336. Wood, p.64.

Gros Ventres tribe of the Rocky Mountain area who were an Algonquian-speaking tribe.) The French called the Awaxawi *Souliers*, but noted that they were part of the *Gros Ventres* nation.

The four HP braves who crossed the river were welcomed by the hospitable Mandans, who befriended them and fed them well. The braves were understood to relate that they would return in four days with the rest of their tribe, and the Mandans made a great effort to prepare a feast for their arrival; but their sign language interpretation was faulty. The HP did return *en masse*, but it was four years later.

Alfred Bowers has concluded that the HP arrived at the Missouri River no earlier than 1615 and did not build round earthen lodges until taught to do so by the Mandans.[337] The Awatixa, who had arrived to the Missouri Valley much earlier, described their first lodges as *atutish*, which now designates the section of their round earthen lodges between the peripheral posts and the outside wall and is used for storage.

The HP lived close to the Mandan villages at first, but altercations broke out between young warriors of the two tribes and several were killed. At the behest of the Mandan chief, the HP agreed to move to a site farther away, north of the Heart River.

The HP later moved to a site on the Knife River. There they quarrelled amongst themselves. One group departed and migrated west and became the River Crow. The River Crow still consider the HP to be part of their tribe, but not the Awatixa or the Awaxawi. The term "Hidatsa" is a corruption of "midah-hutsee-ahti" by the Crow. It means "house made of willows."[338]

The HP had to be reintroduced to corn farming by the Mandans, as they had discontinued most of their agricultural practices, but the HP culture was less influenced by the Mandans than the other Hidatsa subgroups. In historic times the HP were known to frequently leave their gardens for a few seasons at a time and venture onto the Plains.[339]

The HP were more loosely associated as a tribe than the other Hidatsa. Bands of HP ranged north and west along the Missouri, Yellowstone, Little Missouri and Mouse Rivers, and into the Turtle Mountains and Devil's Lake area in eastern North Dakota. In 1837 they were on one of their periodic wanderings

---

337. Wood, p.123.
338. Wood, p.36; and, Baker, p.4.
339. Wood, p.37.

and thus partially avoided the devastating smallpox epidemic that struck that summer.

The HP are thought to have built the village sites Nightwalker's Butte and Rock Village, both of which are north of the Knife River and are now under the waters of Lake Sakakawea.

When a smallpox epidemic struck the tribes in 1781, the HP and Awatixa were living along the Knife River and the Mandan in the Heart River vicinity in six to nine large villages. The Awaxawi were between the two. Bowers estimated that before that epidemic the combined Mandan-Hidatsa population was well in excess of twelve thousand people, the Hidatsa groups constituting about one-third of the total.[340] In 1798, seventeen years after the epidemic, David Thompson surveyed the area for the North West Fur Company and estimated the population to be 1520 Mandans and 1330 Hidatsa.

Prior to 1781, the Mandan-Hidatsa allies were able to repulse the attacks of their enemies. Those enemies were chiefly the Lakota Sioux, but also the Assiniboine, a Nakota Sioux tribe. After 1781, the Mandan-Hidatsa allies were vulnerable. In 1834 the Assiniboine destroyed the Awatixa and Awaxawi villages on the Knife River, killing a large number of the inhabitants.[341]

Following the 1781 smallpox epidemic, the Hidatsa who had not previously moved to the Knife River area did so. The HP established the village site known as Big Hidatsa, the Awatixa the site known as Sakakawea, and the Awaxawi the site named Amahami.

After 1790, the Mandans also moved north to two villages about eight miles south of the mouth of the Knife River. In time the Awatixa, Awaxawi and the Mandans all moved their village sites but stayed in the same general area.

When David Thompson arrived at the Knife River in 1798, he took note of these villages and described a significant mixing of the Mandan and Hidatsa peoples. He counted the population of the Sakakawea village of the Awatixa and found it to have a Mandan majority. The village of Amahami also had a significant Mandan population. He found the population of the upper village of the Mandans to be one-third Hidatsa. Other travelers do not verify Thompson's findings but they are generally regarded by historians as being accurate. The Mandans and Hidatsa were usually martrilocal; husbands lived in the village of

---

340. Wood, p.127.
341. Baker, p.5.

their wives. This supposes that the married Mandans living in the Hidatsa villages and the married Hidatsa living in the Mandan villages were mostly men.

Sakakawea was a young Indian woman of about sixteen years and the wife of French trader Toussaint Charbonneau when Lewis and Clark visited the Knife River villages in 1804. The following spring the expedition departed upstream en route to the Pacific with Charbonneau and Sakakawea as interpreters and guides. Eight weeks before the expedition departed, Sakakawea gave birth to a son at Fort Mandan where Charbonneau was employed as a translator. Their son was named Jean Baptiste and nicknamed "Pomp" by the men of the expedition.

Sakakawea has traditionally been described as a Shoshone woman who lived with the Hidatsa. She was reportedly captured in Montana as a child and brought to live at Sakakawea Village, the Awatixa village on the Knife River. She and Charbonneau had traveled the headwaters of the Missouri in Montana and were acquainted with the geography. "They went so far [that] they were among people who sometimes went to the ocean out beyond there, so she knew that country."

Translators from Hidatsa to French to English recorded that she had a "brother" near the Rocky Mountains and took the word literally. The Hidatsa say that this was an unfortunate error and that Sakakawea was an Hidatsa woman from the Awatixa village. Billy Fredericks, a serious and credible young Mandan-Hidatsa man with whom I have spoken, believes the Hidatsa version and assured me that the Hidatsa did not take captives; but he was not so adamant to state that the Hidatsa theory is absolutely correct. The theory is reinforced by Bull's Eye, an Hidatsa who claims to be Sakakawea's grandson and remembers his grandmother.[342]

Sakakawea has been reported to have died of fever at age twenty-five, but not before having four children. This brave, adventurous and peripatetic young woman is also said to have accompanied Charbonneau, her husband, to St. Louis. The purpose of the trip was to take their son Baptiste to Captain Clark, who would see to it that he obtained an education.

Written records of Sakakawea's death do not exist, and she is said to be buried in four different locations. Bull's Eye relates that his grandmother

---

342. Rave, Jodi, 'A Different Story of Who Sacagawea May Have Been,' article in the Bismarck Tribune, June 8, 2003, p.4B.

Sakakawea died at age eighty-two when she and her daughter, the mother of Bull's Eye, were attacked after visiting a trading post in Glasgow, Montana.[343]

Bull's Eye's story continues to be told and the Hidatsa and Shoshone tribes continue to claim her as one of their own as do the Comanches. To further confuse the issue, the young wife of Charbonneau who visited St. Louis and died at age twenty-five was reported to have been a member of the Snake tribe. Historians can be adamant regarding the tribal origin of Sakakawea. At the Heritage Center of North Dakota I was told that she absolutely was Hidatsa. Not even Billy Fredericks would go that far.

In David Thompson's 1798 report, sixty-one percent (var. seventy-one percent) of the population of Sakakawea Village was Mandan. Perhaps Sakakawea was a Mandan or a Mandan-Hidatsa.

I like the words of the ranger at the Knife River Villages Site best. When I asked her opinion of the controversy of Sakakawea's tribal affiliation by birth, she replied, "It's your choice."

The Arikara

In 1714 De Bourgmont, a Frenchman, spent several years in three Arikara (Riccaree) villages on the west bank of the Missouri River north of the mouth of the Niobrara in southern South Dakota. At that time, he described forty more Arikara or Skidi-Pawnee/Arikara villages farther upstream. He may have traveled to the mouth of the Little Missouri and if so he would have seen the Mandan villages near the Heart River.[344] The Arikara later moved to sites along the Grand (Arikara) River in northern South Dakota. When La Verendrye found them in 1738, they were living near the Cannonball River in southern North Dakota.

There are marked cultural similarities between the Arikara and Mandan tribes. They both lived in the round earthen lodges that they built in the same manner, and both tribes used the Welsh style coracles or "bull boats." When Sioux attacks became menacing, the Arikara sought protection and moved nearer the Mandan villages. The relationship between the Mandans and the Arikara at one time had been close but later deteriorated, and for a long period prior to the Lewis and Clark visit they were enemies, and conflicts between them were common. When Lewis and Clark visited, the Arikara were living over

---

343. Rave.
344. Baker, p.10.

a hundred miles south of the Mandans. The Arikara joined their cousins, the Pawnee, in Nebraska for a brief period in the 1820s. In 1835 they moved north to a site two miles below the lower village of the Mandans or about twelve miles below the mouth of the Knife River in North Dakota. Two years later the smallpox epidemic of 1837 struck and severely affected the tribe. The smallpox epidemic of 1781 had previously wreaked havoc on the tribe, and visitors to the upper Missouri after 1781 described them as "a very small tribe, far inferior to the Mandans."[345] In the early eighteenth century de Bourgmont had described them as a powerful nation of thirty thousand people.[346]

Descriptions given by the Mandan chief Shahaka to Captain William Clark suggested that the Riccarees (Arikara) were treacherous and perhaps slovenly as well, but the Mandans and Arikara were enemies at the time.[347] Others gave a much better description of the Riccarees. Before arriving at the Mandan villages, the Lewis and Clark Expedition visited the Arikara where the soldiers enjoyed the favors of the women. They were often encouraged to do so by their husbands, who believed that they would catch some of the power of the White men from such intercourse, transmitted to them through their wives.

A Sergeant Gass pronounced the Arikara squaws to be "the most cleanly Indians I have ever seen... handsome... the best looking Indians I have ever seen."[348]

In William Clark's journal, he called them "dirty, kind, poor, and extravagant in possessing national pride. Not beggarly." (spelling corrected)[349] Clark tried valiantly to patch up relations between the Mandans and Ricarrees, but was eventually unsuccessful because the Riccarees broke their promise, allied with the Sioux and attacked the Mandans. The infuriated Mandan chief told Clark that he had always known that the Riccarees were "liars, they were liars."[350]

---

345. Olson, Dana The Legend of Madoc and the White Indians, Jeffersonville, Indiana, 1987, p.102; and, Catlin, George, Letters and Notes on the North American Indians, edited by Michael M. Mooney, Clarkson N. Potter, New York, 1975, p.225-6.

346. Baker, p.10.

347. Durrett, Reuben, Traditions of the Earliest Visits of Foreigners, Filson Club no. 23, 1908, p.97; Deacon, Richard, Madoc and the Discovery of America, George Braziller, New York, 1966, p.218-219; Armstrong, Zella, Who Discovered America?, Lookout Publishing, Chattanooga, p.126; and, Ambrose, Stephen E., Undaunted Courage, Simon and Schuster, New York, 1996, p.189.

348. Ambrose, p.180.

349. Ambrose, p.189.

350. Ambrose, p.189.

Shortly after the Lewis and Clark Expedition the Riccarees began attacking White traders, and when Catlin passed through their territory he gave them a wide berth. Catlin surmised that the Riccarees considered themselves abused by White traders in the past. Another possible cause for animosity by the Arikara was the failure of their chief to return after Lewis and Clark had taken him to the east along with Mandan chief Big White. The Arikara chief died of an unknown cause while visiting Philadelphia and Washington. A letter of explanation and condolences to the Arikara from President Jefferson did not assuage them.

The simplest, most direct migratory route the Mandans could have taken from St. Louis to the Heart River would have been up the Missouri River. Catlin thought they had taken this route and substantiated his opinion with the findings of the abandoned villages that he considered to be Mandan. But the Mandans told Maximilian that in their legends they traveled overland from the east to the White Earth (White) River, a tributary of the Missouri in southern South Dakota. This would be evidence that the old villages seen by Catlin below the White River were those of the Arikara, Pawnee, or some other tribe.

The Pawnee were close cousins of the Arikara. They were a Caddoan speaking people whose origins may have been in Central America.[351] They migrated north, probably to east Texas, and split into two groups. The northern group were called the Skidi-Pawnee and were the progenitors of the Pawnee and Arikara. The Pawnee are distantly related to the Iroquois and the Skidi-Pawnee are thought to have followed the Iroquois up the Mississippi. The Pawnee were in the lower Ohio Valley about 1500, the same time that the Cherokee were driving the Welsh Indians out of Tennessee. The Omaha tribe, a Siouan speaking people, were about to take the same route and linked with the Skidi-Pawnee during their move to the Great Plains. It is possible that the Welsh joined these tribes in a loose association in their migration. This would explain the many cultural similarities between the Mandans and the Arikara, which include the round earthen houses, bull boats, agricultural products, matrilineal descent and residence, and various societies.[352] The burial practices of the two tribes were similar and the Arikara were described as burying their dead in a sitting position facing the east in stone lined graves very much like the Stone Grave People in Kentucky and Tennessee.[353] The Arikara were among the first tribes to obtain

---

351. Baker, p.96; and, Pritzker, Barry M., A Native American Encyclopedia, Oxford University Press, New York, 2000, p. 350.

352. Baker, p.116; and, Pritzker, p.299.

horses and both the Arikara and the Mandan were outstanding equestrians. "Arikara" is a Mandan word. The Arikara name for themselves is *Sahnish.*

In addition to exposure to the Yuchean language, which has been linked to Siouan, a Mandan association with the Omaha tribe during their migration would help to explain the addition of Siouan characteristics to the Mandan language. The Omaha also built round earthen structures similar to those that have been identified with the Mandans and Arikara.[354]

Catlin noted that most of the Mandans were able to speak the Hidatsa Sioux tongue, but the Hidatsa never learned Mandan. He stated:

> Notwithstanding the long familiarity in which they (the Hidatsa) have lived with the Mandans, and the complete adoption of most of their customs, yet it is almost an unaccountable fact, that there is scarcely a man in the tribe who can speak half a dozen words of the Mandan language; although on the other hand, the Mandans are most of them able to converse in the Minataree tongue; leaving us to conclude, either that the Minatarees are a very inert and stupid people, or that the Mandan language (which is most probably the case) being different from any other language in the country, is an exceedingly difficult one (for the Hidatsa) to learn.[355]

The logical conclusion from Catlin's observation is that the Mandans had been exposed to one or more Siouan languages in the past, but the basis of their language was not Siouan, and it was quite unlike the Siouan tongues. One can further see that the flexibility in speaking exhibited by the Mandans would lead to an inconsistency in their language.

The Skidi-Pawnee and Omaha tribes are thought to have traveled up the Mississippi River to the Des Moines River. Then they proceeded up the Des Moines River to northern Iowa and southern Minnesota. From there they headed west to the Missouri Valley where they settled in tandem on the Missouri's western tributaries: the Omaha on the Platte and the Skidi-Pawnee on the Loup. The Arikara and presumably the Mandans as well took part in this migration; the Arikara settled on the Niobrara River on the Nebraska-South Dakota border, and the Mandans on the White River in southern South Dakota.[356]

---

353. Shane, Ralph M., A Short History of Fort Berthold, TAT Museum, 1997, p.5.
354. Pritzker, p.346.
355. Catlin, George, North American Indians, Penguin Books, 1989, p.186.
356. Pritzker, p.299.

The round earthen houses built by the Mandans and the Arikara had a cottonwood frame. They lasted only about ten to twelve years before the wood rotted and the whole structure had to be rebuilt. The tribes burned wood, which on the plains was relatively scarce, being found only in the river valleys. When the timber supplies near their villages were depleted, and their houses needed rebuilding, it became easier to move the village site than to remain at the same location.

The Mandans migrated upstream. They may have briefly settled at sites on the Cheyenne River and the Grand River before they reached the Heart River area where they remained for over two hundred years.

The Mandans have said that when they arrived at the Heart River there were no other people living there. I believe that this was probably true, but only for a brief period. That period would have been after the Awaxawi had been driven back to the east by the Awatixa, and the Awatixa had split with the Mountain Crow migrating west and the residual Awatixa tribe moving up the Missouri to the Knife River area. The deserted villages of these tribes were an invitation to the Mandans.

CHAPTER XVII

1837

In the spring of 1837, nearly a century after La Verendrye's visit to the Mandans, a fur trading steamer named *St. Peters* plied upstream on the Missouri River from St. Louis. The steamer had many miles to travel and the summer season was short at its destination, the trading outpost of Fort Clark, which had been built adjacent to the lower Mandan village on the upper Missouri.

Since the first description of the tribe by La Verendrye, the Mandans had moved north to near the Knife River, having been decimated by the smallpox epidemic in 1781 and then forced out of their villages in the Heart River area by attacks from the Sioux. Due to the twin ravages of war and disease, the robust nation of eight villages and 15,000 people had shrunk to just two villages and a population of 1600. The people of the smaller, weaker nation had also changed. Fewer of them appeared to be white as they had interbred more with neighboring Indian tribes, especially the Hidatsa, to sustain their existence.

Slowly but inexorably the steamer chugged against the current, attempting to dodge the logs and snags that littered the swollen river. As the steamer churned the muddy spring waters, the traders eagerly anticipated the lucrative bounty in furs from several tribes that they expected to be waiting for them at the village of the hospitable Mandans.

Near the mouth of the Cheyenne River they may have noted the old village that Catlin identified as Mandan. Above the mouth of the Grand River was the old village site that John Evans had credited to the "Dog Indians." The steamer then passed the Heart River, where a large and powerful Mandan nation had lived for over two hundred years. Square Buttes, the old boundary between the Mandan and Hidatsa nations, soon appeared on the left, and then the steamer passed stealthily into the territory of the pesky Arikara. In June of 1837, eight miles below the mouth of the Knife River in North Dakota, the *St. Peters* at last arrived at Fort Clark and the lower Mandan village of Ma-tutta-hang-kush. Two of the men on board had become ill on the journey, but are presumed to have been undiagnosed with what proved to be smallpox.

The *Pedr Sant*, commanded by Riryd, the full brother of Madoc, is among those ships listed in the Log of Missing ships of Britain in 1172. This log includes ships that failed to return from a voyage the previous year. A cross was drawn next to the name of the *Pedr Sant* indicating that it was lost at sea. It was 666 years later when a vessel with the same name arrived at the Mandan village carrying the tiny but lethal virus that gave destruction to the Mandan Nation. Six-Six-Six is the Biblical symbol for the Devil. The Evil One had come again to battle the First Man.

The *St. Peters* stopped to trade at the lower village on the west bank of the river and the chiefs and others were allowed to come on board. Francois Chardon, the post commander at Fort Clark later claimed that he could not keep them from coming on board. One ill passenger was taken ashore to Fort Clark. The epidemic began and on July fourteenth a young Mandan died of the disease. By that time several others had caught it. The disease was the worst strain of the pox virus and carried up to a forty percent mortality even in the more resistant White population. This variety affects the liver, heart, lungs and blood vessels and can lead to death even before the disfiguring rash begins. Chance be it that at that time the Mandan village was surrounded by several war parties of its powerful enemy, the Sioux. Because of the presence of these war parties the Mandans were imprisoned within the palisades of their own village and could not disperse themselves onto the plains, where they could have escaped exposure to the highly contagious and deadly pestilence. Close contact with those of their village who were initially infected assured that a large innoculum would infect the others and result in the most severe disease.

Smallpox soon spread to the upper village. The disease became so malignant that death sometimes occurred within hours after the first symptoms began. So slight were hopes for survival when the illness struck that some killed themselves by jumping head first from a thirty foot ledge of rock in front of their village. Others ran at the surrounding Sioux and implored that they be killed.[357]

Catlin described how his good friend, Chief Mah-to-toh-pa (Four Bears), sat in his wigwam and watched every one of his family die about him, his wives and little children, as he himself was recovering from the disease. When he finally left his wigwam and walked out into the village, the shock of the suffering of his people threw him into the throes of deep depression. He wept as he witnessed their...

>...continual crying and howling and praying to the Great Spirit for his protection night and day. With only a few living, and those in appalling despair, nobody thought of burying the dead. Their bodies, whole families together, were left in loathsome piles in their own lodges, with a few buffalo robes thrown over them, to decay and be devoured by their own dogs.[358]

Upon comprehending the plight of his tribe and his own scarred face, Mah-to-toh-pa suddenly grew old and embittered. He may have recalled some of the White traders that had attempted to cheat and swindle in their dealings with the Indians. As his people were dying all about him, he spoke:

>My friends one and all, listen to what I have to say. Ever since I can remember, I have loved the Whites. I have lived with them ever since I was a boy, and to the best of my knowledge, I have never wronged the White man, on the contrary, I have always protected them from the insults of others, which they cannot deny. The Four Bears never saw a White man hungry, but what he gave him to eat, drink, and a buffalo skin to sleep on in time of need. I was always ready to die for them, which they cannot deny. I have done everything that a Red Skin could do for them, and how have they repaid it? With ingratitude! I have never called a White man a dog, but today, I do pronounce them to be a set of black-hearted dogs. They have deceived me, them that I always considered brother, have turned out to be my worst enemies. I have been in many battles, and often wounded, but the wounds of my enemies I exalt in.
>But today I am wounded, and by whom, by those same White dogs that I have always considered, and treated as brothers. I do not fear death my friends. You know it, but to die with my face rotten, that even the wolves will shrink with horror at meeting me, and say to themselves, that is the Four Bears, the friend of the Whites. Listen well what I have to say, as it

357. Deacon, Richard, Madoc and the Discovery of America, George Braziller, New York, 1966, p.219.

358. Catlin, George, Letters and Notes on the North American Indians, edited by Michael M. Mooney, Clarkson N. Potter, New York, 1975, p.229.

will be the last time you will hear me. Think of your wives, children, brothers, sisters, friends, and in fact all that you hold dear, are all dead, or dying, with their faces all rotten caused by those dogs the Whites, think of all that my friends, and rise up all together and not leave one of them alive. Four Bears will act his part.[359]

Four Bears never acted on his threat. Instead he wrapped a robe around himself and wandered off in a daze of anguish to the top of a little hill resolving to starve himself to death. After six days he crept back to the horrid gloom of his wigwam, and laying his body beside his family, drew his robe over him. Three days later the Mandan chief was no more[360] (Fig. 36)

Due to the hospitality of the Mandans their villages were the center of commerce in the upper Missouri Valley. White traders looked forward to arriving at the villages and Indians from other tribes could frequently be seen milling about the Mandan villages, having brought their furs to trade. After leaving Fort Clark and the Mandan villages, the *St. Peters* continued upstream to the trading post at Fort Union at the mouth of the Yellowstone River. As a result smallpox also affected neighboring tribes including the Hidatsa, Arikara, Blackfeet, Crow, Cheyenne, and Cree (Knisteneaux). It has been estimated that in all the tribes of the Northern Plains, 25,000 Indians died in the smallpox epidemic of 1837.[361]

The Riccarees and the Minatarees were affected by the epidemic but not as completely as the Mandans. The two former tribes suffered about a fifty percent mortality. Mandan mortality was closer to ninety percent. The Hidatsa proper were away from their village on a nomadic venture when the disease struck and were able to escape the worst of the epidemic. After the disease had run its course, the Riccarees moved about two miles north and into the nearly empty Mandan village of Ma-tutta-hang-kush.

It is true that the Indians of North America were more susceptible to smallpox than the Europeans. This was not due to any genetic difference in immunity, but rather to contact that Europeans had with *Vaccinia* (the mildest

---

359. Baker, Linda, The History and Culture of the Mandan, Hidatsa, Sahnish, North Dakota Department of Public Instruction, Bismarck, 2002, p. 13; and, Catlin, George, Letters..., p. 75. (This quote was taken by Francois A. Chardon, a fur trapper and the post commander at Fort Clark. Chardon's wife and consequently his children were Sioux).

360. Catlin, George, North American Indians, Penguin Books,1989, p.490; and, Catlin, Letters... p.229.

361. Durrett, Reuben, Traditions of the Earliest Visits of Foreigners, Filson Club No.23, p.91, 1908.

strain), *Variola minor* (cowpox), and *Variola intermedia*, which carries a one to two percent mortality. These are all strains of the virus that produce much milder disease but afford immunity to the dreaded *Variola major* or smallpox virus that wiped out huge numbers of North American Indians. Europeans were also somewhat protected by having knowledge of contagion and the quarantine, which the Indians did not. Edward Jenner, an English physician, discovered that inoculation with the milder strains of pox virus produced immunity to smallpox. He published his work in 1798 and the practice of vaccination spread in England and America. In spite of this, smallpox still carried a mortality rate of fifteen to forty percent among White Americans.[362]

When John Evans returned to St. Louis from his wintering with the Mandans in 1797, friends noted that when he was drinking he would talk with indiscretion. At those times a favorite subject of his was to brag about his denial of the existence of the Mandans. Jebez Halliday added a postscript to his memoranda about Evans stating:

> When heavily in strong liquor [he] bragged to his friends in St. Louis that the Welsh Indians would keep their secret to their graves because he had been handsomely paid to keep quiet on the subject. He added that in a few more years there would be no more trace of any Welsh ancestry or language as time and disease would eventually remove all traces.[363]

The words of this derelict young man proved to be strangely prophetic.

---

362. Alberts, Elisa, 'Smallpox and the Three Affiliated Tribes: The Mandan, Hidatsa, and Arikara,' Houghton Mifflin Company, 1999.

363. Deacon, p.148.

Chapter XVIII

The Fate of the Mandan

There shall a star come out of Jacob,
And a scepter from Israel rise up,
And dash in pieces princes and nations.
The star of morning brightly beams,
...of heavenly consolation streams,
...stands beside us, always guides us, truth devining,
Praise the star that still is shining.

Felix Mendelssohn

Although the smallpox epidemic of 1837 resulted in the virtual extinction of the Mandan nation, some Mandans did survive.

Durrett stated that "Some forty of the tribe survived and were adopted by the Riccarees as slaves." After a period of months, the Riccarees and the Sioux clashed in battle and the Mandan slaves either "committed suicide to avoid capture or laid down to die."[364]

Catlin asserted that the Mandans had:

> ...taken an active part in the battle between the Riccarees and the Sioux, fighting desperately in resistance. At the same time the few remaining Mandan had concerted a plan for their own destruction, by simultaneously running through the stockades of the villages and calling out to the

---

364. Durrett, Reuben, Traditions of the Earliest Visits of Foreigners, Filson Club Number 23, 1908, p.91.

Sioux to kill them "that they were Riccaree dogs, that their friends were all dead, and they did not wish to live." They then wielded their weapons as desperately as they could, to excite the fury of their enemy, and they were thus cut to pieces and destroyed.[365]

Shane reported that the Mandan survivors of the 1837 epidemic consisted of twenty-three men, forty women and sixty to seventy children. He was less emotional than Catlin in stating that the Mandans "had trouble" with the Arikara, the few remaining Mandans then settling exclusively with the Hidatsa.[366]

Catlin's work was published in 1842. In it he wrote: "From the best accounts I could get, and although it may be possible that a few individuals may yet be remaining, I think it is not probable. One thing is certain, even if such be the case, that as a nation, the Mandans are extinct."[367]

Thomas L. McKinney and James Hall estimated the total Mandan survivors of the smallpox epidemic at about 125-145. The few remaining Mandans joined the Hidatsa tribe in 1845. The Hidatsa were also severely affected by the epidemic but less so than the Mandans. The remnants of the two tribes built a successful trading village on the Missouri River named "Like-a-Fishhook" adjacent to Fort Berthold.[368]

After 1837, the Arikara suffered constant raids by the Sioux. In 1851 a cholera epidemic killed three hundred of the tribe and another smallpox epidemic struck in 1856. This left the Arikara even weaker and more vulnerable than before. In 1862 they moved upstream to join the Mandans and Hidatsa at Like-a-Fishhook.

It was inevitable that the people of the three previously unrelated and autonomous tribes eventually would become nearly indistinguishable in language and appearance. The metamorphosis of the Mandans was nearing completion and the words of Oconostota were coming true; "they are no more White People, they are now all become Indians and look like the other Red People of the country."[369]

---

365. Catlin, George, North American Indians, Penguin Books, 1989, p.487.

366. Shane, Ralph, M., A Short History of Fort Berthold, TAT Museum, New Town, North Dakota, 1997, p.12.

367. Durrett, p.67.

368. Pritzker, Barry M., A Native American Encyclopedia, Oxford University Press, 2000; and, Deacon, Richard, Madoc and the Discovery of America, George Braziller, New York, 1966, p.219.

369. Deacon, p.187.

The U.S. Census of 1850 recorded 385 living "Mandans." Nearly all were classified as being of mixed blood.[370] The author was told at the TAT (Three Affiliated Tribes) Museum that the last full blooded Mandan passed away in 1993.[371]

Fort Berthold was neglected by the U.S. Army during the Civil War and in the 1860s frequent Sioux attacks made life even more precarious for the residents of Like-a-Fishhook. As their plight worsened they became impoverished and on the verge of starvation. A bell sounded every evening signifying the closing of the village gates as they feared Sioux attacks in the darkness. In 1862 Four Bears, the Hidatsa chief, was killed in a Sioux attack while he was swimming in the river. In 1869 four hundred Sioux made a savage attack on Like-a-Fishhook, in which forty Sioux and about twenty of the Affiliated Tribes' people were killed.

In their war against the United States the Sioux and their chief, Sitting Bull, made several attempts to enlist the Three Affiliated Tribes as allies but were always refused. Instead, between 1868 and 1876 men of the Three Affiliated Tribes (TAT) enlisted as scouts in the U.S. Army Service. In 1876 forty Ree (Arikara) scouts were attached to Custer's expedition and three were killed.[372]

The Fort Laramie Treaty of 1851 recognized a huge contiguous chunk of land in six states for the tribes of the Northern Plains. The Mandan-Hidatsa-Arikara apportionment was combined and consisted of twelve million acres that comprised most of southwestern North Dakota and significant portions of southeastern Montana and northeastern Wyoming. Major and minor chiefs and tribal dignitaries from Northern Plains tribes made the long trek to Fort Laramie on the North Platte River in southeastern Wyoming for the signing. They represented the Sioux, Cheyenne, Arapahoe, Crow, Assiniboine, Arikara and Mandan-Gros Ventres (Hidatsa) Nations. The Mandans were linked with the Hidatsa and were represented by two Hidatsa chiefs, Nochk-pit-shi-toe-pish and She-oh-mant-ho. Mandan signatures are conspicuously absent on the treaty and no Mandans are pictured in the group photograph taken of signers of the treaty. This presupposes a total lack of adult male Mandan tribal leaders living in 1851.

In 1870 the Fort Berthold Reservation was set aside for the TAT; it consisted of eight million acres. This was further reduced to about one million during the 1880s largely through allotments. In 1910 the U. S. unilaterally

---

370. Pritzker; and Deacon, p.219.
371. Pauline Nez, personal communication, Four Bears, North Dakota, June, 2003.
372. Shane, p.18-19.

removed a large section of land from the reservation reducing its size to 600,000 acres. At that time the reservation included a narrow strip of valley land along the Missouri River suitable for farms and homes. The remainder of the reservation was a treeless windswept plain. (Fig. 37)

In 1946 construction of the Garrison Dam was begun on the Missouri River against the tribes' vehement opposition. (Fig. 38) The resulting Lake Sakakawea bisected the reservation and reduced its land size by 155,000 acres by drowning its farms, homes and best agricultural land. (Fig. 39) The flooding destroyed not only the farms and homes of the tribes but also their economic base and infrastructure. It severely damaged their social structure as well. Ninety percent of the tribes' people had lived in the valley flooded by the lake and had to relocate. The huge lake divided the reservation into five districts that could be connected by roadways only by way of long detours. Two hundred thirty miles of new roadways were required to connect the districts.[373]

In 1992 the tribes received 143 million dollars from the U. S. Government for damages caused by the Garrison Dam. They opened a high stakes casino in 1993. More than half of the reservation is owned by non-Indians. Unemployment remains very high.[374]

The Mandans have the distinction of being the only Indian nation never to have been at war with the United States. In bitter irony, the U. S. Bureau of Ethnology classifies the Mandans and their language as Sioux.

---

373. Shane, p.20.
374. Pritzker.

Chapter XIX

Retracing the Dream

I believe we must discern between two phenomena: evidence generated by *a closed interpretation of the archaeological record; and* (evidence) generated by a reading of the linguistic or historical evidence... My experience convinces me that archaeologists play by different rules depending on the nature of the problems confronting them.

J. P. Mallory, *In Search of the Indo-Europeans*[375]

Saturday, June 14, 2003. As George Catlin had done 171 years before, I decided to visit the Mandan country on the upper Missouri River in North Dakota. My wife and I had left our home in Poplar Bluff in Southeast Missouri the previous day and spent the night with our son and his family near Kansas City. June the fourteenth dawned clear and sunny. It was hot even at this early morning hour as we drove through the interstates of the city.

As we passed through Mound City, Missouri, I had to wonder which Indian tribe had built the mounds that gave the town its name, but I did not stop to inquire.

We drove north with the sparkling waters of the Missouri River on our left. On our right were the fertile but highly erodable loess hills, products of the last ice age. We headed toward Sioux City with Sioux Valley, Sioux Center and Sioux Rapids with its Little Sioux Motel nearby. We crossed the Big Sioux River

---

375. Mallory, J. P., In Search of the Indo-Europeans, Thames and Hudson, London, 1989, p.167..

and approached Sioux Falls. This was Sioux country, the home of the enemies of the Mandans.

At Mobridge, South Dakota, we gained sight of the Missouri River again. This is near the Grand or Arikara River where that tribe had lived for many years. Today the Missouri River at Mobridge is swollen by the waters of Lake Oahe, inundating old Indian village sites.

Catlin first disembarked at Fort Union, an American Fur Company trading post at the mouth of the Yellowstone River on the North Dakota-Montana border. Fort Union was built in 1829, three years before Catlin's visit. The fort has been partially reconstructed and is now a National Historic Site. The site of the reconstructed fort is authentic but the river has changed course and is now some distance away. I found it odd that the Department of the Interior has placed the visitor parking lot in Montana several hundred yards away from the fort, which is in North Dakota.

Catlin disembarked from the steamboat *Yellowstone* and entered Fort Union. I had pictured the Yellowstone as a modest, unimposing vessel but in the visitor's center I was surprised to see an 1888 painting by Robert Beck showing the Yellowstone as a sturdy white double-decked sidewheeler in the river approaching Fort Union. The Yellowstone was the first steamer ever to reach Fort Union and made the trip from St. Louis yearly as a trading vessel. At the fort, the Indians traded their furs for several manufactured items. Samples of various furs traded by the Indians and of the Venetian glass beads and other items traded to the Indians are on display in the fort trading post. The ranger at Fort Union explained that in order to manufacture the glass beads for which they became known, the Mandans began with the Venetian beads, crushed them, then melted them and molded them into the Mandan variety.

The fort has two towers at opposite corners. The southwest tower was used by Catlin as his studio where he painted the Crow, Blackfeet, Assiniboine and Cree Indians. (Fig. 40) After several weeks at Fort Union, Catlin and his two trapper guides, Bogard ("a Yankee") and Ba'tiste, boarded two canoes and set off down the river to the Mandan villages below the Knife River.

Lake Sakakawea now fills the Missouri Valley in western North Dakota. Going down river from Fort Union the river soon stops visibly flowing as the lake is entered. Lake Sakakawea is the largest lake in the United States that is located within the boundaries of one state. Upon entering the Fort Berthold Reservation one soon arrives at Four Bears on the western shore of the lake. The naming of Four Bears is not only to honor Catlin's friend Ma-To-Toh-Pa, the Mandan chief, but also the Hidatsa chief of the same name.

The lobby of the lodge at Four Bears is rustic, pleasantly attractive and inviting. Slot machines could be heard humming and ringing in the casino, which is to the left and down the hallway from the lobby. Across the parking lot is the TAT (Three Affiliated Tribes) Museum hosted by Pauline Nez, a pleasant and informative Mandan-Hidatsa woman. I had previously decided that I would be best served by discarding my natural reticent manner and substituting a polite but pushy inquisitiveness. The plan appeared to meet with success with Pauline and the other Mandan-Hidatsa people that I had the good fortune to meet, because they tolerated my many questions and gave me several leads to tribal authorities and reference materials.

One of the questions that I asked Pauline concerned the "Dog Society" that existed in the Hidatsa tribe; the name had raised my antennae. The "Dog Society" also existed in the Arikara tribe and presumably the Mandan as well. It was composed of adult males who gave direction and instruction to young boys, a bit like the Boy Scouts of today. Pauline thumbed through an old reference book and stopped at a page showing a photo of Dog Society members doing the "Dog Dance." She suddenly remembered them and laughingly blurted out, "The Crazy Dogs!"

"Mad Dogs?" I suggested.

"Yes," she chuckled, not fully comprehending the triple entendre.

Before we left, Pauline graciously allowed herself to be photographed with me. (Fig. 41)

A bridge across the lake connects Four Bears with New Town. This community of 1400 people serves as a center of commerce for the reservation and contains a community college. It was built by the residents of three villages flooded by the Garrison Dam. I learned that Wolf's Trading Post in New Town is a hub for all that goes on, past or present, with the tribes.

In the Halliday/Twin Buttes area I met Bessie Starr, a pleasant, talkative Mandan-Hidatsa woman who referred me to Edwin Benson, a linguist and teacher of the Mandan language at the Twin Buttes school. Bessie left no doubt when she described Mr. Benson as *the* authority on the Mandan language; when the other experts were unsure, they contacted Edwin. Bessie Starr was accompanied by Elaine Incognito, an Arikara woman and the principle of the Twin Buttes School. Elaine's quietly competent, forthcoming and polite manner seemed to be the antithesis of the description of the Arikara that Chief Big

White had given Captain Clark. Actually the relaxed competence and politeness of nearly all the people of North Dakota that I met was impressive and unexpected. I had to wonder if this was due to the relative isolation in which they lived or was genetic but somehow contagious, spreading from the Indians to the northern Europeans that began arriving in the late nineteenth century. I found the White and Indian populations of the state to be friendly and compatible and mutually appreciative of the other's presence and contributions.

Near New Town the treeless windswept plain of the reservation has been planted with intermittent windbreaks of elm, ash, cottonwood and spruce. Despite the plantings, at the crest of every hill or small rise the horizon appeared to be limited only by the curvature of the earth. The straightforward attributes of the Mandan-Hidatsa people seem to have been influenced by the openness of the land. On the great plains of North Dakota there is no place for an individual or an untruth to hide.

The spring had been relatively wet in 2003 and the wheat, grass, sugar beet and canola fields were verdant. The cattle and buffalo grazed steadily on the bounty offered by the rich, dark soil composing the gently rolling glacial hills. The massive ice sheets left rocks in the fields, which farmers have placed in stacks so they can be avoided when plowing.

The long, dark, cold and windy Dakota winter had suddenly given way to the short, hot summer. In mid to late June at this latitude, the 18-19 hours of daylight leave such a short nighttime that it jolts one's physiology, giving the body less than the accustomed time to recuperate from the previous day before beginning the next; the twilight of dusk seemed to merge with the twilight of dawn.

Near the mouth of the Knife River are the five old Hidatsa and Mandan village sites. Most of these villages were settled after the smallpox epidemic of 1781 had decimated the tribes. The three villages on the Knife River were Hidatsa. The Mandan villages were a few miles downstream on the Missouri. David Thompson, who surveyed the area for the British North West Fur Company in 1798, had found that the populations of two of the Hidatsa villages and one of the Mandan were mixed Hidatsa and Mandan.[376]

In 1822 the Mandans moved their lower village a few miles downstream to the site called Mah-tutta-hang-kush. This village site was on a bend of the

---

376. Wood, W. Raymond and Hanson, Jeffery R., Reprints In Anthropology, Volume 32, J & L Reprint Company Lincoln Nebraska, 1986,p.5-7.

Missouri River and surrounded by bluffs, making it more defensible. This is the site where Catlin would spend so much of his time painting and getting to know the Mandans and their chief, Mah-to-toh-pah (Four Bears), whom he grew to respect and admire so greatly. Adjacent to the village the American Fur Company built Fort Clark as a trading post in 1831. It was here that the steamer *St. Peters* arrived in 1837, carrying smallpox. A walking tour now leads through the village, which the Arikara inhabited after the epidemic had run its course. The circular depressions left by the round earthen houses are easily seen as they are at the Knife River Indian village sites of the Hidatsa a few miles upstream. (Fig. 42)

At the Knife River Villages Site an earthen round house has been reconstructed with a bull boat exhibited inside. The villages that I have described are actually only the summer dwellings of the Mandan and Hidatsa. The tribes occupied these sites for most of the year, but in the coldest months they retreated to the lower valley among the trees where they could more easily obtain wood for burning and were more protected from the howling Dakota wind. The houses in these winter villages were not as well constructed as in their main villages and lasted only one or a few seasons after which they would be washed away by floods or destroyed by enemies.

Between fifteen and thirty miles downstream from the Knife River Villages and on both sides of the river are remains of a dozen or so Hidatsa villages of the Awatixa and Awaxawi. On the grounds of nearby Cross Ranch State Park sit two identifiable sites and five or six more that have been discovered. None of these sites have been developed and most are now difficult or impossible for a passer-by to find. Double Ditch is a Mandan or Hidatsa site on the east side of the Missouri River which is being investigated, and where depressions representing round houses of the past and two long circular ditches can be seen. The ditches were part of a defensive barrier that included a palisaded wall. Farther downstream, near the cities of Bismarck and Mandan and the mouth of the Heart River, were several villages of the Hidatsa proper and the Mandan.

At Bismarck is the Ward site, also called Chief Looking's Village, named for a Mandan chief who spent much time looking for a favorite son who was killed in battle. The CCC (Civilian Conservation Corps) reconstructed a round earthen house on this site in the 1930s, but it was destroyed by fire and has not been rebuilt.

At Fort Lincoln State Park, five miles downstream from the city of Mandan, which is directly across the river from Bismarck, four round houses have been reconstructed and guides conduct tours through an old village of the Mandan. This village was named "Slant" or "On-a-Slant," as it was built on unlevel ground. Recent carbon datings at the site reveal that it was settled around 1575.

I was fortunate that Billy Fredericks, a Mandan-Hidatsa, was a member of my tour group at the Slant Village, and after the tour I introduced myself to him. We talked for nearly thirty minutes. Billy is a nice looking, dark skinned, dark haired young man with Nordic features. He spoke carefully but in a friendly, unassuming manner. I told him that in my opinion he probably had ancestors who were from Wales. He was quite open to comments about his tribe and agreed that such a pedigree was likely. Billy was aware that studies regarding language and genealogy were being carried out by the tribe, but when I asked if he would agree to DNA being taken from the bones of his Mandan ancestors for study, he backed away and said it would be up to the commission (of the TAT). Upon further discussion he stated that the commission might agree to the study depending upon the researcher and his intentions.

The Mandan-Hidatsa are typical of the Indians of North America in feeling that they have been victimized in the past and they are therefore suspicious of such studies. In their opinion, for much of the past they have been described unfairly and in an uncomplimentary light by media outlets. Now that the law allows them to control the scientific investigation of ancient remains, they want to assure that it be done in a way that meets their approval. I opined that to me, their restricting stance was well justified in some instances, but not when the facts and findings that became publicized were true. He nodded and stated, that was the problem, so much of what has been described as Indian culture and history is untrue and has wounded and angered all Indian people. He did not object to a scientific study that was carried out and presented in a fair manner.

It was my good fortune to meet Billy. My wife took a picture of us together and he gave me his address for future discourse. (Fig. 43)

At Bismarck I was directed to the Heritage Center of North Dakota, a spacious, modern building devoted to the history of North Dakota and staffed by a team of scientific investigators that includes a paleontologist and a historian. After touring the professionally done exhibit hall that includes a Mandan bull boat, a Sioux-type tipi and the skeleton of an ice age mastodon, I was able to speak with Mark Halvorson, a historian on the staff. After a few introductory comments regarding my own research on the Welsh Indians, he abruptly remarked, "You won't find anyone here who agrees with you." To me his comment appeared to be arbitrary and a bit defensive. Although he could not answer most of my esoteric questions, Mark was helpful in directing me to several references.

The search for one of these references eventually led me to the Indian Affairs Office in the State Capitol Building where I met Melanie Luger. After purchasing the book in question, I engaged her in discussion and learned to my no surprise that she is Mandan-Hidatsa. Melanie is a young dark eyed, copper complected, brown haired beauty with Nordic features. She is quiet, polite, and reserved, but also friendly and obviously intelligent. I thought of the comments about the Mandan women by Catlin and the aging General Clark as soon as I saw her.

After leaving Fort Lincoln Catlin's trail turns south past the old village at Huff, which consisted of rectangular earthen houses dating from 1400 to 1450. Similar North Dakota sites on the east side of the Missouri River at Menoken and the Fort Mandan Overlook, and sites on the James, Sheyenne, and Little Missouri Rivers, and at Fort Yates on the Missouri all contained these rectangular lodge structures and date in the period from A.D. 1100-1450.[377] The Menoken and Fort Yates sites have been carbon dated to around 1200. In the legends of the Hidatsa, the Mandans are quoted as revealing that they had built rectangular structures at one time in the past, and all of these sites traditionally are thought to have been Mandan. This creates a problem with the Welsh-Mandan theory and a big problem, because the Welsh could not have been in the area at those early dates. I find that although the origin of these sites is controversial, their early datings provide the best ammunition for those who say the Mandans have no connection to the Welsh Indians. At Fort Yates three sites have been identified: an early site considered to be Mandan, a seventeenth or early eighteenth century site built by the Awaxawi, and a later site occupied by the Cheyenne. The site is now part of the Standing Rock Sioux Reservation.

Due to the carbon dating the structures in the villages with rectangular lodges could not have been built by the Welsh, and I have several objections to the sites being labelled as Mandan: (1) By the time the Mandan arrived in North Dakota they had associated with the Arikara/Skidi-Pawnee and were building the round earthen house. (2) The carbon dating and structure of the houses at the Menoken and Huff sites is similar to sites along the Sheyenne and James Rivers in southeastern North Dakota that were probably Awaxawi. (3)

---

377. J. Signe Snortland, editor, A Traveler's Companion to North Dakota State Historic Sites, second edition, State Historical Society of North Dakota, Bismarck, 2002, p.35 and 97.

Maximilian was told Mandan legends of their history as being previously in the east, possibly in southern Minnesota or northern Iowa. From there he was told that they crossed overland to the Missouri River at the White Earth (White) River in southern South Dakota. After that they remained in the valley of the upper Missouri. The legends do not include them inhabiting the Sheyenne or James River areas of eastern North Dakota.[378] (4) Most Mandans who have been previously questioned about their origins clearly stated that they came from the mouth of the Missouri River. Others translated this as the mouth of the Mississippi. I suggest it could also mean the junction of the Mississippi and Ohio Rivers as the Ohio is the larger stream at this confluence, and the upper Mississippi/Missouri could have been considered the tributary and therefore that river's mouth. (5) Edwin Benson gave another version of this exclusively Mandan legend regarding their origin. He stated that they landed on an island near the mouth of the Mississippi River following an oceanic voyage. From this island they could easily cross to the mainland and proceed up river. If this legend refers to the landing of Madoc, it has survived for over eight hundred years. However, this description does not fit the mouth of the Mississippi as there are no islands there; but it is an accurate description of Dauphin Island, which is located just south of Mobile. From there the Welsh Indian tribe proceeded up the Alabama River and eventually to Tennessee, where they lived until driven away by the Cherokee. It is this tribe that I believe became the Mandan. (6) Wood has found evidence that the Knife-Heart River region supported a "continuous Hidatsa occupation from about 1100 AD to the historic period." 4 One attraction to the Knife River area was the flint deposits. The flint could be chipped into arrowheads and sharp utensils and was mined by the Hidatsa. (7) La Verendrye (1738) and Charles McKenzie (1772) both reported that the nine villages of the Mandan that they visited near the Heart River were the oldest Mandan villages in the area. These villages contained the dome shaped circular lodges.[379]

But the problem persists that the sites with rectangular dwellings date from 1100-1450 and could have no Welsh connection. What tribe(s) could have built them if not the Mandan? It became a giant conundrum for me. I stared at the pictures and drawings of the villages looking for a clue that I thought might be there and would prove the sites were not Mandan. Perhaps that clue is there.

---

378. Snortland, p.35; and Wood, p.78.

379. Baker, Linda, et a.l, The History and Culture of the Mandan, Hidatsa, and Sahnish, North Dakota Department of Public Instruction, Bismarck, 2002, p.6.

The villages at Huff, Menoken and Double Ditch (DD) were protected by an elaborate array of ditches, ramparts, bastions and palisades. The villagers would not have gone to such an effort if the inhabitants were the only tribe in the area and not subject to attack, and the Sioux did not enter the Missouri Valley and attack them until much later. The lodges at Huff and Menoken were rectangular structures, aligned into rows. A large ceremonial house was at the periphery of the village. In contrast the DD site had round houses that faced a central ceremonial building, characteristic of the Mandan. The DD site was abandoned about twenty-five years before the Lewis and Clark expedition. It is estimated to have been occupied for at least three hundred years as evidenced by the huge middens (refuse piles) at the site. At DD a large community inside the outer ditch at one time had precipitously shrunk to a much smaller community located inside the inner ditch.

The Hidatsa proper have said that they did not build the circular based lodges until taught how to do so by the Mandans. It follows that neither the Awatixa nor the Awaxawi originally built circular based lodges, otherwise the HP would have learned to build these structures from their kinsmen. If these tribes did not build circular based houses prior to the Mandan arrival to the upper Missouri Valley in 1575, what shape did their lodges take? The answer is rectangular.

The Awaxawi then would be the builders of the rectangular lodges at the settlements at Huff, Fort Yates, and along the James and Sheyenne Rivers. The Awatixa, whose territory was more to the northwest, settled the DD, Menoken and Little Missouri sites. The Awatixa made war on the Awaxawi and forced them back to the east. The Huff site was vacated around 1450, and this date reflects the time that the Awatixa drove the Awaxawi out of the Missouri Valley. Later the Awatixa at DD quarreled amongst themselves and a large segment of their people departed, going upstream and becoming the Mountain Crow. The DD village correspondingly decreased to the size enclosed by the inner ditch. By 1575, when the Mandans arrived in the Heart River area, the Awatixa had moved to sites near the Knife River. The Mandan settled peacefully near the Heart River, and the Awaxawi soon returned to the Missouri Valley and learned to build the circular dwellings.

The DD site is postulated to originally have been a village with rectangular lodges. But with centuries of Mandan or later Hidatsa occupation, the rectangular depressions were converted to the round depressions, which are visible today. The site was abandoned following the smallpox epidemic of 1781.[380]

This scenario may be right, it may be partially right, or it may be entirely wrong. Researchers at the Heritage Center consider the early sites to be Mandan. They allege that the Mandan are a Sioux tribe that migrated with other Sioux tribes up the Mississippi and Ohio Valleys into the state of Ohio. From there they led the Sioux migration to the west and entered the Missouri Valley of North Dakota around AD 900. They regard the Mandan as the first Sioux tribe to enter the Valley. If true, such an epic journey at so early a date by the Mandan would absolutely negate any connection between them and the Welsh Indians of Madoc. Archaeologically this explanation may seem to be the simplest, but it has so many stumbling blocks so as to render it beyond credulity. I find little to support their theory other than the ancient rectangular dwellings in North Dakota, which I believe have no connection to the Mandan. Chief among the objections to the theory is the mountain of evidence presented by the numerous visitors to the Mandan for nearly a century, which is overwhelming.

As we meandered south, following the river toward busy and impatient St. Louis, the words of George Catlin as he departed from the Mandans kept echoing through my mind.

> I shall leave the Mandans in the morning and with my canvas and easel and paint pots in my canoe, wend my way on the mighty Missouri. Taking leave will be done with decided feelings of regret. The singular customs of the Mandans have raised an irresistible belief that they have had a different origin, [and are of] a different character, from any other tribe that can be in North America.[381]

My thoughts were also on Billy Fredericks, Melanie Luger, Pauline Nez, Bessie Starr, Elaine Incognito and Edwin Benson, the friendly and I think exceptional Three Affiliated Tribes' members that I was fortunate to encounter. The competence, polite friendliness, and hospitality credited to the Mandans of old seems to have spread to all of the people of North Dakota today.

The formerly great Mandan nation of fifteen thousand souls is extinct and the last full blooded Mandan has passed away, but the Mandans are not dead for enough of them intermarried with the Hidatsa to form a new distinct group.

---

380. Snortland, p.83.

381. Catlin, George, Letters and Notes on the North American Indians, Michael M. Mooney, editor, Clarkson N. Potter, New York, p.224-229.

These Mandan-Hidatsa people have grown so that they now number over three thousand. They even have a new name for themselves, *Nu'eta* (or *Nuweta*), meaning simply "ourselves."[382] The Arikara and North Dakota Whites continue to add to the mix, which includes the *Metis* (mestizo) offspring of French traders and I believe also the Yuchi and Creek Indians who formerly occupied the Tennessee Valley.

These people are naturally interested in their history and have begun investigating their heritage and teaching the Mandan language. When inquisitive outsiders like me poke their noses into tribal history they speak freely and help all they can. But in the end, I think it will be the words of Leonard Muise, the Jakatar, as he spoke to Farley Mowat, that will best apply:

> All those early people... they didn't just dry up and blow away, you know. Don't you believe it! Truth is, they're all of them still round about... One of these times scientists will likely show up here looking to test our DNA to see whereabouts we come from. I don't doubt they'll be some surprised by what they find. But us Jakos, now... we won't be the smallest little bit surprised because, you see, we know just who we are.[383]

---

382. Wood, p.49.

383. Mowat, Farley, The Farfarers: Before the Norse, Steerforth Press, South Royalton, Vermont, 2000, p.334.

Epilogue

Conclusions

Before I retired from Medicine and began doing historical research, I was a practicing physician. In my thirty-seven years associated with the medical field I became unfavorably impressed with a certain dogmatism that was not always justified and did not always fit the facts of the matter. Such incidents, although uncommon, seemed especially to involve academics, those whose opinions and diagnoses were not to be questioned by patient, nurse, or other physician in spite of evidence to the contrary. The story of "The Emperor Has No Clothes" was sometimes an obvious and painful analogy.

I have found similar attitudes among some historians, who observe the evidence for a predecessor of Christopher Columbus in the discovery of America, and conclude with a stubborn resolve that such a discovery could not have taken place. Such is the case with some when they learn of the legend of Madoc and the Welsh Indians. But in so concluding they reject the many eminent individuals of the past that have believed in Madoc and have contributed evidence in support of the truth of the legend. An honest observer does not disregard reports brought forth by such people as Francis Lewis, William Henry Harrison, John Sevier, John Filson, General William Clark, General George Rogers Clark and dozens of other observant men of integrity. To ignore the accounts of these eminent individuals while professing objectivity is ridiculous.

In confronting such mindsets, rather than attempting to persuade the naysayers, I have concluded that it is much more productive to look for answers to questions that remain; questions such as what happened to the survivors of the battles fought at the Falls of the Ohio and at Muscle Shoals? Historical accounts raise these and other questions and titillate the researcher with possibilities. My conclusions, which I admit are partly based on conjecture, follow:

On the third voyage of Madoc, the landing place was the mouth of the Mississippi River. Looking for the Welsh who had preceded them by a year, they traveled up that river rather quickly by rowing their ocean going vessels and by using their one sail when winds were favorable. They reached the Falls of the Ohio over which their vessels were unable to pass. They discovered that the Falls had many advantages as a place for habitation and settled there for nearly five centuries. As they increased in numbers and strength, they built the numerous stone fortifications in Kentucky, Indiana, and Ohio.

The journals and maps that La Salle kept describing his journey of discovery to the Ohio River in 1669-1671 were in the possession of Madeleine Cavelier, an elderly niece, until 1756 when they disappeared. At that time the French and Indian conflicts with the British were reaching a boiling point all along the frontier. If La Salle did reach the Falls of the Ohio, it is likely that he visualized and described the stone fortifications which could be credited to the Welsh of Madoc. Political intrigue may have played a part in the disappearance of these journals because they contained material contrary to French interests.[384]

La Salle's descent of the Ohio River in 1669-70 was terminated when his men suddenly abandoned him at the Falls. Something at the Falls may have prompted them to this rash desertion. Nika, the Shawnee guide, may have related frightening stories of the haunting of the place (Shawnee Chief Black Fish told such a tale to Lord Dunmore in 1773), and sun scorched bones of the victims of the Great Battle would have been visible in 1670, less than ten years after the estimated date of the Great Battle.

After the Great Battle at the Falls in about 1660 a small group of Welsh survived. Few, if any, escaped the Great Battle at the Falls and the survivors did not come from there, but rather from one or more sequestered, outlying colonies in Indiana or Kentucky. They may have escaped from the colony in the Big

---

384. Chesnel, Paul, *History of Cavelier de La Salle*, translated by Andrée Chesnel Meany, G. P. Putnam's Sons, New York, 1932, p.46.

Creek-Wiggins Point area. Big Creek flows westward, which would have given the Welsh an exit to the Wabash and into the Ohio well below the Falls and beyond the wrath of the Iroquois. Or they may have come from a colony in southwestern Kentucky. The mummified remains of the white woman found in Short Cave exhibited many Indian type artifacts, indicating that her people had lived as Indians for a lengthy period and had not just gotten off the boat. The stone lined graves of Christian County, Kentucky and the stone walled springs in Middle Tennessee, are suggestive that the Welsh were present in that area.

There are documented accounts from the eighteenth century that tell of encounters with Welsh-speaking Indians of light complexion in the Kaskaskia area of Southern Illinois. A small group of *Asgens* (the Shawnee word for the Welsh at the Falls) may have lived there and built the fortifications pointed out to General George Rogers Clark and identified by George Catlin. The account of Lt. Joseph Roberts is especially intriguing relating to this possibility. In regard to the Roberts encounter with a Chief of the *Asguaws*, one must wonder what the Chief was doing in Washington D.C. In review, the year of the Roberts encounter was 1801. Captain Abraham Chaplain's encounter with the Welsh speaking Indians at Kaskaskia was in the early 1770s. General George Rogers Clark, the older brother of William Clark, had been to Kaskaskia in 1778 on a campaign to seize the forts in the area from the British. He told of meeting a fair-skinned Indian chief who related that large earthworks then present near the Kaskaskia River were built by his ancestors. The chief met by Lt. Roberts could have come east through curiosity, possibly with the assistance and urging of men of the fort after Clark's campaign, the soldiers seeing that he was no ordinary Indian. Roberts' description of his encounter with the Asguaw chief leaves one with the definite and saddened impression that the chief was lonely. It may be coincidental that the chief was met by Lt. Roberts in Washington, but gave the location of his home in relation to Philadelphia (the old capital), that city being recognized as a center for Welsh immigrants.

Father Jacques Marquette first came upon the Kaskaskia tribe in 1673. At that time they were living on the upper Illinois River near the present town of Utica and only eighty miles from Lake Michigan and Chicago. Marquette found them to be friendly and receptive and they implored him to return. In 1675 he did return and started the Mission of the Immaculate Conception near the Kaskaskia village. The Kaskaskia tribe was part of the Illinois Confederation, otherwise known as the *Illini*, a group of related Algonquian tribes that at that time were being attacked by the Fox and Sioux tribes from Wisconsin. At about the same time the rampage of the Iroquois reached Illinois, striking unparalleled fear and dread into the Illini. In 1683 the French built a fort on the upper Illinois River. Seeking safety, thousands of Algonquians from various tribes soon swelled the resident population near the fort to twenty thousand. In 1687, following more enemy attacks, the French moved their friends, the Illini, downriver. The Kaskaskia tribe settled in the environs of St. Louis, Missouri, until 1703. That year French settlers built the village of Kaskaskia near the mouth of the Kaskaskia River and the Mission of Immaculate Conception was moved there. The Kaskaskia tribe set up their village adjacent to the mission and the French village. The Peoria, Cahokia, Michigamea, and Tamaroa tribes, all members of the Illinois Confederation, settled between Kaskaskia and St. Louis.

In 1720 the French built Fort De Chartres on the Mississippi River, eighteen miles upstream from Kaskaskia. Fort De Chartres served as the French military and administrative headquarters and Kaskaskia served as the commercial center.

The British commandeered the French built forts of the area between 1765 and 1778. General George Rogers Clark, in the employ of the state of Virginia, took over in 1778. Illinois became a separate territory of the United States in 1809. Its capitol was Kaskaskia. Major flooding in 1881 caused the Mississippi River to change its course. The Mississippi broke through to the channel of the Kaskaskia River, thereby creating Kaskaskia Island and washing away the site of the old town of Kaskaskia, which is now under the river.

The *laissez-faire* French were typically more successful in making friends of the Indians than were the strict, demanding Spanish or the arrogant, intolerant British. In 1765 the Illini lost the protection of French forts and French guns and became subject to attack. The Illinois tribes began suffering defeats at the hands of the Fox and the Shawnee who had begun invading their territory at will. Under the umbrella of the French the Kaskaskia tribe had degenerated and dwindled in numbers, suffering from epidemics and alcoholism. Their Illini kinsmen suffered a similar deterioration. In 1832 a united Illini tribe was moved to Kansas and later to Oklahoma. At the time of their removal the survivors were primarily members of the Kaskaskia and Peoria tribes.

George Catlin described the Kaskaskia tribe as warlike and stated that they were set upon with "unexampled cruelty of neighboring tribes who have struck at them in the days of their adversity and helped to erase them from existence." In his book, published in 1842, Catlin stated that "It is doubtful whether one dozen of them are now existing. With the very few remnants of this tribe will die in a few years a beautiful language, *distinct from all others about it...*"[385]

Although the Kaskaskia tribe suffered a marked population decline in the eighteenth and early nineteenth centuries, it did not go out of existence as Catlin described. Also, the Algonquian language of the Kaskaskia tribe was not at all unusual, being nearly identical to that of the other Illinois tribes and similar to that of their relatives, the Miami tribes.

Catlin's mention of the disappearance of a tribe with a distinct language may have been in reference to another tribe living in the Kaskaskia area. Between Fort de Chartres and Kaskaskia and across the Mississippi from the old French settlement of Ste. Genevieve is a small village named *Modoc*, population about fifty. The village of Modoc was formed in 1868 and was originally named *Brewerville*, but in 1882 it changed its name to Modoc. When this writer inquired of five area residents about the origin of the name of the town, they were in agreement that it was named for the Modoc Indians, but none was knowledgeable about the Modoc tribe. It was their understanding that the site had been known as *Modoc* before the settling of Brewerville. Three things appear certain: the Modoc tribe was not a member of the Illinois Confederation because all of those tribes have been identified and extensively researched; the Modoc Indians of Illinois had no connection to a tribe of the same name that lived in Oregon and California; the change of the town's name to Modoc in 1882 had nothing to do with the local railroad since the railroad line near the community was not built until 1902. One mile north of the town of Modoc is an archaeological site, which is named the Modoc Site. The site is representative of the ancient Archaic Culture; excavations began there in the 1950s. The site was named from the nearby village and not from the Indian tribe.

A map from the collection of J. B. Bourguignon d'Anville was drawn in the early eighteenth century and describes the regions discovered and explored by La Salle. The names of many Indian tribes have been written over the area on the map that they inhabited. Just above Kaskaskia, in tiny letters, is the inscription "Maroc." [386]

No other allusions to the Modoc Indians of Illinois appear to be in existence. After 1765, the British and then the Americans controlled the area, and they were acquainted with the legend of Madoc. It seems likely that their

---

385. Catlin, George, North American Indians, Penguin Books, 1989, p.67.
386. Chesnel, p. 148

encounters with Welsh-speaking Indians are what led to a colloquial naming of the *Modoc* Indians, a corruption of *Madoc.* That was not what the tribe called themselves, which was *Asguawa,* as related to Lt. Roberts. The Shawnee called them the *Asgens.*

The *Asguaw* tribe would have been a small tribe, merely a remnant of the Welsh colony at the Falls. After the defeat of the *Asgens* at the Falls, the Iroquois chased bands of Shawnee down the Ohio River and into Southern Illinois. There they again encountered the Asgens and resumed their enmity. With the deterioration of the nearby friendly Kaskaskia tribe, the Shawnee began to freely roam their territory. The eventual fate of the Asguaw would likely have been annihilation or capture by the Shawnee. Some of the captured Asgens became de facto Shawnee. The written statement by Shawnee historians that *"What Tallegwa that were left, were with us"* refers to these captured Asgens (Modocs).

As told to Lt. Roberts in his encounter with the chief, the Asguaw strictly adhered to the Welsh language, not allowing their children to learn another language until the age of twelve. In this manner they were able to maintain their native tongue. James Girty and his brother Simon became de facto Shawnee. James had close associations with captured Asgens and compiled his vocabulary words of the Asgen language with their willing help, as they were anxious to preserve their heritage. The Kaskaskia Asgens (Modocs), including Shawnee captives, were the Welsh Indians encountered by Captain Chaplain, Andrew Ward, George Rogers Clark, Francis Lewis and several others who encountered Welsh-speaking Indians near the Mississippi River in the eighteenth and early nineteenth centuries.

The *Asgens* at the Falls strictly adhered to the language of their heritage, but the *Welegens* of Tennessee and Georgia did not. The Welegens mixed freely with the Yuchi and Creek tribes and their language began to change. The Yuchi language, suspected of being Siouan, particularly was inculcated into the language that became known as Mandan. According to Van West, the Muskogean language of the Creek affected the Yuchean language, therefore the Creek language also would have affected the language of the Welegens.[387] Later associations with Siouan (Omaha and Hidatsa) and Caddo (Pawnee and Arikara) languages added words to the language of the Welegens and further altered its structure. French traders may also have been influential in the process

---

387. Van West, Carroll, Editor-in-Chief, The Tennessee Encyclopedia of History and Culture, Tennessee Historical Society, Rutledge Hill Press, Nashville, p.1093-4.

by which Welsh evolved into the hodge podge language known as Mandan and heard by Catlin.

Catlin expressed disappointment that the Mandan language he encountered differed significantly from Welsh, but he found some obvious similarities in the two tongues which reflected a definite relation. Five years after he visited the Mandans smallpox decimated the tribe leaving only sixty-three adults and sixty to seventy children living. The number of adults, especially males, was further reduced after the Arikara moved into the Mandan village and were attacked by the Sioux. The surviving Mandans, who were mostly children, settled with the Hidatsa. The Arikara joined them seventeen years later. There was no way the Mandan children could have maintained stability in their spoken word. No one, not even Edwin Benson or the U. S. Bureau of Ethnology could possibly be aware of the multiple origins and evolutionary paths the Mandan language has taken.

Castalian Springs, Tennessee (the Thruston Tablet), Indian Fort Mountain, Kentucky, and the Pinnacles area in Kentucky had no connection to the Welsh Indians of Madoc, but the sites quite possibly were inhabited briefly by a group of Vikings. Their saga was never written since they never returned. They perished as a result of violent battles with the Indians, capture, and attrition.

Neither does the naming of the village of Tallega reflect the presence of the Welsh. Rather, the Shawnee named the village in reference to the Cherokee who intruded into eastern Kentucky where they established villages in the seventeenth century.

It is not impossible that the stories of Welsh speaking Indians on the Carolina coast or the Melungeons of East Tennessee relate to distant isolates of the Welsh Indians of Madoc, but I do not think that is likely. The former were most likely encounters with the Lumbee Indians, who were descended in part from the Roanoke colony.

The white people described by the Tomahittan Indians were most likely descended from the mix of Iberians, North Africans and black slaves that fled the Spanish colony of Santa Elena when the British attacked in 1587. These people became the Melungeons. If there were any soldiers that remained at Chiaha twenty years after the Pardo expedition, they either joined the refugees from Santa Elena or assimilated with the Indians.

On his second voyage Madoc and his compatriots landed at Dauphin Island. From there they entered Mobile Bay and proceeded up the Alabama

River. They built the fortifications at De Soto Falls, Fort Mountain, and those near the Hiwassee and Tennessee Rivers. They were driven from the area by the Cherokee around 1500.

The Welsh Indians of Tennessee became the Mandan Indians, who were named by early French traders. They left Tennessee and traveled via the Tennessee, Ohio, and Mississippi Rivers at least to the mouth of the Missouri, and probably to the mouth of the Des Moines River. They encountered the Pawnee-Arikara and Omaha tribes on their journey and exchanged customs, ideas and some language. From the headwaters of the Des Moines River they traveled overland to an eastern tributary of the Missouri, down that tributary to the Missouri and then up the Missouri to the mouth of the White River in South Dakota. They briefly stayed near the mouth of the White River before moving to the Cheyenne River area. Then they proceeded up the Missouri to the present site of Bismarck, North Dakota, which they reached around 1575. They built their villages in the Heart River area and remained there for over two hundred years.

I believe that the case for the Mandans being descended from the Tennessee Welsh colony is quite strong. But to accept this postulate only leads to more questions. There is no doubt that they were a mixed breed, but when and with what tribe or tribes they practiced miscegenation in antiquity is open to debate. The Yuchi are a likely possibility, and one must also suspect the Creek Indians of Dallas Island. In their migration they would have encountered numerous tribes including the Omaha, Osage, Pawnee, and Arikara. There can be no doubt that they interbred with the Hidatsa after arriving in present day North Dakota. Any of the other tribes may also have been ancestors, to a greater or lesser extent, of the Mandans seen by Catlin.

Until the steamer *St. Peters* carried smallpox to the Mandan villages in 1837, the Welsh colony had survived for 667 years. The dozens of visitors to the Mandan saw them as an honest, polite, friendly and hospitable tribe. Some described them as civilized. In William Goldings's book *The Lord of the Flies* a group of English boys are marooned on an island. Their behavior rapidly degenerates into barbarism. Golding's thesis was that human nature is held in check by the constraints of civilization, and in its absence an atavistic savagery results. This did not happen with the Mandans, even after thirty generations. They lost track of their history, but they did not lose their manners. Golding's book is fiction; the Mandans are not.[388]

In summary, the demise of the Welsh Indians, the Mandans, the Asgens, the Asguaws, the Kaskaskia area Modocs or Marocs, the Welegens, the Tallega, and the White Indians of Chief Oconostota was due to exposure to a virulent strain of smallpox and to insufficient military strength brought about by an insufficient population. The Welsh tribes were simply overwhelmed by their enemies who greatly outnumbered them. The incipient Welsh colonies were too small and under attack too soon, before they could become powerful enough to withstand the attacks of the Cherokee, Shawnee, Iroquois, and Sioux. The perpetual wars and epidemics that they suffered kept them small.

Would they have survived if Madoc had landed at Mobile Bay instead of the mouth of the Mississippi on his third voyage and the tribes had been united? Perhaps, but not necessarily, and the question is moot at any rate. More poignant are intangible questions regarding the co-existence and survival of civilizations and the teaching of history according to the footprints of a people who have no other voice.

---

388. Golding, William G., Lord of the Flies, Berkley Publishing Group, New York, 1954.

BIBLIOGRAPHY

The Aboriginal Research Club, Detroit, compilers, *Ancient Copper Mines of Upper Michigan, ca. 1941*

Alberts, Elisha, *Smallpox and the Three Affiliated Tribes: The Mandan, Hidatsa and Arikara*, Houghton Mifflin Company, 1999

Ambrose, Stephen E., *Undaunted Courage*, Simon and Schuster, New York, 1996

Angel, Paul Tudor, "The Mysterious Megaliths of New England," *The Barnes Review*, October, 1997, v.3 no.10, p.3

Angel, Paul Tudor, "Who Built New England's Megalithic Monuments?" *The Barnes Review*, November 1997 v.3 no.11 p.17

Appalachian Summit, Chapter Two, *Color of Gold*, http://appalachiansummit.tripod.com/chapt2.htm

Armstrong, Zella, *Who Discovered America? The Amazing Story of Madoc*, Lookout Publishing Co., Chattanooga, 1950

Baird, Clay P., *A Journey to the Falls*, Highway Press, Jeffersonville, Indiana, 1994

Baker, Linda, et al, *The History and Culture of the Mandan, Hidatsa, Sahnish (Arikara)*, North Dakota Department of Public Instruction, Bismarck, 2002

The Barnes Review, editorial, May-June, 1999, v.5 no.3 p.2-3

Benson, Edwin, personal communication, Halliday, North Dakota, 2003

Benthal, Joe, personal communication, Madisonville, Tennessee, 15 September, 2003

Brandenburg Stone Exhibit, Meade County Kentucky Public Library, on loan to the Charlestown, Indiana Public Library, 2002

Brondsted, Johannnes, *The Vikings*, Penguin Books, Baltimore, Middlesex, England, 1960-1965

Brown, Frederick N., *The Voyage of the Wave Cleaver*, www.vinlandsite.com

Bureau of American Ethnology Bulletin 145, *Yuchi, Indian Tribes of North America*, p.145

Burkindine, Katelyn, "Evidence That Muslim Populations Throve in Pre-Columbina America," *The Barnes Review*, Sept-Oct. 2001 v.7 no.5 p.33

Burroughs, W.G., Kentucky Geological Survey, Series VI, 1923, Plate XXXIV

Cahill, Robert Ellis, *New England's Ancient Mysteries*, Old Saltbox Publishing House, Salem, Massachusetts, 1993

Catlin, George, *Letters and Notes on the North American Indians*, Michael M. Mooney, editor, Clarkson N. Potter, New York, 1975

Catlin, George, *North American Indians*, Penguin Books, 1989

Chapman, Paul H., "The Spirit Pond Rune Stones: The Ultimate Crossword," *The Barnes Review*, May-June, 2001, v.7 no.3 p.67

Chapman, Paul H. "They Were Here First - St. Brendan and the Norsemen," *The Barnes Review*, October, 1995, no.13 p.23

Chatters, James C., *Ancient Encounters, Kennewick Man and the First Americans*, Simon and Schuster, 2001

Chesnel, Paul, *History of Cavelier de La Salle*, translated by Andrée Chesnel Meany, G. P. Putnam's Sons, New York and London, 1932

Clift, G. Glenn, *History of Maysville and Mason County, Kentucky*, v.1, Transylvania Printing Company, 1936

Coe, Michael, Snow, Dean, and Benson, Elizabeth, *Atlas of Ancient America*, Equinox, Oxford, England, 1986

Cohat, Yves, *The Vikings Lords of the Seas*, Thames and Hudson, 1995

Collins, Lewis, *Historical Sketches of Kentucky*, Lewis Collins and J. A. and U. P. James, Maysville, Kentucky and Cincinnati, 1847, Reprinted by Henry Clay Press, Lexington, 1968

Collins, Lewis, and Richard H., *History of Kentucky*, Morton Publishing, Louisville, 1924

Corliss, William R., *Ancient Infrastructure, Remarkable Roads, Mines, Walls, Mounds Stone Circles*, The Sourcebook Project, Glen Arm, Maryland, 1999

Deacon, Richard, *Madoc and the Discovery of America*, George Braziller, New York, 1966

Diaz, Bernal, *The Conquest of New Spain*, Penguin Books, New York, 1963

Diaz-Granados, Carol, and Duncan, James R., *The Petroglyphs and Pictographs of Missouri*, University of Alabama Press, Tuscaloosa, 2000

Duncan, James R., personal communication, St. Louis 2002

Duncan, John, "The Origins of the Picts," www.scotshistoryonline.co.uk/ originl.html

Durrett, Reuben, *Traditions of the Earliest Visits of Foreigners,* Filson Club Number 23, 1908

Durrett, Reuben, "Who Buried the Hatchet Under the Sycamore Tree?" Centenary of Louisville, Filson Club, 1893

Eckert, Allan W., *The Fronteirsman, A Narrative,* Little, Brown and Company, Boston, 1967

Eckert, Allan W., *That Dark and Bloody River - Chronicles of the Ohio River Valley,* Bantam books, New York, 1995

Faulkner, Charles H., *The Old Stone Fort, Exploring an Archaeological Mystery,* The University of Tennessee Press, Knoxville, 1968

Faulkner, Charles H., personal communication, Knoxville, 2003

Fausz, J. Frederick, personal communication, St. Louis, 2003

Fell, Barry, *Bronze Age America,* Little Brown and Company, Boston, 1982

Finnan, Mark, *The Sinclair Saga,* Formac Publishing Company, Halifax, 1999

Fowke, Gerard, *The Evolution of the Ohio River,* Hollenbeck Press, Indianapolis, 1933

Funkhouser, W.D., and Webb, W.S., *Ancient Life in Kentucky,* Berea College Publications, 1928

Gibson, Frances M., *The Seafarers: Pre-Columbian Voyages to America,* Dorrance and Company, Philadelphia, 1974

Gilbert, Martin, *The Dent Atlas of American History,* J.M.Dent, London, Third Edition

Glass, Sherman A., *Return to Fox Fields, The Mason County, Kentucky, Ft. Ancient Site,* The Manchester, Ohio, Signal, 1984

Golding, William G., *Lord of the Flies,* Berkley Publishing Group, New York, 1954

Haywood, John, *Civil and Political History of the State of Tennessee,* Heiskell and Brown, Knoxville, 1823

Haywood, John, *The Natural and Aboriginal History of Tennessee...,* F. M. Brooks, Kingsport, 1973

Hendon, Carolyn, personal communication, DeSoto State Park, Alabama, 2001

Herm, Gerhard, *The Phoenicians, The Purple Empire of the Ancient World,* William Morrow and Co., New York, 1975

Homer, *The Odyssey,* Book 13, line 305-315

Howard, James H., *Shawnee - The Ceremonialism of a Native American Tribe and its Cultural Background",* Ohio University Press, Athens, 1981, p.4-5

Ingstad, Helge, *The Viking Discovery of America,* Checkmark Books, New York, 2001

Jennings, Francis, *The Founders of America From the Earliest Migrations to the Present,* Norton Press, New York, 1994

Jones, Gwyn, *The Norse Atlantic Saga, Oxford University Press*, London, 1964

Joseph, Frank, "More Evidence for a Lost White Civilization in Ancient America", *The Barnes Review*, September-October v.7 no.5 p.11

Joseph, Frank, "Wisconsin's Sunken City," *The Barnes Review*, November-December, 2000, v.6 no.6 p.63

Kerr, Judge Charles, ed., *The History of Kentucky*, The American Historical Society, Chicago and New York, 1922, v.1 p.31-37,

Livingood, James W., *A History of Hamilton County, Tennessee*, Memphis State University Press, 1981

Logan, F. Donald, *The Vikings in History*, Routledge, London, 1992

MacDonald, Lorraine, "The Picts," www.siliconglen.com/Scotland/11_5.html

Mallory, J. P., *In Search of the Indo-Europeans*, Thames and Hudson, London, 1989

Martin, Renee C., *Your Script Is Showing*, Golden Press, New York, 1969

Martin, Stephen, "The Kensington Rune Stone," *The Barnes Review*, March-April, 2002, v.8 no.2 p.5

McCutcheon, David, *The Red Record - The Wallum Olum*, Avery Press, Garden City, New York, 1993

McGuire, Helen, personal communication, Beattyville, Kentucky, 2003

McMahan, Basil, *The Mystery of Old Stone Fort*, Nashville, 1965

McNallen, Steve, "Indian Tribal Folklore Reveals Evidence of a Vanished Tribe of Caucasoids in North America," *The Barnes Review*, 1999, v.5 no.3 p.9

Miller, Madeleine S. and Miller, J. Lane, *Harper's Bible Dictionary*, Special Cokesbury Edition, Harper and Rowe, New York, 1973

Mowat, Farley, *The Farfarers: Before the Norse*, Steerforth Press, South Royalton Vermont, 2000

Nugent, John, "Who Were the Original Native Americans?" *The Barnes Review*, May-June, 1999, v.5 no.3 p.5

Olson, Dana, *The Legend of Prince Madoc and the White Indians*, Jeffersonville, Indiana, 1987

Palmer, Olga, personal communication, Tallega, Kentucky, 2003

Parkman, Francis, *La Salle and the Discovery of the Great West*, Signet Classics, published by The New American Library of World Literature, Inc., New York, originally published in 1869

Pauketat, Timothy R., "A Guide to the Prehistoric and Native Cultures of Southwestern Illinois and the Greater St. Louis Area," Illinois Archaeological Educational Series No. 2, Illinois Historical Preservation Agency, 1993

Perry, John, personal communication, Berea, Kentucky, 2001

Pohl, Frederick J., *Prince Henry Sinclair*, Clarkson N. Potter, New York, 1974

Pohl, Frederick J., *The Viking Settlements of North America*, Clarkson N. Potter, New York, 1972

Powell, Richard L., *Geology of the Falls of the Ohio River*, Indiana University Geological Survey Circular Ten, Bloomington, 1999

Pritzker, Barry M., *Native American Encyclopedia*, Oxford University Press, New York, 2000

Pugh, Ellen, *Brave His Soul*, Dodd, Mead and Co., New York, 1970

Rankins, Walter, *Historic Augusta and Augusta College*, 1949

Rave, Jodi, "A Different Story of Who Sacagawea May Have Been," article in *The Bismarck Tribune*, June 8, 2003, p.4B

Roberts, David, and Krakauer, Jon, *Iceland, Land of the Sagas*, Villard Books, New York, 1990

Ryan, William and Pittman, Walter, *Noah's Flood*, Simon and Schuster, New York, 1998

Shackleford, Nevyl, article in *The Lexington Leader*, 14 November, 1957

Shane, Ralph M., *A Short History of Fort Berthold*, Three Affiliated Tribes Museum, New Town, North Dakota, 1997

Shawnee United Remnant Band, article, *Montgomery County, Ohio, Newsletter*, p.91

Sinclair, Andrew, *The Sword and the Grail*, Crown Publishing, New York, 1992

Slaymaker, J.S., "Rediscovering the Forgotten White Ancestors of Many American Indians," *The Barnes Review*, Sept.-Oct., 2001, v.7 no.5 p.5

Snortland, J. Signe, *A Traveler's Companion to North Dakota State Historic Sites*, 2nd edition, State Historical Society of North Dakota, Bismarck, 2002

Taylor, Robert, "Prehistoric Race Left Many Mounds Throughout Ohio River Valley", letter, 1874, reprinted in *The Kentucky Explorer*, February, 1995, p.68

Tiffany, John, "Did Irishmen Discover America?" *The Barnes Review*, September-October, 2001, v.7 no.5 p.9

Tiffany, John, "Did an Unknown 'Pre-Viking' Culture Roam Canada?" *The Barnes Review*, September-October, 2001, v.7 no.5 p.37

Tiffany, John, "The Enigmatic Origins of the Mandan Indians," *The Barnes Review*, September-October, 2001, v.7 no.5 p.53

Tiffany, John, "Eric the Red, Leif Erikson and other Viking Discoverers of America," *The Barnes Review*, October, 1997, v.3 no.10, p.21

Van West, Carroll, Editor in Chief, *The Tennessee Encyclopedia of History and Culture*, Tennessee Historical Society, Rutledge Hill Press, Nashville

Wahlgren, Erik, *The Vikings and America*, Thames and Hudson, London, 1986

Wells, Spencer, *The Journey of Man: A Genetic Odyssey*, Princeton University Press, Princeton, New Jersey, 2003

Wood, Abraham, letter to John Richards, *The Journeys of James Needham and Gabriel Arthur in 1673 and 1674 Through the Piedmont and Mountains of North Carolina to Establish Trade with the Cherokee, http://rla.unc.edu/Archives/accounts/Needham/NeedhamText.html*

Wood, W. Raymond and Hanson, Jeffery R., *The Origins of the Hidatsa Indians: A Review of Ethnohistorical and Traditional Data, Reprints In Anthropology,* Volume 32, J & L Reprint Company, Lincoln, Nebraska, 1986

Woodward, Grace Steele, *The Cherokees,* University of Oklahoma Press, 1982

Wright, William, *Born That Way,* Alfred A. Knopf, New York, 1998

SECONDARY RREFERENCES

Barton, Benjamin S., *New View of the Origin of the Tribes and Natives of America,* 1797

Boland, Charles Michael, *They All Discovered America*

Burroughs, W.G., *Geography of the Kentucky Knobs,* 1926

Caradoc, Humphrey Lloyd and David Powell, *The Historie of Cambria, Now Called Wales,* 1584

CBS Interview on "*60 Minutes,*" with Leslie Stahl, 25 October 1998

Davies, Nigel, *Voyage to the New World,* 1979

DuTemple, Octave, *Ancient Copper Mines of Northern Michigan,* Marlin Press, Barrel Michigan, 1962

Filson, John, *History of Kentucke,* 1784

The Gazeteer of Georgia, 1837

Hakluyt, Richard, *The Voyages, Navigation, Traffiques and Discoveries of the English Nation,* v.3, Bishop, Newberrie and Barker, London, 1582

Herbert, Thomas, *A RElation of Some Years Travaile, Beginning Anno 1626,* William Stansby, London, 1634

Lewis, Benjamin F., "The Madog Tradition," *Utica Morning Herald,* 11 April, 1894

Mackay, James: His Manuscript Notes in the E.O. Voorhis Memorial Collection, *Archives of the Missouri Historical Society,* St. Louis

McKinney, Thomas L. and Hall, James, *The Indian Tribes of North America*

McMurtrie, Henry M., *Sketches of Louisville,* 1819

Nielsen, Dr. Richard, "A Response to Dr. James Knirk's Essay on the Kensington Rune Stone," *Scandinavian Studies,* v.72 no.1

The Palladium, newspaper article, 12 December 1804, Frankfort, Kentucky

Pickett, Albert J., *History of Alabama,* 1845

Priest, Josiah, *American Antiquities and Discoveries,* 1833

The Sagas of the Iclanders, numerous translators, Penguin Books, New York, 2001

The Saturday Evening Post, "They Signed Away Their Lives for Yours," article, 9 July, 1947

Severin, Timothy, "The Voyage of Brendan," *National Geographic*, December 1977

Smith, John, Captain, *General History of Virginia*, 1621

Starnes, *Missouri Historical Review*, v.17 p.345

Stoddard, Major Amos, *Sketches of Louisiana*, Philadelphia, 1812

Thruston, Gates P., *Antiquities of Tennessee*, 1890

Wallace, Birgitta, *Dossier of Archeology*, No. 27, March/April 1978

Winsor, Justin, *Narrative and Critical History*, v.7 p.90

Young, Colonel Bennett H., *Prehistoric Men In Kentucky*, Reprint Services Corp., 1910

INDEX

A

Adam, 5–6
Adena, 99, 114, 152
Advocate Bay, 35
Africa, 5–6, 12, 16–18, 28, 118
Ainu, 12, 153–154
Al Idrisi, 24
Alabama, 15, 2–3, 72–74, 77–78, 84, 103, 155, 192, 203, 208–209, 212
Alaska, 8, 14, 101, 106, 153
Alec Mountain, 16, 76
Algonquian, 26, 31, 102, 105, 107–108, 110, 127, 142, 145, 167, 199, 201
Allen, Penelope, 72
Amahami, 168
Anatolia, 7, 23
Andaman Islands, 6
Andress, Gene, 73
Anishinabe, 105
Annesta, 58–59
Apache, 106, 139, 153–154
Aramaic, 18
Arapahoe, 106, 183
Archaic Culture, 201
Ari Marson, 32–33
Arikara, 18, 85, 105, 137, 142, 144–146, 151–152, 162, 165, 170–174, 176, 178, 182–183, 186–187, 189, 191, 195, 202–204, 207
Aristotle, 16
Arkansas, 53–54, 91, 105, 116, 118
Armstrong, Zella, 64
Arnold, Benedict, 52
Arthur, Gabriel, 86, 212
Asgens, 12, 17, 125, 199, 202, 205
Asguaw (a), 125, 202
Ashmolean Museum, 122
Asia, 6–8, 12–13, 23–24, 28, 30, 42, 101, 153
Assiniboine, 148, 165–166, 168, 183, 186
Athapaskan, 106, 139, 153
Atlan, 52

Attiwandeton, 19–20
Augusta (Kentucky), 98
Australia (-ns), 6, 12, 153–154
Avalon, 32, 35
Avebury, 25, 28
Awatixa, 165–169, 174, 189, 193
Awaxawi, 143, 165–168, 174, 189, 191, 193
Azore, 40, 63–64
Aztec (-s), 64–65, 107–108

B

Baal, 25
Baffin Island, 43, 50
Balkans, 8, 30
Baltimore, 138, 208
Baptiste, Jean, 148, 169
Barthinus, 39
Bartow County, 76
Basque (-s), 18, 24, 27–28, 31, 35–36
Bat Creek, 18
Battle Creek, 96
Beatty, Charles, 135
Beck, Robert, 186
Bel, 25
Benson, Edwin, 7, 156, 162, 187, 192, 194, 203
Benthal, Joe, 7, 2
Beothuk (-s), 3, 31, 33–35, 37
Berea (Kentucky), 7, 18, 210
Bergen, 32, 48, 53
Bering Strait, 12–14, 101–102, 106
Big Bellies (see Hidatsa), 20, 143, 145, 166
Big Creek, 97, 199
Big Eddy, 92
Big Four Bridge, 96
Big White (see Shehaka), 144–145, 172, 188
Bimbutas, Marija, 7
Binion, Mr., 134
Bismarck, 7, 18, 140, 189–190, 204, 207, 211
Black Fish, 125
Black Sea, 7, 23, 42

Blackett, Brian, 95
Blackfeet, 19, 106, 148, 178, 186
Bodmer, Karl, 133
Bogardus, Dr. Carl, 97
Borden, William W., 97
Bosporus, 7, 23
Bougainville, 132
Bourbon County, 99
Bourne Stone, 26
Bowles, William, 137
Brachycephaly, 13
Bracken County, 114
Brackenridge, Henry M., 145
Bradbury, John, 145
Brady, John, 94
Brandenburg Stone, 12, 17, 95, 207
Brecon, 123
Brenda, 58–59
Breton, 35, 123
Brewerville, 201
Bristol, 32, 36, 49, 67
Britain, 16, 18, 20, 24, 27–28, 31, 42, 68, 72, 74, 90, 94, 138–139, 148, 160, 176
British, 25–27, 36, 40, 42, 67, 80, 85, 104, 118, 122–125, 138–139, 141, 157, 188, 199–201, 203
Briton (-s), 24
Brittany, 18, 24, 28, 63
Bronze Age, 13–14, 15, 19–21, 28, 209
Bullitt, Thomas, 125
Byblos, 15

C

Cabot, John, 3, 36
Caddo, 105, 202
Cadiz, 18, 26
Cadwaldr, 58
Cahill, Robert Ellis, 18
Cahokia, 7, 12, 17, 77, 106–109, 200
Caledonia (-ns), 28
California, 12, 14, 201
Cannonball River, 20, 170
Cape Breton Island, 36, 44, 48
Cape Cod, 15, 47–48
Cape Girardeau, 141
Cape Verde Islands, 63
Caradoc, 60, 121, 212
Carn Fadrun, 80
Carrollton (Kentucky), 98
Carthage, 16–18, 26, 91, 117
Cascade, 11
Castalian Springs (Tennessee), 17, 203
Catawba, 84, 105
Catlin, George, 13, 19, 144–145, 147, 156, 159, 185, 194, 199–200
Cavelier, Madeleine, 198

Cayuga, 103
Chaplain, Captain Abraham, 125, 199
Charbonneau, Toussaint, 159, 169
Chardon, Francois, 176
Chatsworth (Georgia), 75
Chattanooga, 7, 64, 72, 76, 78–79, 84, 104, 207
Chatters, James, 71
Cherokee, 15–16, 3, 71–76, 78–79, 83–84, 86, 90, 103–104, 108, 112, 172, 192, 203–205, 212
Cheyenne, 20, 105–106, 139–143, 145, 151, 174–175, 178, 183, 191, 204
Chiaha, 77, 79–80, 203
Chicamauga, 15, 76
Chickasaw, 84, 103, 108
Chief Looking's Village, 189
Chiles, Gordon, 7
Chippewa, 19–20, 105
Chiwere, 162
Choctaw, 103, 135
Chrisiant, 58–59, 94
Christian County, 113, 199
Christianity, 30, 32, 43, 47–48, 65–66, 149
Chrochan, George, 134
Churchill, Winston, 11
Clark, George Rogers, 125, 127, 197, 199–200, 202
Clark, William, 143, 148, 171, 197, 199
Coelbren, 17, 77, 95
Collins, Lewis, 208
Columbia River, 11
Columbus, Christopher, 3, 40, 42, 50, 64, 67, 118, 197
Conasauga (Conestoga), 87
Conception Bay, 31–34
Connecticut, 148
Coosa River, 71–73
Coracle, 161
Corn Island, 95, 110
Cornish, 123
Cornwall, 16
Coronation Gulf, 49
Cortez, Hernando, 107
Cox, E.T., 97
Crecelius, Craig, 95
Cree, 106, 148, 178, 186
Creek, 16, 18, 76–78, 80, 84–85, 87, 93, 95–96, 98–99, 103–104, 113, 137, 195, 199, 202, 204
Cross Ranch, 189
Crow, 19, 148, 152, 167, 178, 183, 186
Cruithne, 28–29
Crusade (-s), 42
Cumberland, 90–91, 116–117
Cymric, 57, 123
Cyprus, 16, 20

D

Daedalus, 51

Dakota, 7, 3, 104, 156, 162, 165, 170, 173, 186, 188–191, 194, 211
Dallas Island, 16, 76–77, 80, 84, 204
Dane (-s), 42, 54, 118
Danube River, 7–8
Darien, 52, 118
Dauphin Island, 73, 192, 203
David, brother of Madoc, 58–60, 64, 67
Davis Strait, 17
De Bourgmont, 170
De Soto Falls, 7, 12, 16, 2, 72, 74–75, 203
De Soto, Hernando, 77
Deacon, Richard, 20, 1
Dearborn County, 99
Deheubarth, 57
Delaware, 103, 105, 108–109, 157
Des Moines, 173, 204
Diana Island, 12, 14
Diaz, Bernal, 107
Dillehay, Tom, 12
Dinwiddie, Governor, 134
Dog Indians, 20, 142–143, 175
Dog River, 20, 72, 142
Dolichocephaly, 13
Dolmen (-s), 12, 14, 25
Dorset (-s) (see Tunit), 31, 37, 47
Double Ditch, 189, 193
Drogio (Drogeo), 14, 33, 35

E

Eastern Settlement, 48
Edwall, 67
Edward, Lewis, 160
Egypt (-ians), 8, 17, 26
Einon, 67
Elizabeth, 73, 208
Elk River, 84
Emma, 64, 67
England, 7, 14–15, 18, 24–26, 29, 32, 35–36, 43–45, 49, 51, 57, 60, 64, 116, 122, 124, 133, 179, 207–208
Eperios, 17
Erie, 103, 109, 112
Erik the Red, 32, 42–43, 51, 63
Eriksson, Leif, 15, 43, 63
Eskimo (-s), 31, 49
Estotiland, 14, 33–35, 51
Ethiopia, 5
Etowah, 12, 16, 75–76
Europe (-eans), 3, 6–8, 12, 16–21, 23–25, 27–28, 30–31, 34–37, 39, 42, 45, 48–49, 51, 54, 58–59, 63, 86, 112, 131, 136, 145, 154–155, 178, 188
Evans, John, 20, 137–138, 140, 152–153, 175, 179
Eve, 5
Evil One, 150, 176

F

Faeroe Islands, 14, 17, 63
Falls of the Ohio, 12, 16–17, 79, 89–90, 92, 108, 125, 127, 198, 211
Faulkner, Charles, 81
Fayetteville (Tennessee), 93
Fell, Barry, 13–14, 42
Filson, John, 127, 197
First Man,, 149–150, 176
Florida, 78, 123
Follins Pond, 15, 47
Fort Ancient, 12, 18, 98–99, 108–109, 113–114, 152
Fort Berthold, 19, 162, 182–183, 186, 211
Fort Charles, 139
Fort Clark, 175–176, 178, 189
Fort De Chartres, 200
Fort Laramie, 183
Fort Lincoln, 18, 189, 191
Fort Mandan, 13, 18, 143, 159, 169, 191
Fort Meigs, 126
Fort Mountain, 12, 15–16, 2, 75–76, 81, 115, 203
Fort Serof, 73
Fort Toulouse, 77
Fort Union, 13, 19, 148, 178, 186
Fort Yates, 142, 166, 191, 193
Four Bears, 7, 13, 133, 145, 149, 177–178, 183, 186–187, 189
Fowke, Gerard, 97
Fox Field, 12, 18, 98, 113–114, 209
France / French, 3, 20, 24, 28, 35–37, 41, 58, 60, 63, 68, 72, 76–77, 84, 105, 110, 118, 126, 131–134, 138–139, 141–142, 145, 149, 152, 156, 161, 166, 169, 195, 199–202, 204
Fredericks, Billy, 7, 13, 19, 169–170, 190, 194
Freemason (-ry), 52
Freydis, 15, 43–44
Fundy, Bay of, 35

G

Gadsden, 73–74
Gael (-ic), 26, 35, 123
Galatia (-ns), 24
Garrison Dam, 13, 19, 184, 187
Gass, Sergeant, 171
Gaul, 28
Gentlemen's Magazine, The, 133, 137
Georgia, 16, 2, 75–78, 103, 155, 202, 212
Gibson, Frances, 17
Girty, James, 157, 159, 202
Glasgow (Montana), 170
Glass, S.A., 18
Gnupson, Eric, 36
Goeral, 67
Goldring, William, 204
Grand Banks, 35

Grand River, 142, 174–175
Grave Creek, 18
Great Bahama Bank, 40
Great Battle at the Falls, 79–80, 96, 109, 111, 114, 126–127, 198
Great Britain, 15, 24, 27–29, 123
Great Miami River, 92, 98
Great Plains, 102, 104–106, 172
Great Stone Fort, 17, 96–97
Greenland, 14, 17, 24, 30–32, 35–36, 42–53, 63
Griffith, Maurice, 136
Grimolfsson, Bjarni, 47
Gros Ventres (see Hidatsa), 20, 142, 145, 166, 183
Guadaloupe, 67
Gudleif Gudlaugson, 32
Gudrid, 46
Gunn, James, 35
Gwynedd (Gwynet), 57–58, 61, 63–64, 73, 123–124

H

Habersham County, 76
Hakluyt, Richard, 60
Hall, James, 182
Halliday (North Dakota), 7, 207
Halliday, Arthur T., 138
Halliday, Jabez, 138, 140, 143
Hamilton County, 16, 80, 210
Hancock County, 125
Hanno, 26
Hanseatic League, 32
Harrison, William Henry, 98–99, 197
Hawk Wing, 110–111
Haywood, Judge John, 78
Heart River, 20, 140, 166–168, 170, 172, 174–176, 189, 192–193, 204
Hebrew, 18
Hebrides, 29, 63
Helluland, 43
Herjolfsson, Bjarni, 43
Herodotus, 16
Hicks, Levi, 135
Hidatsa, 9, 18–20, 105, 137, 140, 142–143, 145–146, 149, 151–152, 159–160, 162, 165–170, 173, 175–176, 178, 182–183, 187–194, 202–204, 207, 212
Hiwassee, 16, 2, 72–73, 76–78, 83–84, 87, 204
Holston River, 86
Homer, 15, 209
Hop, 15, 45, 47–48, 51
Hopewell, 81, 83, 99, 108–109, 114, 152
Horn Shelter, 13
Houma, 108
Howell, 59, 64
Hrafn the Dueller, 42
Hudson Bay, 53

Huff, 191, 193
Hvitramannaland, 31–32, 46, 51

I

Iberia (-ns), 18, 24–28, 31, 203
Icaria, 14, 34
Icarus, 51
Ice Age, 6–8, 92, 101
Iceland, 14, 17, 29–30, 32, 39, 42–43, 48–52, 54, 63, 118, 211
Ieuan Brechfa, 58
Illini, 199–200
Illinois, 7, 17, 107, 110, 118, 199–202, 210
Incognito, Elaine, 187, 194
India, 6, 8, 12, 23
Indian Fort Mountain, 12–13, 18, 115–118, 203
Indiana, 17, 20, 2, 89, 92, 94–99, 103, 113, 198, 207, 211
Indo-Europeans, 8, 28, 30, 185, 210
Ingstad, Helge, 20, 50
Innu, 31
Inuit, 24, 30–31, 36, 49
Iowa, 107, 173, 192
Iowerth, 58–59
Iran, 8, 30
Ireland, 18, 24, 28–29, 31, 39–40, 44, 51, 58, 60, 63–64, 67, 73, 118, 121
Irish, 26, 29–30, 35, 39–40, 51, 57–58, 63, 118, 123, 138
Iroquois, 79, 103, 105, 108–112, 117–118, 127, 172, 199, 202, 205
Isle Royale, 19–20, 41
Israel, 6, 181

J

Jackson, Andrew, 104
Jakatar (-s), 36–37, 195
James River, 191
Jamestown, 121
Jefferson, Thomas, 101, 131, 141, 159
Jeffersonville (Indiana), 17, 93, 207, 210
Jericho, 6
Jessaume, Rene, 139, 159
Jimenez, Marcos, 80
Jon (Priest), 36, 211
Jones, Dr. Sam, 138
Jones, Reverend Morgan, 122
Joseph, (Chief), 20
Julius Caesar, 41

K

Kansas, 185, 200
Kansas City, 185
Karlsefni, Thorfinn, 12, 15, 44
Kaskaskia (Illinois), 125
Kaskaskia River, 127, 199–200

Keewenaw, 19–20
Kelly, Mary Louise, 111
Kelt (-s) (ic), 15, 19–20, 24–26, 28–30, 63, 123–124
Kennewick (Washington), 11
Kennewick Man, 12, 153–154, 208
Kensington RuneStone, 7, 12, 15, 53
Kentucky, 7, 17–18, 1–2, 12, 75, 78–79, 89–90, 92–93, 95, 97–99, 109, 111–116, 118–119, 121, 124–127, 136, 172, 198, 203, 207–213
Kentucky River, 18, 92, 115–116
Kinniconick, 93
Kittanning, 157
Kjalarnes (Keel Point), 44, 48
Knife River, 18–19, 140, 142, 159, 166–171, 174–176, 186, 188–189, 192–193
Knife River Villages Site, 170, 189
Knights of the Templar, 33
Knisteneaux (see Cree), 178
Knutsson, Paul, 53

L

La Chapelle, 145
La Tene, 23
La Verendrye, Sieur de, 132–133, 140, 149, 156, 170, 175, 192
Labrador, 17, 31, 43, 51
Ladd Mountain, 16, 76
Lafferty, Mrs. W.T., 126
Lake Oahe, 186
Lake Sakakawea, 13, 19, 168, 184, 186
Lake Superior, 18–19
Lakota, 104, 168
Lee County, 18, 115–116, 125
Lee, Tom, 14, 27
Leifsbudir (Leif's Camp), 15, 20, 44
Lenape, (Lenni), 102, 105–109
Levant, 6, 15
Lewis Meriwether, 141, 143, 145, 152, 159
Lewis, Captain, 125
Lewis, Francis, 126, 157, 197, 202
Licking River, 92
Like-a-Fishhook, 182–183
Little Miami River, 94
Little Missouri River, 191
Little River, 15, 74
Little Tennessee River, 76
Lloyd, Humphrey, 60, 212
Lloyd, Thomas, 122
Llwyd, Edward, 122
London, 133, 137, 160, 209–212
Lookout Mountain, 72, 74
Louis VII, King, 60
Louisiana, 20, 103, 108, 138, 153, 213
Louisville, 17, 79, 89, 92–94, 115, 124, 127, 208–209, 212
Lovelock, (Nevada), 12

Luger, Melanie, 191, 194
Lumbee, 123, 125, 203

M

M-130, 6, 12, 153–154
M-168, 6
M-175, 6
M-20, 6
M-45, 6, 154
M-89, 6
Mackay, James, 139–141, 212
Madison (Indiana), 93
Madoc, 9, 11, 15–17, 20, 1, 3–4, 40, 55, 58–60, 63–64, 66–68, 71–74, 77, 79, 89–94, 116, 118, 121, 123, 127, 135, 137–138, 155–157, 160, 176, 192, 194, 197–198, 201, 203, 205, 207–208, 210
Maine, 25, 45, 54
Mallory, J.P., 161, 185, 210
Manchester (Ohio), 93, 209
Mandan (-s), 9, 13, 18–20, 3, 105, 126, 129, 131–134, 136–145, 147–152, 155–157, 159–163, 165–176, 178–179, 181–195, 202–205, 207, 211
Manx, 123
Marble Hill (Indiana), 97
Marine Men, 19–20
Markland, 31, 43, 46, 50–51
Marmara, Sea of, 7
Marquette, Father Jacques, 199
Mason County, 18, 113–114, 208–209
Massachusetts, 25–26, 35, 208
Ma-to-toh-pa (Four Bears), 13, 19, 149
Ma-tutta-hang-kush, 176, 178
Maya, 13, 17, 108
McAlpine Dam, 92
McChord, Wendell, 7, 1
McKinney, Thomas, 182, 212
Mediterranean Sea, 7
Melanesia (-ns), 6
Melungeon (-s), 85, 125, 203
Mendelssohn, Felix, 181
Menoken, 191, 193
Menominee, 18, 106
Meredith ap Rhys, 59
Metis, 195
Mexico, 64–66, 74–75, 102, 105, 107
Mexico City, 64
Miami, 93, 98, 110, 118, 201
Michigamea, 200
Michigan, 19–20, 41, 103, 105, 199, 207, 212
Micmac, 18, 26, 33, 35–37
Mill Creek, 93
Minnesota, 15, 53, 105, 173, 192
Mississippi (state), 16–17, 67–68, 79, 86, 89–93, 99, 102–103, 109, 116–117, 125, 131, 134–136, 138, 151, 155, 172–173, 192, 194, 198, 200–

202, 204–205

Mississippi River, 16, 67–68, 90–91, 116–117, 125, 131, 135–136, 151, 155, 173, 192, 198, 200, 202, 204

Missouri, 7, 19, 72, 86, 105, 107, 126, 131, 134–145, 148, 151–152, 155, 159, 165–167, 169–175, 178, 182, 184–186, 188–189, 191–194, 200, 204, 208, 212–213

Missouri River, 19, 72, 126, 131, 134, 136, 138–139, 141–142, 144–145, 148, 151, 155, 159, 166–167, 170, 172, 175, 182, 184–186, 189, 191–192

Mitochondrial DNA, 5

Mobile, 15–16, 66–68, 71–73, 89–90, 155, 192, 203, 205

Mobile Bay, 15–16, 66–68, 71–73, 89–90, 155, 203, 205

Modoc (-s), 75, 201–202

Mohawk, 103, 109

Montana, 105, 148, 169, 183, 186

Monte Verde, 12

Montezuma, 64–65

Moore, David, 115

Mound City (Missouri), 185

Mount Desert Island, 15

Mountain Crow, 166, 174, 193

Mouse River, 167

Mowat, Farley, 14, 24, 27–28, 31, 37, 195

Muise, Leonard, 37, 195

Muscle Shoals, 15, 78–79, 86, 90, 93, 198

Muskogee (-ean), 73

Mystery Hill, 25

N

Na Dene, 153–154

Nacoochee Valley, 75–76

NAGPRA, 153

Nahathaway (-s), 165

Nakota, 104, 166, 168

Narragansett, 15, 47–48, 51–52

Nashville, 84, 90, 210–211

Natchez, 90, 107–108

National Museum of Canada, 154

Navajo, 153–154

Nebraska, 171, 173, 212

Needham, James, 86, 212

Nevada, 12

New Hampshire, 25

New Jersey, 7, 211

New Orleans, 104, 135, 141

New Town, 187–188, 211

New York, 103, 109, 117–118, 122, 126, 135, 207–213

Newfoundland, 14, 20, 3, 24, 31–36, 39–40, 43–45, 49–51, 63

Newport (Rhode Island), 51–52

Nez Perce, 20

Nez, Pauline, 7, 13, 19, 187, 194

Nielsen, Richard, 53

Niobrara, 170, 173

Noah, 7, 23, 211

Nochk-pit-shi-toe-pish, 183

Norse, 14–15, 20, 29–36, 41–43, 45–52, 54, 61, 118, 210

North Carolina, 84, 115, 117, 123, 125, 212

North Dakota, 7, 18–19, 3, 132, 134, 140, 142, 148, 165–167, 170–171, 176, 183, 185–186, 188, 190–191, 194–195, 204, 207, 211

North Salem (New York), 14

Norwegian (-s), 41–42, 46, 48, 52–53, 118

Nova Scotia, 14, 31, 33, 35–36

O

Oconostota, 71–73, 78–79, 83, 86, 104, 155, 182, 205

Ogam (-ic), 25

Ogygia, 17

Ohio, 7, 13, 17, 19, 1, 78–81, 85–86, 90, 92–99, 108–110, 112–114, 118, 127, 134–135, 138, 151–152, 155, 159, 172, 192, 194, 198–199, 202, 204, 209, 211

Ohman, Olaf, 15, 53

Ojibwa, 106

Okak, 31

Okipa, 13, 19, 149–150

Oklahoma, 54, 91, 104, 116, 200, 212

Olamico, 80

Old Stone Fort, 80–81, 83, 93, 209–210

Olmec (-s), 17, 66, 108

Omaha, 139, 145, 151, 162, 172–173, 202, 204

Oregon, 13, 201

Orkney Islands, 14, 29, 32–33

Osage, 204

Oto, 107

Ottawa, 106

Owain Gwynedd, 15, 59, 94

Owen, Reverend N., 123

Owen, William, 137

P

Padouca (-s), 137–138, 141

Paiute, 12

Paleo-Americans, 11, 13, 11–14, 77, 101–102, 153–154

Palladium, The, 124, 136, 212

Pamiok Island, 14, 27

Pamlico River, 123

Papar, 30–31

Pardo, Juan, 80

Parris Island, 80

Patursson, Trondur, 40

Pawnee (Skidi-Pawnee), 85, 105, 145, 151, 171–173, 202, 204

Payne, General John, 114

Pedr Sant, 68, 90, 176

Pcepy, Joseph, 125
Peg (a Cherokee) 72
Pendleton County, 99
Pennsylvania, 12, 118, 147, 157
Peoria, 200
Pettaquamscutt River, 15, 48
Philadelphia, 125, 134, 137–138, 140, 143–144,
    148, 156, 172, 199, 209, 213
Phoenicia (-ns), 11, 15–18, 21, 24–26, 31, 41, 64,
    66, 118, 209
Pickett, Albert, 74
Pictones, 28
Picts, 18, 28–29, 209–210
Pillars of Hercules, 16, 29
Pima, 17
Pinnacles, The, 13, 18
Pitman, Walter, 23
P-Keltic, 123
Plutarch, 16–17, 26
Polk County, 76–77, 87
Polynesia (-ns), 12, 153–154
Poplar Bluff, 7, 185
Portsmouth (Ohio), 93
Potowatomi, 106
Powell, David, 60, 212
Priest, Josiah, 74
Pritzker, Barry M., 84, 156, 162, 211
Promontorium Winlandia, 50
Pumpkintown, 16, 76
Punic Wars, 18, 24
Pygmy (Pygmies), 14
Pyramid Lake, 12
Pytheas, 29
Pyvog, 59

Q

Q-Keltic, 123
Quetzalcoatl, 65–66

R

Rave, Herman, 96
Red Indians, 13, 3, 6, 12–14, 33, 37, 95, 101, 109,
    114, 127, 141, 152, 154
Red River, 53, 165
Renfrew, Colin, 7
Rhode Island, 15, 48, 138
Rhodri, 59, 64
Ricarree (Ree, see Arikara), 145, 161, 183
Riryd, 67–68, 90, 176
Roanoke Island, 123
Robert of Rhuddlan, 132
Robeson County, 125
Rock Creek, 90
Rock Lake, 20
Rock Village, 168
Rockcastle Hills, 116–117

Rockcastle River, 116
Roman (-s, Rome), 26, 28–29, 51, 74, 80
Rose Island, 13, 17, 20, 96–97
Ross, John, 104
Rune (Runic), 49–50, 52–54, 91–92, 116, 118,
    208, 210, 212
Russell, Dr. John, 103
Ryan, William, 23

S

Sakakawea, 159, 168–170, 186
Sakakawea Village, 169–170
Sakarya, River, 7
Salt Lick Creek, 93
San Blas, 52, 118
Sand Island, 92, 95, 111
Sand Mountain, 16, 76
Sanders, John, 127
Santa Elena, 80, 85–86, 203
Sargasso Sea, 40, 60
Sauk, 106
Savannah Fort, 16, 2–3, 76–77, 81
Savannah River, 78, 86, 118
Scioto River, 93
Scotland, 14, 24, 27–30, 44, 51–52, 210
Scotti, 29, 51
See-pohs-ka-nu-mah-ka-kee, 156
Seminole, 103–104
Semites, 8
Seneca, 103, 157
Severin, Tim, 40
Sevier, John, 71–72, 74, 104, 155, 197
Sevier, Joseph, 73
Shawanoe, 118
Shawnee, 17, 79, 84, 108–111, 115, 118, 125, 135–
    136, 157, 159, 199–200, 202–203, 205, 209,
    211
Shawnee Town, 135
Shetland Islands, 14, 34
Sheyenne River, 142, 166, 193
Shoshone, 106, 169–170
Siberia (-ns) Clan, 6, 8, 14, 154
Sidon, 15
Sinclair, Prince Henry, 14, 63, 211
Sioux (Siouan), 84, 104, 107, 145, 162, 165, 172–
    173, 202
Sioux, (Siouan), 104–106, 133, 139–140, 143–
    144, 146, 151–152, 162, 166, 168, 170–171,
    173, 175–176, 181–185, 190–191, 193–194,
    199, 203, 205
Sitecah, 12
Sitting Bull, 183
Skidi-Pawnee (see Pawnee), 85, 170, 172–173,
    191
Skinner, Dr., 127
Skraeling (-s), 33, 44–46
Slant Village, 190

Smith, John, 121
Snake, 170
Snowden, 124
Solomon, 16
South America, 13–14, 155
South Carolina, 12, 80, 85, 122
South Dakota, 142, 151, 170, 172–173, 186, 192, 204
Southern Isles, 63, 118
Spain, 23–24, 28, 118, 138–139, 141, 208
Spanish, 20, 33, 36, 52, 64–65, 67, 72, 79–80, 85–86, 134, 138–143, 153–154, 200, 203
Spirit Cave, 12
Spirit Pond, 54, 208
Square Buttes, 176
St. Brendon, 11, 39–40, 61, 118
St. Finbarr, 11, 39–40, 61, 118
St. Francis River, 53
St. George's Bay, 31, 36–37
St. Louis, 106, 138, 140, 144, 148, 169–170, 172, 175, 179, 186, 194, 200, 208–210, 212
St. Peters, 175–176, 178, 189, 204
Starr, Bessie, 187, 194
Stoddard, Amos, 73, 131, 213
Stonehenge, 25, 28
Strata Florida, 60
Straumsey, 15, 45, 48
Straumsfjord, 15, 45–46, 48, 51
Stuart, James, 73
Sudan, 5
Sunrise Sea, 19
Surinam, 123
Sutton, Benjamin, 135
Swede (-s), 42, 53

T

Tallapoosa, 3, 77
Tallega (Tallegewi, etc.), 7, 106, 108, 112, 115, 125, 203, 205, 210
Tamaroa, 200
Tartessians, 18, 24, 28
TAT (Three Affiliated Tribes), 183, 187, 190, 194, 207, 211
Tecumseh, 159
Tellico, 78
Tennessee, 7, 15–17, 2–3, 14, 18, 71–73, 76–81, 83–87, 90–91, 104, 117–118, 125, 155, 172, 192, 195, 199, 202–204, 207, 209–211, 213
Tennessee River, 76–78, 80, 84, 90, 204
Tenskwatawa (The Prophet), 159
Teotihuacan, 17
Texas, 13, 68, 89, 103, 172
Thompson, David, 168, 170, 188
Thorgest, 42
Thorhall, 63
Thorstein, 63
Thorvald, 15, 43–44, 47

Thruston Tablet, 12, 17, 91–92, 116–118, 203
Thruston, Gates P., 90
Thule (Tule), 29, 49, 52
Tlaloc, 17
Tobacco (Chief), 111, 127
Toltec (-s), 64, 66, 74, 108
Tomahittan, 203
Tombigbee River, 90
Toronto, 20, 41
Torquemada, Juan de, 66
Tula (Tulla), 65, 73
Tunica, 108
Tunit, 31, 33–34, 36–37, 47, 49–50
Turner, John, 157
Turtle Mountains, 167
Tuscarora, 103, 117, 135
Tutelo, 105
Twin Buttes, 162, 187
Tyre, 15

U

Ukraine, 7
Umatilla, 153–154
Ungava, 14, 30–31, 36, 51
Uto-Aztecan, 106

V

Vaccinia, 178
Variola, 179
Victoria, Queen, 148
Viking (-s), 11, 15, 17, 20, 18, 29, 34, 40–42, 46–47, 50, 52, 54, 57–58, 60, 63, 67, 91, 94, 116–118, 203, 208–211
Vinland, 15, 31, 36, 43–45, 50–53, 63
Virginia, 12, 86, 101, 105, 117, 122–123, 125, 134, 136, 200, 213

W

Wabash, 92, 199
Wales, 9, 11–12, 15, 17–18, 57–58, 60, 64, 66–67, 73–74, 77, 80, 89–90, 94–96, 113, 121, 123–124, 126, 132, 134–135, 137, 149, 153, 161, 190, 212
Wallum Olum, 102–103, 105–106, 108, 210
Wampanoag, 52
Ward, A.H., 126
Ward, Andrew, 126, 202
Washington, 124, 144, 148, 160, 172, 199
Welegens, 12, 87, 202, 205
Wells, Spencer, 5
Welsh, 12, 15–17, 1–4, 57–58, 60, 64, 67, 69, 71–73, 75–81, 83–85, 87, 89–96, 98, 103–104, 108–114, 116, 121–127, 131, 133–138, 140–142, 145, 149, 153, 155–163, 170, 172, 179, 190–192, 194, 197–199, 201–205
West Virginia, 18, 112, 114

Western Settlement, 48
Westport (Massachusetts), 14
White (Earth) River, 172–173, 204
White Indians, 20, 1, 4, 52, 68, 73, 78, 83, 86, 90,
   95, 104, 114, 121, 126–127, 131, 136, 153, 205,
   210
Whittall, James, 14, 165
Wiggins (Wiggam's) Point, 97–98, 199
Williams, Captain David, 91
Williams, Edward, 134
Williams, John, 135
Wilson, Alan, 95
Winnebago, 162
Wisconsin, 20, 105, 107, 118, 199, 210
Woden-Lithi, 41
Woodford County, 99
Woodland Culture, 77
Wright, William, 57
Wyandotte, 103

Wyoming, 183

X

Xerxes, 16
Xualae, 112

Y

Yellowstone, 148, 167, 178, 186
Young, Bennett H., 115
Yuchi (Yuchean), 78–79, 83–86, 93, 105, 162,
   173, 195, 202, 204, 208
Yukon, 106

Z

Zeno, 12, 14, 34–35, 51
Zollicoffer, Felix, 116
Zuni, 17

Printed in the United States
22336LVS00001B/375

9 780875 863009